The Savage Country

by Walter O'Meara

Illustrated by Philip B. Parsons

Houghton Mifflin Company, Boston
The Riverside Press, Cambridge

BOOKS BY WALTER O'MEARA

The Trees Went Forth
The Grand Portage
Tales of the Two Borders
The Spanish Bride
Minnesota Gothic
Just Looking
The Devil's Cross
The First Northwest Passage
The Savage Country

THIRD PRINTING

The Savage Country

Contents

	INTRODUCTION	vii
I	THE GRAND PORTAGE	1
II	THE RENDEZVOUS	15
III	THE NORTHWEST ROAD	43
IV	PEMBINA	79
V	RUM, WOMEN AND RATIONS	103
VI	BLOOD ON THE PRAIRIE	137
VII	THE BLOND INDIANS	157
VIII	THE SASKATCHEWAN	197
IX	VERMILION	211
X	THE HAUNT OF THE MAMMOTH	233
XI	ASTORIA	247
	THE SOURCES	298
	INDEX	301

To my old friends and canoemates,
Robert T. Herz, William T. Comstock
and Joseph C. Taylor

Introduction

ABOUT three hundred years ago, the forests of North America were invaded by a new species of predatory animal — the fur trader. From the viewpoint of an industrious and harmless little rodent called the beaver, at least, he was a predatory animal; and none was ever more slaughterous. Before long the fur brigades were spreading havoc over thousands of square miles of wilderness among the ugly little beasts with the precious coats. To the north, their deadly canoes drove to the Rocky Mountains and beyond the Arctic Circle. Farther south, they reached the headwaters of the Missouri. Eventually, they arrived at the Pacific Ocean.

All over North America, the fur hunters ruthlessly killed beaver. And quite as ruthlessly, at times, they killed one another. The scramble for beaver became a grim, silent struggle in the lonely bush. *"Pro pelle cutem"* was the motto of the greatest and grandest of the trading companies; or, less delicately, "A skin for a skin." It could have served them all.

Royal coffers were filled and dynastic fortunes — like the Astors' — were founded on the trade in beaver. The very history of nations, including our own, was powerfully affected by the struggle in the remote fur country. Never, indeed, has so small an animal caused so much furor in the world, so much toiling and daring, such a vast expenditure of energy. And for what reason? A fashion in hats! For in the elegant seventeenth and eighteenth centuries, it must be understood, the pelt of the beaver was seldom worn in its natural state; that is, simply as fur. It was made into felt, and the felt into hats — the famous beaver hats of Restoration England, Louis XIV's France, and indeed all of Europe for several generations. But the vogue for the big hats with the rolling brims was more than a fashion, really; it was a mania. To appear without one of the elaborate affairs of felt, plumes, jewels, braid and embroidery was to be quite hopelessly out of style. To own a fine "beaver" was to prove one's standing as a man — or woman — of the *beau monde*. Like our cashmere coat or foreign sports car, it was a status symbol of its time.

There was only one kind of fur out of which a beaver hat could be made; and that, quite naturally, was the beaver's. But the reason is a curious one. Like all pelts, that of *Castor canadensis* is composed of two kinds of hair: the under hair, which is silky, gray and closely knit; and the guard hair, which is coarse, long and reddish brown. In one very important respect, however, the beaver's fur differs from that of other animals. If you examine it under a microscope, you will find that each under hair is covered with tiny barbs. And it is these barbs that make it better than any other fur for making hats.

It is not hard to see why. When the long, coarse guard hairs are plucked, only the soft, smooth fur remains. This fur is sheared from the hide and sifted until a sort of soft down is left. Then the downy fibers are matted together by heat and moisture, and rolled, shrunk and beaten into felt. And nothing works up so well, clings together so tightly, and makes such smooth, lustrous, silky felt as the fur of the beaver, with its millions of microscopic barbs.

You don't often see a hat of genuine beaver nowadays; and when you do, it is priced at a figure that only a Texas oilman could afford to pay. Most of us are quite content, indeed, with our fedoras of cony or rabbit; but in the days of Beau Nash, the rage for "beavers" was so intense that a gentleman of fashion would have pawned his sedan chair, if necessary, to possess one. So, as the demand for beaver soared, the search for the costly — and profitable — pelts spread. Northern beaver was the finest of all, and the French traders pushed their quest for the rich, dark Canadian skins almost to the Rocky Mountains. And especially they ransacked the wilderness for the beaver robes of the Indians.

These robes, worn with the fur next to the body, acquired not only a certain aroma and well-greased pliability, but other characteristics that made them a superior material from which to make hats for milord and milady: the fur became soft and downy, or, as the French traders said, *cotonné*. It took from fifteen to eighteen months of constant wearing, however, to produce a well-seasoned robe; and this made it necessary to go deeper and deeper into the continent, to meet new tribes and tap fresh sources of *contonné* pelts.

Driven by this necessity, as well as by wars, politics, and an insatiable curiosity to know what lay around the next bend of the river, the French built trading posts as far west as the Upper Saskatchewan. When, after the conquest of Canada in 1760, the British gradually took over the fur trade, they extended the search for beaver all the way to the shores of the Pacific.

This book tells about these British fur traders — the Gentlemen of the North West Company, as they came to style themselves. More particularly, it tells about the adventures of a fur trader named Alexander Henry the Younger — to distinguish him from a celebrated uncle, Alexander Henry of the Colony of New Jersey, who wrote a famous book about his travels in the Indian country — and his activities as an officer of one of the most extraordinary organizations in the whole history of North American business enterprise.

The Savage Country

I

The Grand Portage

SLOGGING along the north coast of Lake Superior, the canoes from Montreal fetched up at a small bay near the western end of the Great Lakes system, where the North West Company had its field headquarters. From a stockaded post near the shore, an ancient trail wound over nine miles of rough, wooded terrain to the upper reaches of the Pigeon River. This footpath was the famous Grand Portage — or, as it was sometimes called, the Great Carry.

It was not the longest of portages; Portage la Prairie was almost twice as long. It was not the most difficult; the terrible Grande Allumette was much worse. It could not match the spectacular beauty of the lovely Portage la Loche. But of all portages in the Northwest, it was by far the most important — for one enormously simple reason. Only the Grand Portage offered a way through the red bluffs that frown down on the northern shore of Lake Superior. Only by the Grand Portage trail could you pierce the continuous barrier of hills to the navigable water of the Pigeon River, and thence proceed to any corner of the continent you wished to visit.

"Give me a north canoe and a little lyed corn and grease," a Nor'wester could say, "and there's no place I can't go from the Grand Portage." And he would not be far from right. By way of well-traveled routes, a determined man could paddle and portage to the Atlantic Ocean, Hudson Bay, the Arctic Sea, the Gulf of Mexico — even, if the Blackfoot decided to let him through alive, to the Pacific Ocean.

Actually, the Nor'westers did fan out in all these directions. Regularly, and as a matter of everyday business, they came and went by canoe through the whole country north and west of Lake Superior, and southward toward the headwaters of the Mississippi. More than a hundred of their forts dotted the wilderness that we know today as the Canadian provinces of Ontario, Manitoba, Saskatchewan, Alberta, British Columbia, and much of the North West Territories, as well as the states of Minnesota, North Dakota, Montana, Idaho, Washington and Oregon. And the jumping-off place for all this far-reaching activity was the beautiful little bay on the eastern end of the Grand Portage trail. Here the North West Company had built its principal fort and trading post. Here, long before such struggling settlements as Chicago and St. Paul were even thought of, a thousand men and more gathered every year for the great spring Rendezvous; and what is today a little cluster of fishermen's cabins off U.S. Route 61 was for a brief interval each summer one of the most populous — and certainly the most uproarious — spots west of the Appalachians.

2

FRENCH explorers, looking for the Western Sea, discovered the Grand Portage.

First among them, in all probability, were those enigmatic travelers and brothers-in-law, Radisson and Chouart, who coasted the north shore of Lake Superior in 1660. A few years after them came that intrepid captain of the wild *coureurs du bois*, Daniel Greysolon, Sieur Duluth. And others, no doubt, followed them. But the first Frenchman who, as far as we know, actually traveled the canoe route to the Interior was young Jacques de Noyon, of Quebec. Late in the seventeenth century, de Noyon learned from a party of Assiniboine about a great sea far to the west. "Its waters rise and fall," the Indians told him. "On its shores are fortified towns with stone walls, where white bearded men ride on great beasts, with the women behind." They themselves, they added, were on their way in that direction, to fight a race of dwarfs "about three feet and a half tall, and very stout."

De Noyon decided to go along and join the fun — and possibly find the long-sought passage to the Western Sea. He went as far as Rainy Lake, where he built a fort and wintered.

Not long after this thrust of de Noyon's, Louis XV approved the establishment of three posts in the *pays d'en haut* to serve as bases for the never-ending search for a Northwest Passage. An expedition headed by de la Noue, a native of Montreal, built a fort at Kaministiquia, about thirty miles east of the Grand Portage, and began trading with the Indians. The French explorers never missed a chance to trade a few beaver pelts along their routes.

It was just such a combination of exploring and trading, in fact, that enabled Pierre Gaultier, Sieur de la Vérendrye, to finance the most important discoveries yet to be made in the Northwest. A fur trader by profession, Vérendrye was at heart an explorer; and finding the elusive passage to the Western Sea and the Spice Islands was his dream. Unable to get money from the king for his explorations, he turned to the merchants of Montreal. They agreed to finance him if he would mix a certain amount of trading with his voyages of discovery.

Vérendrye then headed west with his three sons and about forty men. At Michilimackinac they picked up a Jesuit missionary. In the summer of 1731, they all passed over the Grand Portage and, following an Indian map that showed "the whole course of a river from the height of land beyond Lake Superior to above California," they set out to find the Western Sea. For ten years they probed the wilderness, extending their explorations to the Lake of the Woods, Lac Winipic, the Red River of the North, and the Assiniboine; then overland to the upper waters of the Missouri, and finally — almost a century before Lewis and Clark — to the eastern slope of the Rockies.

True to his compact with the Montreal merchants, Vérendrye built trading posts wherever he carried the fleur-de-lis: Fort St. Pierre on Rainy Lake, Fort St. Charles on the Lake of the Woods, and others on Lac Winipic, the Red River, and even the Saskatchewan. Collectively, these and later posts became known as "the Post of the Western Sea." And if there seems to be a tinge of irony in that term, Vérendrye and his stalwart sons could feel, at least, that they had made a good try. They had not got to California, to be sure; and they had found no Northwest Passage — for the simple reason that there was none. But they had ventured deeper into the howling wilderness than any white man had ever gone before. They had contributed immensely to the world's knowledge of its own geography. And they had firmly established the French fur trade — one of the most critical factors in the colossal eighteenth century struggle for political power in North America.

3

WHAT the French were up against was the necessity of finding a new route by which to tap the riches of the beaver country before the English did. The old way was through Hudson Bay; but in 1713, by the Treaty of Utrecht, that was lost forever. Now the English were sitting securely on the Bay in their laced suits and cocked hats, and even the prairie Indians were making the long journey eastward to trade at their posts.

The French, blocked everywhere in the north, sought desperately to find a new gateway into the *pays d'en haut;* and Vérendrye, as we have seen, found it at last, through the Grand Portage. From his time until the Conquest, French traders followed in the wake of his canoes, some by way of the Grand Portage, some by a branch of the same route, through Kaministiquia. Forts sprang up everywhere. Soon the French commandants had a chain of strong points and trading posts from Montreal to the foot of the Rockies. The westernmost, Fort à la Corne, was 3000 canoe miles from Montreal and within sight of the mountains.

To maintain such a far-strung and often hazardous system

of communications, young and daring men were needed. They were to be found aplenty in Montreal and the sleepy little towns along the St. Lawrence. So eager was the exodus to the *pays d'en haut*, in fact, that both government and church became alarmed at the drain on the colony's best youth and set up an elaborate system of regulations and licenses to stem it. What bothered the authorities most, however, was the natural ease with which the young men from the quiet rural towns went native. "It is not necessary to examine the cause," Sir Alexander Mackenzie commented sagely, "but experience proves that it requires much less time for a civilized people to deviate into the manners and customs of savage life than for savages to rise to a state of civilization." And the French required very little time indeed. They quickly married Indian girls, took to Indian ways, accepted the Indian code of morals. They swiftly became all but savages, in fact; and the church complained bitterly that they were a disgrace to the Christian religion. The government, for its part, considered shipping them off to Martinique or San Domingo. "They might be employed to advantage on the privateers," one official suggested, "as the majority are resolute men."

Yet, these *coureurs du bois*, or bush rangers, formed the solid base on which the French fur trade rested. Dirty, licentious, superstitious, drunken and lawless they might be; but they *were*, after all, "resolute men," and nobody could bear the unimaginable toil and hardship, the cold and hunger of the *pays d'en haut* so cheerfully as these *habitant* lads — half wild and half Indian at last — who had deserted the quiet hamlets along the river for the wide freedoms of the wilderness.

And when, in the course of history, the blow fell that ended the French regime forever, it did not silence their paddle songs on the wide lakes and long rivers of the north. For the British bourgeois (as the moguls of the fur trade were called), no less than the French commandant, found it quite impossible to carry on the trade without the Canadian voyageur.

4

THE end came in 1760, with Wolfe's conquest of Canada by a single battle atop the Rock of Quebec. But the trade did not pass immediately into British hands. For a time there was no trade. For a little while the beaver in his snug winter quarters was unmolested. The French posts fell into ruins or were burned by the Indians. The portages became choked with windfalls and brush. The very canoe routes were forgotten. "Not an army officer, not a priest, not a fur trader," it was said, "remained beyond Kaministiquia."

A few daring merchants, to be sure, ventured into Lake Superior the very year that Montreal fell to British arms — among them Alexander Henry the Elder. Then Pontiac took the war road, and after the sack of Michilimackinac — which Henry almost alone survived — the trade again stopped. It was not picked up until the end of the great chief's war in 1765. In that year Henry was again sending his canoes with gewgaws and rum to the ancient French posts. Soon others besides Henry began to filter into the abandoned beaver country, most of them by way of the old Grand Portage route. They were often plundered and sometimes scalped; but the lure of 400 per cent profit kept them coming, and gradually a regular trade was re-established.

Among the early visitors to the Grand Portage was the

gullible American, Jonathan Carver. Supposedly in search of a Northwest Passage at the behest of Major Robert Rogers, the famous organizer of Rogers' Rangers, Carver stopped at the Portage to provision. The Indians fed him tall tales, which he swallowed whole; but the traders had no food to spare, and so he turned his canoes homeward.

Another was Peter Pond. Also an American, Pond had a large streak of curiosity in his make-up, and it — perhaps as much as his strong trader's instinct — lured him to the farthest point yet reached by anyone in the Northwest. He crossed the great Methye Portage and built a fort thirty miles south of Lake Athabasca — which still looks terribly far north on modern maps — and from there, he probably pushed up the Peace River. Pond drew up a map of his wanderings, perhaps the most elaborate and detailed map that ever a fur trader had made. It was his intention, he said, to present it to the Empress of the Russians, who were busy establishing their own trading posts on the Pacific Coast and in what is now Alaska.

Like his famous map, which was the topic of much argument and dispute around the lonely fires of the fur country, Peter Pond's career had always been a controversial one. On his first foray into the beaver lands, he had killed a man in a duel. "We met the Next Morning Eairley & Discharged Pistols," he wrote of the incident, "in which the Pore Fellowe was Unfortenat." Later, he was guilty of the murder of at least one rival trader, and perhaps responsible for that of another. Yet, Pond's stormy career was but a reflection of the general discord and dissension — and not infrequently violence — that had begun to erode the British fur trade. For the cutthroat competition among the Montreal merchants had reached such a point, at last, that the very existence of the trade was threatened.

The demoralization of the bourgeois infected all hands, down to the lowliest canoeman. Drinking, fighting, quarreling with the Indians along their routes, the brigades seldom reached winter quarters — except, perhaps, by dog sledge. Winter was one long brawl, often marked by bloodshed. Hatred and ill-will hung like an evil miasma over the remote reaches of the *pays d'en haut*.

The Indians, as a consequence, lost all respect for the whites. They often held up the fur brigades and forced them to pay tribute, so that thirty or forty canoes had to travel together, with armed men for protection. The posts, often attacked, were in a continual state of alarm. Pillage and murder were common. Even at the Grand Portage, matters came to such a pass that the commandant at Michilimackinac had to send an officer and half a dozen soldiers to keep peace among the quarreling traders. Thus things went steadily downhill until the summer of 1787; and then came the pay-off.

That summer, Roderic McKenzie and William McGillivray, exhausted and dour, arrived at the Grand Portage from distant Athabasca. They had not been expected at the Rendezvous that year. What, the traders wondered, had caused them to make the grueling seventy-day trip down from Fort Chipewyan?

The answer was a grim one. John Ross, a bourgeois of considerable importance in the north, had got into an argument with Peter Pond's men over some fish nets. A scuffle had ensued. Ross had been shot. He was dead.

The first reaction at the Grand Portage was a round of

accusations and recriminations. But even the worst of the hotheads could see that the dog-eat-dog era in the Northwest had at last come to its sordid end. Simon McTavish gently reminded the warring traders that this was the last straw. Unless a stop was put to bloodshed and murder, unless they could find a way to work together, they were all finished separately. Quebec's patience could be stretched only so far. McTavish was a powerful figure in Canada — a rich, fabulously successful merchant, whose adventures had taken his men and ships across two oceans. No one matched his personal influence in the fur trade. No one but he, perhaps, could ever have brought order out of all this chaos.

McTavish not only cleansed Augeas' stables, but in the process founded one of the most remarkable business organizations of all time: the great North West Company. For it was in a partnership of the feuding merchants — to be called the North West Company — that McTavish found a solution to the troubles besetting the fur trade. The new concern was not the first North West Company. Twice before, loose coalitions, dominated always by the powerful Montreal merchants, had been put together under that name. Neither had lasted long. But this new North West Company endured to see its trade empire spread to the Pacific Coast, Hudson Bay, the British Isles, China and the Sandwich Islands — thanks almost wholly to the powerful personality, energy and business genius of Simon McTavish, sometimes called "The Premier."

By the charter of the North West Company, McTavish and Joseph Frobisher were given management of the Concern's affairs in Montreal and England, and they were to be styled Agents. All the other traders, to be called Wintering

Partners, would remain in the *pays d'en haut* with the Indians. Peter Pond, incidentally, was shipped back to Milford, Connecticut, where he could cause no more mischief.

Each summer, the charter further specified, every Nor'-wester who could manage it must leave his wintering station and come to the Grand Portage for the Concern's great annual "board meeting." The Partners had just begun to gather there when, in June of 1801, Alexander Henry the Younger arrived for the Rendezvous.

5

HENRY had just completed a hard, fast twelve-day trip from his post in the Interior. He had spent two years in the *pays d'en haut*, the first near Lake Winnipeg, the second on the Red River of the North, in the extreme northeast corner of what is today the state of North Dakota, then territory still held vaguely by the French. He was not yet a full-fledged Wintering Partner of the North West Company, although he had seen seven years of service with the Concern, most of it in Montreal and such near-in posts as Detroit and Michilimackinac. He was still a Clerk — by no means an inferior rating, however — but his responsibilities as chief of the Red River post were clearly on the order of a Partner's.

Henry was a native of Montreal; and, like so many Montrealers of his day, he was born to the north canoe and the trading wicket. Besides his famous uncle, he had at least three other close relatives in the fur trade. One of his cousins ranged the beaver country as far west as the Coast and gave his name to Henry House, a fort he built high up the Atha-

basca. Another was murdered by Indians on the Liard River.
A third was killed while trading at Fort Nelson.

So it was natural that Alexander Henry himself should go
into his uncle's business at an early age and spend all his life
in the trade — at least fifteen years of it in the Northwest, or
the *pays d'en haut,* as the country beyond Lake Superior was
termed. During those years he went everywhere and did
everything that a Nor'wester normally would. He made vast
journeys by canoe, by dog sledge, and by foot over the mountains. He built forts on the prairies and in the forest belts,
and traded with a dozen tribes, from the Chippewa to the
Chinook. He froze, starved, suffered sickness, and endured
the terrible loneliness of the wintering station. He debauched
the Indians with rum, fought with them, doctored them, and
married one of their women after the fashion of the country.

Henry never became famous, like his uncle; nor rich, like
some of the other bourgeois. But nobody, it is certain, lived
more fully the hard, lonely, dangerous, often sordid and
sometimes heroic life of the trader. None was more a Nor'-
wester.

But if, in all these ways, Alexander Henry the Younger
was no different from any other Nor'wester, in one respect
at least he was apart from them all. He alone not only lived
the life of a Nor'wester, but kept a meticulous day-to-day
record of it.

It was every Nor'wester's duty, of course, to note the weather, the trade, and other routine matters pertaining to the
conduct of his post in a "fort journal." But, for the most
part, only the barest of facts ever found their way into these
scribbled diaries of busy and sometimes illiterate post masters.
Henry, on the other hand, omitted absolutely nothing.

Night after night, he set down in a big book bound in rawhide covers the longest, most circumstantial, and by all odds the frankest account that has come down to us of life in that vast and lonely wilderness sometimes called the *pays sauvage* by uneasy traders. The very first page of his remarkable journal gives us this vivid picture of Henry's strange, almost compulsive drive to describe his experiences in exact and uninhibited detail:

> I was accustomed to sit up late, with a candle burning in my tent, for some time after the fires had been put out. Some of my people, who had occasion to sleep away from home, assured me that from their camp, which was about 12 miles E. of us, they could distinctly perceive this light, which they observed to be extinguished about midnight, when I went to bed.

Henry wrote this in 1799 — his first year as master of a small post on the Rivière Terre Blanche, about a hundred miles west of the present city of Winnipeg. During his next fifteen years in the Northwest, he never for a day — with the exception of two inexplicable lacunae — failed to keep the record; and it ends only on the night before his death — with an unfinished sentence.

In the pages of his journal, we shall accompany Alexander Henry the Younger on his vast wanderings across the continent; and we must join him now at the great summer Rendezvous of the North West Company.

II

The Rendezvous

HENRY FOUND the Grand Portage already in an uproar of
human and animal turmoil. Several hundred Indians had long
ago pitched their mushroom birchbark lodges on the lake
shore, to await the coming of the traders; and now they were
joined by as many canoemen from Montreal. Suddenly,
where there had been nothing at all to disturb the sandpipers
running along the water's edge, almost a thousand men,
women and children — and innumerable dogs — were mill-
ing around the little wilderness fort called, after the trail,
Grand Portage. Only at the canoe dock was there anything
like ordered activity. Here the big *canots du maître* were in;
Henry watched them unloading.

Early in May they left Lachine, these big, high-prowed
craft, with goods and provisions for the Interior. Carrying a

cargo of five tons, including a crew of ten, they traversed the ancient route — up the Ottawa, across Lake Nipissing, down the French River, then through the Sault Ste. Marie into Lake Superior — and arrived at Grand Portage late in June.

The 500-pound miracle that made this long and always perilous journey possible — and, indeed, allowed the fur trade to function at all — was the heavy canoe, called variously the *canot du maître*, the Grand River canoe, and the Montreal canoe. It was built at Three Rivers during the winter season and, as soon as the ice permitted, brought to Lachine and loaded for the trip west. Nothing like the Grand River canoe was known before the coming of the traders — the Indian craft were small and fragile by comparison — and it is unlikely that, pound for pound, a better answer to the peculiar transportation problems of the Nor'westers could possibly have been devised. Streamlined as a jet fighter, it was about thirty-six feet long and six wide amidships. It was constructed entirely of white-birch bark, cedar splints, and the roots of the spruce tree. Its sides and bottom were nowhere more than a quarter of an inch thick. Six men could easily carry it; and it could carry the equivalent of, let us say, two American automobiles.

Stowing that weight of cargo in such a flimsy vessel was an operation that called for almost mathematical precision. To make it easier, all trade packs were made up in *pièces* of exactly ninety pounds each. Thus the distribution of weight could be calculated almost to the ounce. When all the packs — about sixty in all — had been lowered onto the long poles laid in the bottom of the canoe, they fitted together like the pieces of a jigsaw puzzle; and the gunnels of the canoe sank to within six inches of the water. The management of such a heavily laden craft was, as one might imagine, a very delicate business; the canoemen, it was said, had to be careful how they parted their hair!

After loading at Lachine, the big craft with their high, gaily painted prows, were ready to shove off at dawn for the Grand Portage, two thousand miles away. Some of the miserable village, including a few sleepy prostitutes, would be at the dock to see them off. But the leave-takings were brief, most of the voyageurs having already said good-by to their girls and families in Montreal.

"Allez!" The guides barked out the orders and the canoemen, each carrying his own vermilion-tipped paddle, sprang to their places with an almost military smartness. The flashing blades dipped into the clear water of Lake St. Louis.

"Adieu! Bon voyage! Bon voyage, mes voyageurs!" The ragged group on the quay loosed a halfhearted cheer. From the doorway of the little dockside inn, somebody might fire off a gun. The voyageurs raised a song, perhaps the one about love and springtime:

> *Tous les printemps,*
> *Tant de nouvelle,*
> *Tous les amants*
>
> *Changeant de maîtresses;*
> *Le bon vin d'endort,*
> *L'amour me reveille.*

Once into the brown waters of the Ottawa — then called the Grand River — they took the bright feathers out of their caps, lowered the big flag at the stern of the bourgeois' canoe, and got set for one of the most heartbreaking trips in the history of overland navigation.

For two months they paddled, pushed, pulled, sailed and manhandled their big egg-shell craft and four tons of lading through a complex of rivers, lakes and portages that nobody but a voyageur, bred for generations to the job, could ever have traversed. Sometimes, in the boiling water of a Calumet or Long Sault, they came to grief: at one portage on the Ottawa thirty crosses commemorated lost canoemen. Sometimes they were swamped by the sudden squalls and great seas that swept Lake Superior. But usually they managed to outwit fate — and, perhaps, a few unfriendly Indians — and, firing guns and shouting their ancient songs, to finish their long journey with a wild dash into Grand Portage Bay, each canoe in line, every paddle stroke in unison.

The last of the 1801 brigades — and Simon McTavish with it — had just put in when Alexander Henry the Younger arrived at the Rendezvous. As was the custom, the Premier had been carried ashore on the shoulders of his men and borne through a shouting throng of traders and Indians to his quarters in the Great Hall. And now, the huzzas and salutes having ceased — although the smell of gunpowder still lingered in the air — the canoemen were unloading at the wharf.

They worked feverishly, gaily, noisily in the manner of voyageurs, some tossing up the packs with a shout, some trotting with them up the easy slope to the fort. The Chippewa girls hung about, watching the operation, getting in the way of the workers, laughing and shrieking at their obscene sallies. All the dogs barked excitedly. And beyond this French, Indian, English and canine din, this violent and incessant agitation of half-naked bodies in and around the fort, lay Grand Portage Bay, serene, sparkling, and — except for a few small Indian canoes slipping across its surface — empty under the gentle June sun.

2

IN ALL North America, perhaps, there was not a lovelier little bay. Its outlines — as you would have noted in the year 1801 — were very like a firesteel's: an almost perfect oval with a broken outer edge. The horns of the firesteel were Pointe aux Chapeaux (today's Hat Point) and Pointe à la Framboise. And it was beyond Pointe aux Chapeaux that the Montreal brigades camped on their last night, so that the voyageurs could shift and shave, and put on their feathers and finery to make a brave arrival at the Portage.

Directly opposite the fort lay a green wooded island, like an emerald on a lady's hand mirror. Landward, to form a natural amphitheater, rose high, rocky hills, fire-swept and covered, as they are still, with stunted timber, and blueberry, raspberry and gooseberry bushes growing between the fallen, fire-blackened trees. If you climbed the highest of these hills, called the Sugarloaf, you could see the hazy outlines of Isle Royale. And beyond Pointe aux Chapeaux, the islands that people living at Grand Portage today call the Susies. And everywhere, around and beyond these, the vast expanse of "the mother and mistress of all the lakes" — so clear and transparent that, on a fine day, bottom could be seen in thirty fathoms.

At the edge of this exquisite little bay, surrounded by a

few acres of meadow and cleared land, stood the principal establishment of the North West Company. "This," Daniel Harmon wrote in his journal, "is the Headquarters and General Rendezvous for all who trade in this part of the world."

Yet, notwithstanding its importance, and despite the British ensign flying against the clear summer sky, the Grand Portage was not a very impressive post. The fort itself consisted of but sixteen buildings enclosed by a palisade with a bastion and a heavy gate. The buildings were constructed not of logs, but of solid planks, some whipsawed on the spot, some brought from Sault Ste. Marie in the Concern's sloop, the *Otter*. Their roofs were covered with heavy cedar shingles; their doors and windows painted that strong shade of red called Spanish Brown.

Half a dozen of these rather ramshackle buildings served as storehouses for the Concern's property — rum, trade goods, and provisions going up; furs coming down. The rest comprised living quarters, shops, sheds, a counting house, and a mess hall in which a hundred men could eat at once. The only other structures inside the palisade were: the powder magazine, stone-walled and tin-roofed, like the houses in Montreal; the "butter tub," into which refractory voyageurs were tossed; the "cantine salope," where the canoemen squandered their winter's wages on liquor and the fort girls.

All this inside the high, vermilion-tipped stockade. Outside, the fields in which a few horses and milch cows grazed; the squalid village of Indian lodges at the water's edge; the canoe yards, where the famous north canoes were made; the tent camps of the canoemen behind the fort; and, at a prudent distance, a few huts of the XY Company, the Nor'westers' only competition at Grand Portage.

And over everything now, the raucous, steadily mounting uproar of the Rendezvous.

3

A THOUSAND white men — Porkeaters from Montreal, North Men from the upper posts, a handful of free trappers and XY men — would soon be on the ground: a thousand whites and nobody knew how many Indians — three thousand souls in all, perhaps, would gather for this Rendezvous.

The Indians and Montrealers had already arrived. Soon the North Men would come roaring over the portage trail, each with a hundred and eighty pounds on his back, and in his simple voyageur's heart an immense craving for rum, women, and the other artless divertisements of the Rendezvous. First, however, there was work to do: the packs to make up, and supplies and provisions got over the portage. For the trade goods, as they came from Montreal, had to be repacked for the Interior. A single Montreal canoe might bring a cargo — worth £500, incidentally — made up of rum, twist tobacco, point blankets, vermilion paint, Spanish beads, brass or iron kettles, sugar, axes, knives (butcher and scalping), guns, shot and ball, gunpowder, china bowls, printed cottons, flints and firesteels, drugs. These various articles must be sorted and repackaged to meet the special needs and tastes of the Indians at Pembina, Fort des Prairies, Bas de la Rivière, Fort Chipewyan, and all the other posts, far and near.

On long deal tables in the warehouses, the Montreal packs were broken open and their contents done up in new ninety-pound *pièces*. Each taut, canvas-wrapped pack was then marked with the Concern's trade-mark, a big "N. W." Another letter — as "Q" for Bas de la Rivière — was added to designate the department for which the pack was intended. This work took about two weeks. The Montrealers always pushed it, so as to finish it before the North Men arrived.

They were well along with the job when Alexander Henry reached the Rendezvous. Crossing the Grand Portage from the west, he had encountered scores of Porkeaters on the trail with trade goods for the Interior. They had passed him at the tireless portage trot, sometimes forcing him off the path, into the underbrush or mire. But, aside from a few curses, he had made nothing of it; the Big Carry was on, and even a bourgeois must make way for it.

4

IT TOOK a hundred men a fortnight to get the supplies for the Interior across the portage, and the furs back. And, since all the trade goods must be carried over before the North Men arrived, this part of the work fell to the Porkeaters.

The Porkeaters were the Montreal canoemen. They were called Porkeaters, it is supposed, because their regular rations while en route to the Grand Portage were lyed corn and grease. It was not a very complimentary tag; and, as a matter of fact, they hardly deserved it. Compared to the North Men, perhaps, the Porkeaters — who never, except in rare cases, went farther into the *pays d'en haut* than Rainy Lake — were the rather colorless work horses of the fur trade. They had little glamour, and apparently they weren't even very clean. Contrasting their encampment at the Grand

Portage with that of the North Men, Gabriel Franchère perceived "an astonishing difference between these two camps, which are sometimes 300 or 400 men each; that of the pork-eaters is always dirty and disorderly, while that of the winterers is clean and neat."

Yet, one could not deny the dangers and terrible difficulties of the long route they traveled from Montreal. They were superb canoemen; and, to judge from their regular performance at the Grand Portage — the carrying of almost a thousand pounds apiece over the nine-mile, man-killing trail — they did not lack strength and stamina. Each man was required to take eight trade packs of ninety pounds each from one end of the Grand Portage trail to the other. Ordinarily, he set off with two packs. Some, according to Alexander Mackenzie, had returned and were ready for two others in six hours — eighteen miles of uphill and downhill packing, often in mud up to the knees, under a 180-pound load. For this the voyageur received six livres Grand Portage currency for each *pièce* carried over, with a Spanish dollar for each additional one over the prescribed right.

This crippling, and even killing, work was lightened a little by two techniques of portaging. The first was the use of the portage collar or tumpline. This was simply a leather sling, broad in the middle and tapering to the ends, to which a pack was fastened and settled on the voyageur's back. The wide part of the strap was then passed across the forehead, and another pack tossed on top of the first. By leaning forward, into his tumpline, the packer took some of the weight off his back; and occasionally he was tempted to add a third pack to his load — and an extra Spanish dollar to his pay.

Another help was the system of *posés*, or resting places,

used on all long carries. It was general in the Northwest, indeed, for a portage to be measured by the number of *posés* into which it was divided. The length of a *posé* depended, naturally, on the nature of the ground; but the distance had gradually become fixed at six hundred yards to half a mile. The Grand Portage was divided into sixteen *posés*. Yet, despite tumplines, *posés*, the extra Spanish dollar for "overtime," and an occasional issue of rum, the work of portaging over the Grand Portage was more fit for draft animals than human beings. Ordinarily, the Canadian voyageur was full of good cheer and high spirits, and he sang a lot as he dipped his vermilion paddle into the clear waters of the north. But there is no record of anything but grousing on the Grand Portage.

"The portage road," wrote the Nor'wester François Mahliot, "is truly that to heaven, because it is narrow, full of overturned trees, obstacles, thorns and muskegs. Men who are obliged to carry baggage over it certainly deserve to be called *men*." Mahliot happened to be speaking of another portage, but what he said was true of many in the Northwest — and not least of the Grand Portage. Those who sweated their 720 pounds or more over its tortuous, mucky nine miles of uphill, fly-infested trail deserved indeed to be called *men*.

5

Now the canoe hands from the *pays d'en haut* were arriving. They swarmed in almost daily from the far-off departments — Athabasca, the Upper Fort des Prairies, Fort Dauphin, the Upper English River — long of hair, bare of thigh, almost indistinguishable from the savages in their working gear. As

they roared over the portage, they flung ribald insults at the
Porkeaters. These were the North Men — the elite of the
voyageurs. They had been more places, seen more sights,
suffered more hardships, risked more dangers, known more
women, could brag harder — "I had twelve wives in the country and six running dogs" — than any canoeman from Canada. They shouted their raucous boast, *"Je suis un homme"*
— and looked hopefully about for someone among the Montrealers to deny it.

Often enough they were obliged. The Porkeaters, for all
the contempt in which the North Men held them, were not
averse to an occasional battle; and the toughest mining town
in the West never saw so many brawls, perhaps, as the annual
Rendezvous at the Grand Portage. And the Nor'westers, far
from forbidding these broils, encouraged, even promoted
them. For by such rivalry was the famous *esprit de corps* of
the Northwest Bullies — as the Hudson's Bay people wryly
termed them — developed. Through the lumps got at the
Grand Portage were the Concern's men conditioned for more
serious frays in the *pays d'en haut* with rival traders.

But there was still another reason why the bourgeois
blinked at the violent "frolics" of their men. The Rendezvous
was a period of blowing off steam — the two or three short
weeks in the whole year when a man could get drunk, not in
moody solitude, but properly, in the company and companionship of hundreds. It was a time when he could raise the kind
of hell that only crowds make possible; when he could make
up — perhaps with a little interest — for long, dark months
of loneliness. The bourgeois understood this need: they felt
it themselves.

And so, as soon as the North Man had crossed the portage

and flung his neat, square packs of furs down on the warehouse floor, he was issued a *régale*. This consisted of a loaf of white bread, half a pound of butter, a few gills of rum, and a little tobacco. He then settled his account with the Concern, drew his pay — if any — and signed up for another stretch in the *pays d'en haut*. He was now ready for his fling. He donned his best short shirt, deerskin leggings, blue capote, and the gaudy sash that was his voyageur's trade-mark. Thus resplendent, he headed for the "cantine salope," where more bread, pork, butter, tobacco and liquor — at eight dollars a quart — could be bought; and where, it is easy to guess, the fort girls got most of both his *régale* and his wages.

Prostitution was not popular with the Indians, since all the men were married — some to several wives. But the tribes quickly saw its possibilities among the white traders, and around the big posts it was likely to thrive — sometimes, as at Astoria, to the acute annoyance of the bourgeois — on a rather organized basis. The Chipewyan, for example, took their women hundreds of miles to Hudson Bay, for no other purpose than to barter them to the Gentlemen of the Great Company.

At the Grand Portage, of course, circumstances were just about ideal for the dusky daughters of joy; and the Chippewa, with little else to trade, flocked with their wives and daughters to the Rendezvous. The Chippewa girls, if we may believe the testimony of the bourgeois, were not without allure. They were often pretty, sometimes beautiful. "They have a softness and delicacy in their countenance," hard-boiled Peter Grant observed, "which rivals the charms of some of our more civilized belles."

Many another visitor to the Grand Portage agreed with

him; and if even the bourgeois found so much to notice and admire in the daughters of the Chippewa, perhaps the common canoehand should not be censured too severely if he paid extravagantly for their favors at the "cantine of the harlots."

It probably took him a very short time, indeed, to go broke. He was soon back in his tent village behind the fort, living on his daily allowance of a quart of lyed corn and three ounces of fat, and deep in debt to the Concern to boot. And there were some cynical enough to suspect that this cycle was one over which the Nor'westers lost little sleep. A voyageur who had pledged a year's wages for a few days' fling at the Rendezvous was a voyageur well anchored to his job. Ah, well, it was the life!

"I spent all my earnings in the enjoyment of pleasure. Now I have not a spare shirt to my back, nor a penny to buy one. Yet, were I young again, I should glory in commencing the same career. There is no life as happy as a voyageur's life, no place where a man enjoys such freedom as in the Indian country. *Huzza! Huzza! pour le pays sauvage!*"

6

IN THE midst of all the hell-raising, the Partners gathered in the Great Hall to carry on the business of the North West Company. At the head of the long, baize-covered table sat Simon McTavish himself. This was his first visit in five years to the Grand Portage. That he had found time, between trips to London and New York, to make the long journey betokened the importance of the 1801 Rendezvous. It was, indeed, a grave moment in the affairs of the Concern.

McTavish looked tired. He was fifty now, and had lost some of the persuasiveness and charm that had contributed so much to his power and success. He was prone to snap out questions and make short, occasionally rude answers. The past few years had dealt him some hard blows. And it was one of these, really, that had brought him to the Grand Portage: the defection of Alexander Mackenzie from the Concern.

Of all the Nor'westers — not excepting the Olympic McTavish himself — Alexander Mackenzie had the truest stamp of greatness. While still in his twenties, he had wrested leadership from the older and far more experienced Wintering Partners. But his restless mind and the immense energy that had got him the nickname of "Perpetual Motion" found no fulfillment in the fur trade. He turned to exploring, and went in search of Vérendrye's elusive old star — the Northwest Passage. He didn't find it, of course; but he discovered what is now the Mackenzie River and followed it to the Arctic Ocean. A few years later, he crossed the continent by canoe and afoot — the first man ever to do it — and on a high rock overlooking the Pacific wrote in vermilion paint:

ALEXANDER MACKENZIE, FROM CANADA
BY LAND, THE 22ND OF JULY, 1793.

His fellow Nor'westers, busy dealing out rum to the Indians and gathering in beaver pelts, paid little heed to his great exploits. So Mackenzie went to England, where he was feted by society, had his portrait painted by Sir Thomas Lawrence, wrote a best-selling book about his travels, and was knighted by George III. Now, as the Partners met with Simon McTavish, he was still in England . . . and no longer a Nor'wester.

Abruptly, at the 1799 Rendezvous, Mackenzie had quit the Concern. Some said it was out of pique, because so little had been made of his epochal discoveries. But for a long time, all knew, there had been bad blood between him and McTavish. The reasons for this enmity between two strong-willed, ambitious, intensely egocentric men were complicated; but Mackenzie's reaction was elementary enough. In a raw outburst of pent-up anger, he suddenly stalked out of the Great Hall and went back to Montreal.

This alone was shock enough to McTavish; but right on top of it came another. A new company was forming to challenge the Nor'westers' hold on the fur trade. And at the head of it, as soon as he returned from abroad, would be Alexander Mackenzie. The new Company, known — from the letters on its packs — as the XY Company, was backed by strong and respected Montreal merchants, whose energies were equal to their ample resources. Its posts were already building throughout the beaver country. Its canoes were everywhere. In a single season, the "Potties," as the Nor'westers disdainfully called them, had become a serious threat — so serious indeed that Simon McTavish had summoned to the 1801 Rendezvous every Winterer who could possibly leave his station in the *pays d'en haut*.

7

ABOUT a score were able to respond. They represented only half the total roster of Partners; but perhaps a truer cross section of the Concern had never gathered in council. If you wished to know what kind of man a Nor'wester was, you had only to look about you in the Great Hall at Grand Portage on, let us say, the thirtieth of June, 1801.

Very conspicuous, as always, was John McDonald of Garth — so called to distinguish him from the innumerable other McDonalds in the fur trade — who had come down from Upper Fort des Prairies. He was a huge, violent man, six feet four inches tall, with a bushy beard and long hair, both flaming red. His speech, especially when he was excited, was an odd mixture of Gaelic, French, English and various Indian dialects. He had a withered left arm, and so the voyageurs — who must have nicknames for everyone — called him Bras Croche. His bad arm, however, never interfered with Garth's enjoyment of a good battle. He loved fighting so much that he sometimes accompanied the Blackfoot on their raids against other tribes. He was a great builder of forts, and always sought the most dangerous spots in which to build them . . . He was also famous for his braggadocio.

From the Upper English River department came Angus Shaw, called Monsieur le Chat by the voyageurs, perhaps because of his small voice, perhaps as a pun on his name. He had spent many years in desolate northern posts, yet had managed to keep his high spirits and sense of humor. He was noted for his generosity. "Mr. Shaw, being a dashing bourgeois," a trader's journal recounts, "gave the men of my fifteen canoes a dram out of a big keg he had on tap." Such a man was naturally well liked by everyone.

Also from the Upper English River came Donald McTavish, a gay devotee of women and wine, who one day, in a distant land, was to be the companion of Alexander Henry the Younger in death.

"Big John" McDonnell, sometimes called the Priest because

of his piety, arrived from the Assiniboine with his wife *à la façon du pays*, pretty Magdeleine Poitras. A steady, slow-moving man, dressed in dark broadcloth and wearing a sword, he imparted a note of sober respectability to the gathering in the Great Hall.

From Fort Alexandria, in the rich Swan River department, an enigma: Archibald Norman McLeod. Long in the fur trade, he had once been respected, even loved, by his voyageurs. But the *pays d'en haut* sometimes played tricks with men. McLeod it had turned into a harsh, cruel autocrat, who recognized no law but his own. Ruling like a despot, he even forced his men, it was rumored, to renew their contracts by threats and tortures. He was one of those, the Nor'wester François Larocque observed, "who can never think themselves forgiven . . . because they themselves are incapable of forgiving."

A puzzle of another sort was Roderic McKenzie. Cousin of the great Sir Alexander and bourgeois of the largest and richest department in the Northwest, Roderic had built Fort Chipewyan on Lake Athabasca. It was his strange ambition to make this lonely post a kind of cultural center for his vast subarctic district, and he had collected a library from which the men at his outposts could draw books. "The Athabasca Library," as the traders called it, was not a very large one — for every copy of the classics must compete with a quart of rum for space in a north canoe. But its quality was good, with titles ranging from Herodotus and Tertulian to Adam Smith's *Roman Antiquities* and Goldsmith's *Geography*.

During the long, dull winters at Chip, Roderic busied himself not only with reading, but with his own extraordinary *magnum opus*. This was no less than an anthropological account of all the Indians in his territory, and an analogy of their customs with those of ancient peoples. In this stupendous undertaking he employed the strikingly modern research technique of sending out a printed circular to all his post masters, requesting data on a specified list of subjects.

He got back a great mass of material, which he broke down, cross-indexed, and attempted to relate to the anthropology of European and Asian races. But he got no farther, alas, than the first chapter of his book, precisely penned in a big ledgerlike volume which may still be seen in the dusty files of the Canadian Archives at Ottawa.

Another McKenzie — of whom there were almost as many as McDonalds in the fur trade — was that old reprobate Daniel, who was so fond of the bottle that a trust fund finally had to be set up for his support. He was down from his distant post of Upper Fort des Prairies, on furlough in accordance with the North West Company's system of "rotation." Peter Grant, of Lac la Pluie, and William McKay, of Lac Winipic, were also on their way to Montreal for their sabbaticals.

And lastly, among all these Highlanders, an echo of the old days when the French commandants blazed the long trails which the men of Inverness and Loch Lomond were merely following: Charles Chaboillez, master of the Red River department and technically Henry's bourgeois. He was from an illustrious family of traders, the third of his name to distinguish himself in ventures reaching back to the French regime. One of his sisters had married Simon McTavish, another Roderic McKenzie. He himself, when he retired, would bring his four métis children to Montreal, see them properly baptized — then marry the daughter of a British army officer.

Such were the Nor'westers. Such, good and bad, great and small, but not one of them ordinary, were the men who had gathered on the last day of June, 1801, to hear, first of all, what Simon McTavish had to say about the Concern's affairs.

8

WHAT he had to say was not very good. The Potties, with plenty of capital back of them — perhaps more than the Nor'westers could scrape together — had stepped up competition to a point where everybody was losing money. Rum was flowing like water in the *pays d'en haut*. The Indians, thoroughly debauched, were no longer good for anything as beaver hunters. And, on top of everything else, some of the best fur country was showing signs of playing out. But he wasn't licked yet, McTavish said, with a flicker of his old fire. There were ways the upstarts could be beaten. But first, they'd have to do a little housecleaning themselves.

For one thing, there were too damned many drunken Clerks and interpreters — not to mention Partners — in the wintering grounds. From now on, the rum pots would get something to sober them up: Clerks and interpreters, loss of a year's wages; Partners, expulsion from the Concern. Any objections? Resolution adopted!

Next, the extravagant habits of the bourgeois would have to be curbed. No more of this dashing about in light canoes, trying to set new records. Hereafter every canoe would carry a pay load of furs or provisions. Agreed? So record it!

Then, there was the matter of women and children. The hordes of Indian women and their half-breed offspring living at the posts was an evil, the Premier insisted, that had to be suppressed . . . Or at least checked, he added over the sudden growls of protest. "Let it be resolved," he read out, "that no man — whether Partner, Clerk or engagé — shall take any woman or maid from any of the Indian tribes to live with him after the fashion of the North West, that is to say, in the Company's houses or forts at the expense of the Concern."

At this point he remembered, perhaps, what had happened when he pushed Alexander Mackenzie too far. He hastily amended the resolution: "It is, however, understood that taking the daughter of a white man, after the fashion of the country, shall not be considered a violation of this resolve."

In that form the resolution was adopted (the Nor'westers had no intention of observing it, anyhow) and McTavish switched from his housecleaning program to certain moves he had in mind against the Potties. Some of them amazed Henry, as they must have every other Nor'wester. What, for example, could you say of a man who proposed to send an expedition into Hudson Bay and establish posts right under the noses of the English, as the Nor'westers called their rivals there?

Yet, McTavish was planning to do just that. He also was going to build a fort and win a foothold for the Concern on the Pacific, and had already dispatched his nephew Duncan McGillivray on that errand. He had great plans for the China trade. He was dickering for a lease on the rich "King's posts" on the St. Lawrence . . .

In all these ways, and more besides, the embattled Premier was plotting the future of a bigger, stronger, and, no doubt, more ruthless North West Company — and the Potties be damned. But above all, he told the Nor'westers, with a dash of his old guile, they had one thing the newcomers could never match: they had *men*.

It was on the superiority of the North West Company's personnel — its matchless corps of hardened Wintering Partners, Clerks, guides and canoemen — that McTavish was depending for final defeat of the wealthy but inexperienced XY Company. And it was his plan, now, to select half a dozen of the Concern's toughest and most capable Clerks, give them full-fledged Partnerships, and send them into the critical areas — with orders to take care of the Potties in their own way.

Alexander Henry the Younger was pleased, but by no means surprised, to hear his name read off from McTavish's list. News traveled with astonishing speed in the North West Company — sometimes even before it happened! Henry had counted on his promotion: who, he wondered, were the others? The Premier called them off.

Hugh McGillis, a Clerk stationed at Fort Dauphin, was one. He had married an Indian woman, by whom he was having — to his disgust — a great many children.

Jean Baptiste Cadot was another. This extraordinary half-breed had been educated in Canada. He spoke Latin, French, English and Nipissing fluently — it was said. He was also an accomplished drunkard.

John McGillivray, second son of Farquhar McGillivray, who led the remnant of the Clan Chattan from the field of Culloden, was also on the list. Anyone could see that he would go far in the Concern.

James McKenzie's name added no luster to the roster of new, young and hopeful Partners. A brother of Roderic McKenzie, his buying and selling of women at Athabasca, together with the sardonic tone of his dealings with other traders, had given him a bad reputation — even among Nor'-westers.

And last on the list, an American, Simon Fraser of Bennington, Vermont. Already a veteran of Athabasca, he was headed for distant stations beyond the Rockies, where he would be the first to navigate the river that now bears his name.

"Each of these Gentlemen," it was unanimously resolved, "should be admitted Partners of the North West Company for one Forty-sixth share each, their Interest in the same to Commence with the outfit of the year 1802."

It was characteristic of Alexander Henry the Younger — who tells us very little indeed about himself — that he felt no necessity of mentioning his promotion in his journal.

9

AFTER business, pleasure — in the fashion of the Northwest. The meetings in the Great Hall had dragged on for a couple of weeks; and now, at last, the routine affairs of the Concern had finally been concluded: the annual reports, assignment of posts, granting of leaves, infliction of penalties — all the paperwork of the trade, made out in triplicate, and duly signed, sealed and delivered. The Partners got up, for the last time, from the long table littered with papers, crude maps, inkpots and tobacco jars. They were impatient to get back to their wintering stations ahead of the ice . . . But first, the big fling of the year — the annual ball of the Nor'westers, and the climax of the Rendezvous.

Dancing was for the voyageur as natural as breathing. Along with drinking, hunting, fighting and wenching, it was a popular diversion throughout the Northwest; and there was no post so poor that it couldn't manage an occasional ball. The holidays — particularly St. Andrew's Day, New Year's Day, Christmas, and All Saints' Day — were always good for an extra issue of rum and a frolic in the evening; and every voyageur aimed to be at headquarters for these festivities. But even Sunday, or perhaps the arrival of a canoe brigade — or even a single canoe, if it came to that — was also an excuse for a dance; and the traders' journals are full of such brief entries by sleepy Clerks as: "Dance lasted all night. Very little work done today." And not infrequently: "The men were very quarrelsome and had 4 or five battles."

When Indians were encamped in the vicinity, their women were invited to the ball; and by all accounts they were no mean match for the traders in the energetic jigs and reels that went on and on to the scrape of a single fiddle, and perhaps some banging on a pan, until daylight stole into the swamp. If no women were available, the men paired off, sometimes striving to dance one another down. More often than not, the sweaty frolic wound up in a general brawl. "Finally two battles were fought," Daniel Harmon concludes one description of a New Year's dance, "which put an end to this truly genteel North Western ball."

But the dances of the *pays d'en haut* — at one of which 72 men, 37 women and 65 children were packed into a room twenty-two feet square! — were the uncouth frolics of semi-savages, compared to the great annual ball at the Grand Portage. This the Gentlemen of the North West Company themselves attended; and for it they dressed, as they would for a glittering ball in the Château de Ramezay in Montreal, the Partners in their small clothes and swords, the Clerks in the somber suits that were issued as part of their pay. And when they sat down together in the Great Hall for the traditional feast before the dance, the tall candles cast their glow over a kind of rustic replica of the Beaver Club's celebrated dinners in Montreal.

Was not Simon McTavish himself, the founder of that famous society, at the head of the table? And were they not all Wintering Partners, as every member of the Beaver Club must be? No one, to be sure, wore the big gold medal with the motto, "Fortitude in Distress:" and there were no such distinguished guests as John Jacob Astor or Sir John Johnson to honor their board. Yet there was nothing lacking in food or wines — or the ability to drink in true Highland style — that the diners of the Beaver Club themselves could boast.

So, a little ill at ease perhaps in the presence of so much silver, crystal and Irish napery, they sat down to the roasts of venison, the smoked hams, the baked whitefish from the icy water of Lake Superior, the Indian corn puddings, and boiled potatoes from the Grand Portage garden, and the loaves of fine white bread they'd never see again until another Rendezvous. And they drank that strange toast of the Nor'westers: *"To the Mother of all the saints!"*

Of the drinking capacity of the Nor'westers, there are a number of well-authenticated accounts; and by all of them it was enormous. A guest at one of the Beaver Club's all-night feasts reported awesomely that a dozen diners had put away 120 bottles of wine by morning. "Three and four-bottle men," he added, "would have been milksops among these hardy northern topers."

Alexander Mackenzie was one whose prowess at the bottle
was widely respected. The Nor'westers never tired of telling
about a great drinking match in Montreal when, all the numerous toasts of the Beaver Club having been drunk, only
Mackenzie and William McGillivray remained on their feet.
"To our memory!" Mackenzie proposed. But before that
ultimate toast could be pledged, both warriors slipped under
the table, to join their fallen friends and foes. By the time
darkness had fallen and the Great Hall was cleared for
dancing, it can be assumed that every Nor'wester had arrived
at that fine stage when all men were his friends, and every
Chippewa girl, in her white doeskins or sheathlike dress of
blue cloth, was vaguely beautiful.

Only one direct description of the ball has come down to
us, the one written by Daniel Harmon, of Vermont — a puri-
tanical young man just arrived in the Indian country. "In the
evening the gentlemen of the place dressed," Harmon wrote,
"and we had a famous ball in the dining room. For musick we
had the bag-pipe, the violin, and the flute, which added much
to the interest of the occasion. At the ball there was a number of the ladies of this country; and I was surprised that they
could conduct with so much propriety and dance so well."

But while the bourgeois danced "The Flowers of Edin-
burgh" and "The Dashing White Sergeant" and "The Reel
of Tulloch" with a select — although somewhat tipsy and
excited — group of "the ladies of this country," something
quite different from their decorous rout was taking place outside the great barred gates of the fort.

In the camps of the North Men and Porkeaters, in the
birchbark village along the water front, the common canoe-
hands and the Indians were having their own last frenetic

fling; and that orgy, devoid of even the most elementary restraints, filled the darkness with such shrieks, roars, shouts, gunshots and drum-beating — not to mention the incessant howling of hundreds of dogs and the cries of terrified children — that the music of the bourgeois' elegant ball was quite smothered in the night.

When the hot July sun rose above the metallic reaches of Lake Superior, the Rendezvous was all but over. It remained only for the Porkeaters to load the winter's harvest of furs into the big *canots du maître*, and turn back to Montreal; for the Winterers to cross the Portage and launch their north canoes on the long, long journey to their stations in the *pays d'en haut;* and for the Chippewa to bury their dead, roll up their birchbark lodges, and fade into their hunting grounds until the time for another Rendezvous rolled around.

III

The Northwest Road

AT FORT CHARLOTTE, a batch of ramshackle warehouses on the swampy west end of the Grand Portage trail, Henry's canoes were loading for the long journey over the never-ending maze of waterways called the Northwest Road.

The classic north canoe, the standard freight carrier of the fur trade, was about half the size of the *canot du maître* and was built along different lines — lighter, narrower, more easily manageable in fast water. It was from twenty-four to thirty feet long, about five feet wide amidships, but less than three feet fore and aft. Often, its high prow and stern were decorated with paintings: a horse's head, the Union Jack, a geometric design. Besides its crew of four or five and their provisions, the north canoe could carry better than a ton of pay load. When light-loaded, it was capable of amazing speed.

Henry, for example, once covered the distance between the Forks (modern Winnipeg) and the Grand Portage in twelve days. Roderic McKenzie made the 2000-mile trip from Rainy Lake to Fort Chipewyan in a month and four days. The north canoe *had* to be fast: the lives of its crew, fighting to get to their wintering station ahead of the frost, often depended on speed.

It was constructed of birchbark and white cedar, sewed with watap (the young roots of the spruce), and gummed with pine resin. In a pinch, a fur trader could make a canoe out of almost anything — raw buffalo or deer hide, poplar bark, cedar wood. But the bark of the white birch, peeled from the tree in large sheets and thoroughly dried, was the material par excellence. So highly was it valued by the Nor'-westers that the Concern once shipped rolls of bark, bundles of watap and kegs of gum all the way from Montreal to London, and thence around the Horn to Fort George, in case none was to be found on the Pacific Coast!

Henry's journal does not describe his 1801 trip over the Northwest Road, but his record of the previous year's journey gives us a vivid picture of what travel over that famous highway of the voyageurs was like.

Arriving at Fort Charlotte at the late hour of five o'clock in the morning, Henry inspected his canoes — saw that the bark was new and free of wrinkles, the gum fresh and amber-colored, the frames and sheathing sound. Satisfied, he ordered his voyageurs to proceed with the loading.

Twenty-eight packs, all marked with the big "O" of the Red River department, were then lowered into each vessel. Henry tells us exactly what went into his rather heavily loaded craft: five bales of merchandise (of 90 pounds each); three bales each of Canal tobacco, kettles and guns; a case of iron works, two rolls of new twist tobacco; two bags each of lead balls and shot; a bag of flour and another of sugar; two kegs of gunpowder, and ten of high wine.

In addition to these trade goods, each canoe carried equipment and provisions for the voyage, and packs containing the personal belongings of the men — including trinkets for their wives and children, and their own "Sunday clothes." For the voyageur did not wear his finery — the blue capote, red woolen cap, bright feathers, gaudy sash, and leggings of scarlet cloth — to work. All these he wrapped in waterproofed bundles and stowed carefully in his canoe. What he wore on the job was a pair of deerskin leggings reaching from the ankle to a little above the knee, an Indian breechclout, moccasins, and the inevitable beaded pouch in which he kept his pipe, tobacco and firesteel. In the mosquito or black-fly season, he might add a short, loose-hanging shirt which, with his long hair, gave him some protection against the worst torment of the *pays d'en haut*.

"When all hands were embarked," Henry noted, "the canoes sunk to the gunnels." At ten o'clock they were all off. At three, Henry followed in a light canoe.

2

His route lay along what are today the Boundary waters between the United States and Canada, canoe country beloved by thousands of summer vacationists. The same lakes and streams, the same portage trails, even the same camp sites that were used by the Nor'westers, and long before them by the French, are still in use today. And in most cases — often with French turned into English — they bear the same ancient names.

Thus, Portage Perdrix is still its English equivalent, Partridge Portage; Portage Orignal is Moose Portage; Portage Bois Blanc is Basswood Portage; L'Escalier and Cheval de Bois are Stairway and Wooden Horse portages. The lakes sometimes keep their French or Indian names, as: Maraboeuf, Lac la Croix, Saganaga, Namakan; but Lac Pierre à Fusil is now Gunflint Lake, Lac Croche is Crooked Lake, and Lac des Couteaux is known to us as Knife Lake.

Henry's brigade was hardly on its way when the first carry was reached. At Partridge Falls, a mile and a half upriver, it was necessary to lift both canoes and lading out of the water and carry them 600 paces. It was an easy portage, and the men, fresh and eager to get to their camping place and the usual *régale*, performed it with the smooth dispatch of a boat drill.

Generations of usage, indeed, had reduced the work of portaging to an almost ritualistic routine. Just before touching land, the guide leaped into the water and eased his craft ashore. Then he and the steersman unloaded it, hoisted it up, and shouldered it upright — unlike the *canots du maître*, which were carried bottom up — across the portage. Hard on their heels came the men, each with his load of two packs. If the portage was long, or there was danger of an Indian raid, they stopped every 600 feet at a *posé*, dropped their packs and went back for two more, until all were deposited at the first *posé*; then on to the next, in the same fashion, until everything was across. If the portage was short, they made the whole trip at a dog trot, leaning into their tumplines, heads down, without stopping.

But stereotyped as the process of portaging may have been, the actual performance — especially when two or more brigades happened to converge at a carry — was likely to be one of utter confusion. The curse of the voyageur was vanity. With him, all was "anxiety as to who shall lead the march." He was obsessed by a spirit of competition that drove him to almost unbelievable feats of endurance and strength. He would paddle a hundred miles a day, or carry 500 pounds for half a league, if necessary, to make good his boast, "*Je suis un homme!*" So every portage was a challenge and the occasion of such haste and disorder that even the veteran Henry could marvel and write:

> Everyone was anxious to get ahead and show his activity, as is generally the case in the Northwest. This produced a scene of bustle and confusion which cannot be conceived by anyone who has not been an eye-witness of the great exertion of which the North Men are capable . . . Everything went over the portages in one trip. Canoes and all at a full trot; embarked all hands helter-skelter, pushed off, and all paddled as if chased by an enemy.

The inevitable result of such haste was damage to the packs, and the North West Company tried to cut down the loss by packing the trade goods in a special way, with stout safeguards against breakage. Thus, each individual pack for the Interior contained a more or less complete assortment of merchandise, so that if a pack were lost, the trader would not arrive at his post completely out of some essential item. Further to reduce losses, everything possible was transported in kegs — powder, sugar and rum. Drygoods were packed in double canvas, securely corded and waterproofed. But in spite of everything, bourgeois after bourgeois echoed this familiar plaint of Henry's:

This day passed in repairing the boats and canoes, making setting poles, and examining the different baggage; found small packages much damaged and kegs of wine not more than half full, having been cracked by falling on the rocks and the liquor leaked out. The Canadians are certainly smart active men as voyageurs, but very careless with the property committed to their care.

Still, William McGillivray could say that a half of one per cent would cover all the losses suffered in the transportation of his goods. The voyageur did not get off so lightly. He was the real loser — in the coin of wrenched backs, broken legs, rheumatic pain, and hernia, all common consequences of his mad but lighthearted exertion.

The Partridge Portage was crossed in an hour. The canoes were again launched on the Pigeon River, and after two and a half miles of easy paddling, the brigade arrived at the Prairie Portage. Here, on a delightful meadow where there was "plenty of elbow room for the men's antics," the voyageurs prepared to enjoy their customary *régale* and a little friendly fighting. But first, before the small kegs that each man carried with him from the Grand Portage could be broached, there was camp to make, the fires to build, and the great kettles slung for the evening meal.

3

THE housekeeping of a canoe brigade on the march was of the simplest. A stop for the night was made just before dark. The canoes were unloaded, pulled up, and turned over to serve as shelter for their crews. For the Partner or Clerk, a small tent was pitched. Wood was gathered and a fire built. While the cook prepared supper — a mess of lyed corn, or hominy, boiled up with a little grease in a big tin kettle — the canoemen, often by torchlight, tended to the gumming of their craft while the bourgeois wrote down the record of that day's progress in his journal.

Supper over — and it was a lightning performance — the canoeman was ready for bed. "Nor ghosts, nor rattlesnakes, nor spiders, nothing," one bourgeois wrote, "can prevent the fatigued voyageur from sleeping." And the sooner the better!

Yet Jean Baptiste, sitting on a shelf of clean pink granite sloping down to the dark water, might smoke a quiet pipe before he rolled himself into his blanket and fell into oblivion beneath his north canoe. For a time he might listen to the eerie cries of the loons and watch the mist gathering in restless patches on the suddenly chilled water, while the cook got ready tomorrow's breakfast in a pool of light around his immense fire. He might think of the *habitant* girls he had known in Pointe-Claire or Contrecoeur . . . *Sacré!* Why did I let that wily agent sign me up for three long years in the *pays sauvage?* Why did I leave Lizette . . . and Annette . . . and that little Marie . . . ?

Alerte! Lève, lève, nos gens! The thundering shouts of reveille were likely to blast through the camp as early as midnight, although the usual time of embarkation was three o'clock. If the rapids was ahead, the canoes would not shove off until daylight. If a strong headwind was blowing up, they might not leave until it had died down. It was possible, on the other hand, that a whole night might be spent on the march, without going ashore at all.

Breaking camp was even simpler and faster than encamping. Breakfast, precooked, was the same as supper, lyed corn and grease, and dispatched with even greater speed. In fifteen minutes the canoes were reloaded and launched.

4

THE first leg of the Northwest Road — the traders called all canoe routes roads and all canoe trips marches — terminated at Lac la Pluie, or Rainy Lake Fort. Thus far and no farther the Porkeaters could go with goods for Athabasca, pick up the furs from that distant department, and race back to Montreal before the freeze-up. Hence it was by all odds the busiest and most traveled canoe route in the whole Northwest, and the canoemen on its portages were thicker than the flies in Montreal at shad time. In some places, indeed, the rocks still show the abrasion of their innumerable moccasined feet. And the canoeist who today pitches his tent at the end of a portage trail is camping where, for two centuries, thousands of weary voyageurs stopped the night before him.

On this 600-mile stretch of the Northwest Road — all of it on the present boundary between Minnesota and Ontario — there lay twenty-five good-sized lakes, many more small ones, and several navigable streams. By the bourgeois John McDonnell's count, there were thirty-six portages at low water. The voyageur traversing this section of the Road was thus confronted by almost every problem known to canoe travel; and he solved them not infrequently at the peril of his life.

The portages he took in stride, although some of them were so long and rough as to "greatly fatigue and even lame the men." The Stairway Portage, almost straight up and down and negotiable only by means of footholds cut into the rocks, called for special portaging skills, as well as tremendous exertion. And some, like the Wooden Horse Portage, were just plain ugly.

It was not difficult to break a leg, or rupture yourself, or even to get killed on a portage. "L'heureux was near being killed by a fall, carrying his canoe," runs the entry in a trader's journal. "He was senseless for some time . . . Four men were obliged to carry him up the hill in a blanket."

It was not always necessary, however, to undergo the toil and often the danger of carrying both canoe and lading overland. Frequently a *décharge* could be made. At a *décharge* part, or perhaps all, of the load was carried around a rapids, while the lightened or empty craft was towed past it. For this purpose every north canoe carried sixty yards of cordelle, a tracking cable composed of twisted strands of fine, strong line. The cordelle sometimes broke, occasioning the loss of canoe and cargo — and some of the finest profanity in the Nor'-wester's repertory.

There were also times when a rapids could be run, or saulted. Much depended on the height of the water. Even a dangerous stretch of river could sometimes be saulted during the rainy season. Henry himself tells with a certain glee of having gone down the tricky Little Portage rapids in the Lake of the Woods under full sail!

The most difficult rapids were "interdicted" by the Concern; but the Canadian canoeman could not always resist temptation — especially if he had a skinful of high wine — and not a few died in white water, taking foolish chances. Other rapids, while not interdicted, were decidedly "passable but dangerous," as the road signs say. Scores of canoemen lost their lives in them. "When you are in the worst rapids," an ancient *chanson à l'aviron* advised, "let the Virgin Mary be your guide." It was as good a rule as any. But not all canoe travel was downstream, of course, and working *up* a rapids was quite as dangerous — and a lot more laborious — than saulting down one. The job was done with long steel-tipped poles called "setting poles," and by towing or tracking from the shore.

But a good deal of the Northwest Road — in fact most of it — was not rivers at all, but a succession of lovely lakes, granite-rimmed and pine-walled, and sparkling beneath a sky so blue that it seemed to come right down to the water. To swing down Maraboeuf or Gunflint on a fine day, singing a lively paddle song in unison with a hundred other voyageurs, pausing occasionally to light your pipe and enjoy the comfort of good Brazil tobacco, with a dram before supper, and a belly full of corn pudding at the end of the day — that was not such a bad life, really. There were worse ways for a man to pass his little time on earth!

5

THE crew of a north canoe numbered six or eight men — men, it must be added, of a very special stamp, who had been bred for generations, as it were, to the incredibly hard life of the voyageur. They were small, short, thickset, seldom more than five feet five inches tall; for there was no room for beef in a north canoe, and along the St. Lawrence, indeed, it was counted the worst of luck for a woman to bear big sons. They had powerful arms and backs, and weak, often bandy legs.

Their skins were as dark as a half-breed's — which they often were.

Yet, despite his lack of stature, the Canadian voyageur was a man of amazing physical strength and endurance. Who else could paddle a canoe for eighteen hours a day on a quart of lyed corn or a handful of pemmican? Or trot over a mile-long portage with two hundred pounds, then hurry back for another load? Or keep going, if it came to that, on nothing to eat but a few strips of toasted leather?

Even those aloof aristocrats of the fur trade on Hudson Bay were aware of the sterling qualities of the Canadian canoemen — and frankly envious of them. Andrew Graham, Master of York Fort, described them as "chosen men, inured to hardships and fatigue" under which the Hudson's Bay Company's hired hands would have gone to pieces.

In all respects, indeed, they were a remarkable if not always estimable breed — filthy, ignorant, obscene, superstitious, lecherous, drunk whenever possible; yet tough as Indians and cheerful under trials that would have tried the heart of a Jesuit martyr. Travelers sometimes noted a certain dignity, courtesy and Gallic charm. The Nor'westers took a somewhat dimmer view of their graces. "All their talk is about horses, dogs, canoes, women, and strong men who can fight a good battle," Harmon observed contemptuously. And he added that he would rather have fifty drunken Indians in his fort than five liquored-up Canadians.

But they did not all conform to a pattern, of course. There were cowards among the brave ones, and sad ones with the gay. There were even some giants. Henry himself had one — the great Negro, Pierre Bonga. Bonga, who was from a famous family of voyageurs, weighed almost two hundred pounds. He could carry five packs — more than twice his own weight — over a portage, and easily. There was no one who could measure up to Bonga.

In a north canoe the crew disposed itself as follows: in the bow, the bowsman, who was also the guide in charge; in the stern, the steersman who, alone among the canoemen, stood while the craft was under way; between these, the middlemen, two on a seat.

On the open stretches of the Boundary lakes they hit up a cadence of about forty strokes a minute, every man except the steersman keeping exact time with the bowsman's pace. At this rate, from four to six miles an hour could be logged in calm water, and as many as a hundred miles could be covered in a day.

If you make that out to be from twelve to sixteen hours of paddle work, you are right. The voyageur's regular day began at three o'clock in the morning. After six hours of paddling, he stopped for breakfast. Again at noon he paused for dinner and was on his way in an hour. After that it was hard, steady going until nightfall — or perhaps long after dark. He could keep this up — as much as twenty hours of paddling and portaging, with an occasional assist from the wind, when a sail was hoisted — for two or three weeks at a time.

Like all heavy workers, he consumed vast quantities of food, his diet varying with his progress into the *pays d'en haut*. Thus, between the Grand Portage and Rainy Lake he subsisted on lyed corn and melted fat. After reaching Rainy Lake, the corn-and-grease diet gave way to one of wild rice and grease. Beyond Lac Winipic, the main subsistence was pemmican, until the fresh-meat country was reached. To these basic rations the voyageur added, when he was lucky and could get them, wild fruit or berries, a bit of fish, a few birds' or turtles' eggs, or perhaps a small dog bought from the Indians. He also consumed quantities of rum and tobacco. And it was this Spartan diet, perhaps, that brought him — although often greatly underweight — safely to his wintering station. That and the system of *"pipes."*

Nobody is quite sure of what a *"pipe"* was. Some think it was the distance covered while a voyageur smoked a pipeful of tobacco. Others maintain it was the pause — possibly at two-hour intervals — during which he opened his *sac-à-feu*, got out his tobacco, and rested for five or ten minutes while he smoked his clay.

Alexander Henry himself defines the *"pipe"* most accurately, perhaps, with a casual reference in his journal: ". . . when the men stop to rest and light their pipes, which they frequently do in the course of the day." The voyageur, in other words, probably smoked incessantly, and the *"pipe"* was merely a pause for recharging and relighting, followed by a few minutes of rest and chat. Very like our own coffee break. Distances, incidentally, were often reckoned in terms of *"pipes,"* instead of miles or leagues.

Sometimes a canoe brigade had to make a *dégrade*. This was simply to go ashore, or remain ashore after camping, because of high winds. The modern canoeist's version of the term is "to be windbound"; and as every modern canoeist knows, it is one of the most exasperating experiences of canoe travel — especially if it is also raining. The voyageur, who could make a joke about almost anything, had a standard one about a crew windbound in a tiny lake with sheer sides and a narrow exit scarcely as wide as a canoe. But he too loathed to sit out a stubborn gale; and often he chanced disaster because of his impatience. As many men were lost in the stormy traverses of the inland lakes, perhaps, as in the chutes and rapids.

But such were the risks, and such was the toil and almost unbelievable exertion that a voyageur must accept as part of the endless struggle against space and time — against the savage leagues that lay between him and the relative security of some little post in the wilderness; against the freeze-up that could strand him, helpless to move and certain of death, in a trap of iron lakes and rivers. It was a grim, unrelenting, one-sided struggle that wore down and destroyed the strongest; and few, in fact, lived beyond their fortieth year to prolong it.

6

ON THE lower end of the Northwest Road Henry's brigade ran into a series of bothersome portages, one of which was longer than the Grand Calumet, the longest on the Ottawa. Packing, towing, and wading up to their waists on slippery rocks, they got around Caribou, Fowl, Moose and the three Cherry portages, and dropped their canoes into the Lake of the Mountains. They coasted down that lake with a fine breeze aft, came to the Watab Portage, crossed it, and worked through a narrow passage to the New Grand Portage. Here, his men being dead tired and the carry 3000 paces long, and a mankiller, Henry broke one of the rules of canoe travel and camped at the near end of a portage.

They were up before daylight, however, and by ten o'clock had everything over the worst carry on the Northwest Road.

At the other end Henry found scores of canoes, some embarking, some finishing the portage, and all in great confusion. He decided to pitch his tent and wait for his brigade to catch up with him. They arrived and that evening all got pleasantly drunk on their small kegs of rum.

They were off early the next morning, so early that Henry pauses to remark pridefully in his journal that they "crossed Rosa lake to Petite Peche, where were some canoes not yet stirring." He does not mention — perhaps because it was so familiar an experience — one of the strangest phenomena encountered by the voyageur on the Northwest Road, or anywhere else: the "heavy water" of a little lake just beyond Rose. Sir Alexander Mackenzie was the first to describe it.

Except along the south shore, Mackenzie comments in his *Voyages*, the water "has a peculiar suction or attractive power, so that it is difficult to paddle a canoe over it . . . I have indeed been told that loaded canoes have been in danger of being swallowed up, and have owed their preservation only to other canoes, which were lighter." He adds that he himself had found it difficult to get away from this "attractive power," although in no apparent danger of being sucked under. To their bewilderment, incidentally, canoeists on the Boundary waters still experience this odd phenomenon. Marine engineers have an explanation for it in the muddy bottom of the lake, and point out that even battleships are sometimes affected by a similar "drag" when passing over certain areas of the ocean bed, as off the coast of Maryland.

Next stop was the Height of Land, where the men "generally finish their small kegs of liquor and fight many a battle." Henry's voyageurs, we may assume, were no exception. The occasion for the Height of Land frolic was the brigade's arrival at the place where the rivers no longer flowed southward into Lake Superior and the St. Lawrence River system, but northward into Hudson Bay. From here on, therefore, all travel would be downhill. No more toilsome poling against the current, no more tracking the canoes upstream. What better excuse for getting a little drunk and fighting a few friendly battles?

But the voyageur must make a ceremony out of everything — especially if the ceremony could be made to include an issue of rum. Thus, at a similar spot on the Ottawa route, he threw away his setting pole, put on a ritual song and dance, and was rewarded by his bourgeois with a few extra drams. His horseplay at the Height of Land included the initiation of all tenderfeet into the elite company of the North Men. A cedar bough was dipped into a northward-flowing stream and the water sprinkled over the initiate, from whom traditional oaths were extracted — among them a solemn promise never to kiss any other voyageur's wife against her will. The broaching of a keg of rum and the firing off of guns "in the Indian manner," that is, one after another, completed the ceremony.

Next day, with a fine following wind, they were on Gunflint. They sailed up the lake under a sparkling, cloud-heaped sky and soon reached the Stairway Portage (although not the same one that bears that name today). They clambered down its sixty paces, lowering the canoes painfully, and:

> We embarked and proceeded to the Cheval de Bois, an ugly portage of about 400 paces. Thence to Portage des Gros Pins, which is about 700 paces, to a small lake. Through this we passed to a chain of rapids and small lakes and down to Maraboeuf portage, which is about 200 paces. This is succeeded by several small rapids, through which

we passed to Pointe à la Framboise, where we camped after dark. The men were much fatigued. We found the air very cold. Gummed our canoes by torchlight, as they had received some damage in coming down the last rapid.

But all was not such toil and travail on the Northwest Road. In fine weather, when the long lakes glinted for miles ahead, and the warm fruity smell of ripe blueberries was wafted to them from the shore, they maintained their steady beat of forty paddle strokes a minute, sometimes hoisting a small sail, and logging an easy six miles an hour on quiet water.

They drove from the ale-brown lakes of the south to the clear, glass-green ones of the north, through water thick with the "bloom" that appears in summer, and ponds gay with white or yellow water lilies, where the moose browsed on the succulent roots. They "thridded" streams choked with wild rice, out of which blue herons rose on ponderous, beating wings. They slid down quiet rivers, where the eyes of deer burned in the shore shadows, and swept across the easy reaches of Maraboeuf, Big Sag, Lac des Couteaux and Lac Bois Blanc; and the life of a voyageur was no worse than it might have been.

But sometimes they ran into trouble. The big lakes were not always calm, nor the skies above them always clear. Sudden rain squalls were frequent, and often a brigade was drenched so thoroughly that it was necessary to put ashore, open all the packs, and dry the wetted merchandise on the rocks and bushes. Or, as the Henry's journal now reminds us, much worse could happen:

> The wind now abating a little, we embarked, and with great difficulty reached Petit Detroit sometime after dark. Just at this moment a black thunderstorm was collecting;

we could not reach land, as a reef of rocks prevented
approach to the shore; and, before we could reach a proper
landing, the storm burst upon us, with thunder and
lightning, rain, and a terrible squall from the W. . . . We
got under the lee of a large stone, where, all hands clinging to it, with much trouble we kept our canoes from
being blown out upon the lake, where we must inevitably
have perished. The thunder and lightning were horrid;
every flash served but to show us our danger, and instantly
left us in utter darkness. Toward day the storm abated,
but we did not think it proper to stir from our large stone
till daybreak.

After putting ashore "to refresh themselves," the brigade
was again on its way by ten o'clock. And so, in fine weather
and foul, sometimes blessed with fair winds and vibrant days
of brilliant sunshine, sometimes cursed with ill luck on the
portages, the bloody scourge of black flies, the inevitable afflic-
tion of boils, they slogged on.

Occasionally they met a band of beggarly Indians offering
their women and a few scraps of moldy dried meat in trade.
Often they encountered other brigades. On Lac des Couteaux,
three canoes from Rainy Lake, loaded with packs from the
Athabasca department, passed them, and Henry gave them
his dispatches for Montreal.

In Lac Croche — which today has a long bay named for
every day of the week — they ran under the painted rocks
shot full of arrows by the Sioux, it was said, as a reminder to
the Chippewa that their forest fastness was not secure from
invasion by the warlike plains tribes. And here they met nine
more canoes loaded with the dark, rich furs of the Athabasca
department.

Now, entering Lac la Croix, a beautiful lake full of high,

wooded islands — like tall ships under sail — they came to the *mai*. The *mai* was a tall spruce tree sheared of all its branches, except those near the top. This lobstick — soon to be the most famous landmark in the Northwest — marked the place where the "New Road" to Lake Superior branched off from the old Grand Portage route.

There was nothing new about the "New Road," really. Long ago, the French had regularly used this more northerly route to their headquarters at Kaministiquia. Then, after the Conquest, it had been entirely forgotten until Roderic McKenzie, quite by accident, had rediscovered it. And now the Nor'westers, apprehensive that the Grand Portage was in United States territory, had begun to build a new field headquarters on the site of the old French post. Soon the Grand Portage route would be abandoned altogether, and the North West Company's flag would fly over their "New Fort" on the Kaministiquia.

From Lac la Croix, it was but a short paddle down the quiet little Rivière la Croix to Lake Vermilion and then into Namakan, a big body of water swept by headwinds that forced the canoes to make a *dégrade*. Here, for the first time, Henry left the present international boundary and, groping his way down a crooked passage, found the entrance to Lac la Pluie.

By far the largest lake he had yet encountered, Lac la Pluie — now Rainy Lake — wandered in an intricate maze of bays, estuaries and islands for almost a hundred miles westward and northward. Henry's goal, Rainy Lake Fort at the western end, was forty miles away. Driven about by strong winds that at one point almost brought disaster, it took him two days to make the traverse. The journal records its successful completion:

This evening my brigade arrived all safe. The gentlemen danced until daybreak, all very merry.

They had finished the trip from the Grand Portage in exactly two weeks: no men, no canoes, no goods, and very little time lost.

7

PERCHED on the high bank of the mist-driven outlet of the lake, Rainy Lake Fort was one of the oldest — and still one of the most important — posts in the Northwest. De Noyon had probably wintered on the spot in the 1680's; and Vérendrye had certainly built a fort there in 1731. At least one trading establishment had occupied the site of Vérendrye's old Fort St. Pierre ever since.

Now there were two: the North West Company's post, in charge of Peter Grant; and the XY Company's rival establishment, under one M. Lacombe. Between the permanent white and Indian populations of these two posts and the great influx of canoemen every summer, the place was almost as thronged as the Grand Portage. Through it passed the brigades going to or from their wintering stations all over the Northwest. To it — but no farther — came the North Men from Athabasca, and even Great Slave Lake, with their precious dark pelts. And from Montreal, came the crack brigades of Porkeaters, to pick up the Athabasca furs and hurry back to Canada.

Only a large and roomy post could accommodate these swarming hundreds, and Rainy Lake House was indeed an impressive establishment. Like Bas de la Rivière, Fort de la Montée, and Cumberland House, it was a huge depot as well as a trading center. To it vast quantities of wild rice were brought by the Indians, to be stored and rationed out to the northern brigades. Here birchbark, which grew abundantly in the vicinity, was gathered and fashioned into north canoes — as many as a hundred each winter. And here, also, tons of fish were caught and dried or frozen.

The fort itself was built on the usual plan, but was far larger and more elaborate than anything Henry had yet seen in the Northwest. Inside a strong stockade pierced by heavy gates and flanked by bastions, a number of solid wooden structures formed a hollow square. High above them, a platform ascended by a ladder served as a lookout or *guérite* — not so much, however, for spotting hostile Indians as for spying on the XY people. And higher even than the *guérite*, the Union Jack snapped on the breeze from Lac la Pluie.

The post buildings consisted of the usual Indian Hall, quarters for the men and their families, stores, warehouses, shops, canoe sheds, a smithy, icehouse, powder magazine, and stables. In addition, however, there was one large structure that was unique to Rainy Lake House: the building in which the North Men from the bleak, subarctic Athabasca department lodged during their short visit here. For good and colorful reasons, Athabasca House was famous throughout the fur country.

None of the Rainy Lake houses, it might be noted, were constructed in the familiar notched-corner style that we associate with the traditional American log cabin. Like most wooden houses in the *pays d'en haut*, they followed the French pattern of building called *poteaux-sur-sole*, or posts-in-the-sill. It was a type of construction that, although it originated in the French-Canadian colonies, derived from the ancient timber-and-plaster architecture of northern France.

To build a posts-in-the-sill house, you first mortised square uprights into a foundation frame of heavy logs. Then, into grooves in the uprights you slipped horizontal logs, one on top of the other, until the walls were as high as you wished them to be. The roof you made of small logs and covered it with cedar bark. You laid a floor of spruce poles, adzed flat on the upper side. Into the windows you fitted "panes" of deer parchment, scraped paper-thin. You built chimneys of stone and mud; and you plastered your whole house, inside and out, with clay and the white earth that, in most parts of the fur country, served as whitewash.

Fort buildings constructed in this manner were often of considerable size. The Great Hall at Fort Gibraltar, built by John McDonald of Garth at the Forks of the Red and Assiniboine Rivers, was 64 feet long and 30 wide; the man's quarters 34 by 28 feet; and the store 32 feet long. At Pembina, Henry himself was to build a storehouse 100 feet long and 20 feet wide.

Rainy Lake House was not only a commodious post, but it provided its two-score men and their Indian wives and families with comforts not often found in the *pays d'en haut*. Each room in the dwelling houses had its own fireplace and — the ultimate in wilderness luxury — was furnished with beds.

To support itself, in addition to meeting the insatiable demands of the North West Company's commissariat, the post had to keep very busy indeed. Every day, all winter long, the sawing crews went out to cut, square and haul timber. Houses and stables were raised, roofs covered with split shingles, floors laid. Hay was cut, fish seined by the ton, vast quantities of wild rice and maple sugar traded and stored. Barrels and shingles, canoes, snowshoes, dog and horse *traineaux*, wheelbarrows and traps were fashioned by men and women whose skills seemed equal to almost any task.

Besides all this, the fort must be kept clean and cleared of snow in the winter; the kitchen gardens and extensive potato, corn, oats and barley patches tended during the summer months; the livestock — cows, horses, hogs and sheep — looked after; immense reserves of firewood cut, hauled and split. And, since Rainy Lake was a trading post as well as a supply depot, the beaver must not be neglected; for M. Lacombe competed fiercely — although on the whole decently — for the fruits of the Indians' hunts.

At this busy post — which, incidentally, appears to have had plenty of time left over for dancing, holiday festivities, and the proliferation of métis offspring — Alexander Henry the Younger tarried only long enough to enjoy a glass or two with hard-drinking Peter Grant, dance with his people until daybreak, and sample the new potatoes from the post's famous garden.

On the day after his arrival — which happened to be a Sunday — he set all hands to repairing their canoes, and at noon they were off again.

8

THERE were two things that even the dourest of the Nor'-westers could, and did, grow lyrical about: one was the lovely Portage la Loche, and the other was the Rainy Lake River. Most beautiful in the North, by all accounts, Rainy Lake River reminded homesick travelers of the English parklands, with its "fine, rich, sloping banks of grass and luxuriant verdure interspersed with oak trees." It was the kind of wide, sweet-flowing stream that any canoeman could be happy on; and now its high-wooded shores echoed, with fine effect, the paddle songs of Henry's brigade.

Like all voyageurs, Henry's crews sang a great deal. They sang partly out of natural high spirits, partly because singing helped to while away tedious hours of paddling; and partly for the same reason that seamen sang their chanteys at the capstan and windlass — it helped, by some occult magic, to make the work easier.

The Canadian canoeman's *chansons à l'aviron,* for all their occasional delicate, haunting beauty, were work songs. The rhythms were those of the vermilion-tipped paddles, of backs bending in cadence, of the canoe's thrust at the end of each strong stroke. The words did not matter much — they were often meaningless, even to the singer.

The best-known and most beautiful of all voyageurs' songs, and by far the most popular with the men, was "*A la Claire Fontaine,*" which begins:

> *A la claire fontaine*
> *M'en allant promener,*
> *J'ai trouvé l'eau si belle*
> *Que je m'y suis baigné.*
> > *Il y a longtemps que je t'aime,*
> > *Jamais je ne t'oublierai.*

> At the clear fountain
> As I walked idly by,
> The beautiful water
> Said, Come bathe in me.

Long have I loved you,
Ne'er forgot will you be.

How does it happen that this lovely song was such a universal favorite with half-savage canoemen, and even with drivers of dogs and horses, throughout the Northwest? Where did it come from? To the first question we can only answer, perhaps: Who can explain the mysterious power of beauty? And to the second: Nobody knows, it is very old.

Most of the voyageurs' songs, in fact, were versions — often illiterate and garbled — of ancient Old World folk melodies. They ranged from pastoral ditties and tragic love songs to heroic ballads and even lullabies. "They were composed," Nicholas Garry, who heard them many times, explains, "during the old French times, representing scenes in France."

Their mere titles suggest both their antique origin and oddly incongruous subject matter: "The Lovely Lisette," "The First Day of May," "I Have Plucked the Lovely Rose," "The Dumb Shepherdess," "The Three Captains," "The Fair François," "Roll, My Ball!" And, more like what you'd expect a voyageur to sing: "My Birchbark Canoe" and "I'm Plenty Scared of Those Wolves!"

But it would be a mistake to think that the voyageur always sang so sweetly and innocently. The songs that have come down to us, we may be sure, are only the printable ones; and even they, perhaps, were more often parodied obscenely than sung in their pure form. Thus, most of the songs of Pierre Falcon, one of the most famous ballad writers of the *pays d'en haut*, have been lost, simply because they would not have looked very good in print. Another famous song writer was Willard Ferdinand Wentzel, a Clerk of the North West Company, whose talent as a musician "brightened the long dreary hours, and contributed to keep all cheerful around him." He too composed many ballads — "mostly obscene and unfit for publication."

Yet, the words mattered little, one way or the other; what really counted was the music. And, since music almost always sounds good over water, *"La Belle Lisette"* coming from a hundred throats across the dancing surface of Lac la Croix or Namakan must have sounded very fine indeed.

The voyageurs did no harmonizing, apparently; they simply sang in unison, led by the steersman, who sometimes carried the air alone, followed by the crew in chorus. A good voice, incidentally, was worth money to a voyageur. The canny bourgeois, recognizing that song, like liquor, spurred men to greater effort, were willing to pay for it. "Of such use is singing, in enabling men to work eighteen or nineteen hours a day through forests and across bays," wrote one diarist, "that a good singer has additional pay."

No one knows what songs Alexander Henry's men sang as they swept down "the most beautiful river of the North," but it is certain that they did sing, as all voyageurs by nature must. And so, singing and paddling, they passed an old Hudson's Bay Company post, ran the Long Sault, arrived at the entrance of the Lake of the Woods, and camped on a big island at its mouth. "A terrible storm during the night," Henry wrote.

9

Now the Northwest Road wound for seventy-five miles through an immense confusion of low, rocky islands — some so large as to be easily mistaken for the mainland — called the

Lake of the Woods. On one of these islands, in ancient French times, the Sioux had fallen on the camp of Father Auneau, killing him, nine voyageurs, and Vérendrye's son Jean Baptiste. Henry's men became silent as they passed this awesome spot on which no voyageur had ever since camped. A cloud of great, ungainly pelicans followed them as they hurried by.

They were now in that part of the lake shown on our maps as the Northwest Angle, a curious fragment of Minnesota completely detached from the rest of the state and seemingly surrounded on all sides by Canada. Ahead was the point where, after the American Revolution, it was decided that the boundary between the United States and the Dominion should leave the old canoe route and become a line running due west until it struck the Mississippi. Something that could never happen, as the Nor'westers — who knew their geography better than the statesmen — pointed out, since the Mississippi rises far south of such a line!

Progress down the lake was not without its annoyances, all meticulously noted in Henry's journal:

> We found a number of Indians who had made canoes and were all intoxicated with the liquor received for them. They were much inclined to be insolent, and talked about firing on us.

> The wind came on so strong as to oblige us to put ashore, where we passed the rest of the day drying our goods on L'Anse de Sable.

> The wind continued to blow all day, which kept us in our quarters. I caught one of the men stealing flour out of a bag, and another stealing sugar; these two rascals had formed a scheme to feast their women.

But troubles come to an end, and even a headwind dies down in time. Soon the brigade was cruising along under full sail, or creeping through narrow channels filled with beds of wild rice, or portaging occasionally between pondlike divisions of this mazy lake.

They met other brigades; this part of the Northwest Road was so well traveled that it was not unusual to see fifty or sixty canoes, all under sail perhaps, on their way to or from winter quarters. Often they made a *dégrade* or camped for the night together, or landed on a sandy beach to mend their craft which, because of the hot weather, needed frequent gumming. Then letters were given for delivery to friends below or above, and the news and gossip of the Northwest was exchanged.

Twenty-four Athabasca canoes, one learned, had passed on their way to Rainy Lake, the crews almost starved; they had eaten nothing for four days.

A young English lord named Selkirk, it was reported, had hatched a mad scheme for founding a colony on the Red River, of Scotch and Irish settlers.

So-and-so of the Swan River brigade had lost a year's wages for grog drinking; so-and-so of the English River department had been sent down to Montreal in irons for theft.

At Fort Vermilion everyone was laughing at a homesick bourgeois who had built himself a *cariole*, or sleigh, such as they had in Montreal; but when finished, it was much too large to be got through the door of the building in which it was made!

On the Red River, Henry learned, the mosquitoes were so bad that the horses had to be kept in leather tents with smudge fires.

A dwarf beaver, no bigger than a rat, had been caught at Le Pic; an albino one, with pink toenails and pink scales on its tail, had been taken at Chipewyan . . .

But such pleasant bits of gossip and rumor were not all that was exchanged at these accidental meetings of the brigades en route. The North Men — a naturally boastful and combative lot, particularly after a few drams of high wine — were just as quick to trade blows; and it was a rare encounter that did not end up with a few battles or, in the quaint idiom of one trader, with "the men dusting each other's jackets."

Sometimes, out of the boasts and arguments of rival crews camping together, grew a canoe race, like the one described by Duncan McGillivray. McGillivray's Saskatchewan brigade raced the Athabasca canoes for two whole days and nights without once putting ashore. When one of his men fell asleep and rolled out of his canoe, nobody would stop to save him until, at last, his own canoemates reluctantly turned back and fished him, more than half drowned, out of the water. Only after forty-eight hours of unremitting paddle work did the exhausted voyageurs decide to call it quits. "At length, being entirely overcome with labor and fatigue," McGillivray wrote in mixed admiration and disgust, "they mutually agreed to camp and cross the rest of the lake together."

Despite frequent stops to gum the canoes, Henry made good progress. Favored by fine weather and high water, he arrived at the Portage du Rat (near the modern towns of Keewatin and Kenora) and began his descent of the Rivière Winipic, the water of which he describes as "very high and rapid, and rather dangerous."

On this river he suffered his first loss of the outward voyage: one canoe, one man.

10

"The White River," the Nor'westers sometimes called the Rivière Winipic, and with good reason. Rapids, rips, chutes and falls interrupted its whole course of almost two hundred miles, giving its swift water a turgid milkiness that spelled danger, and often disaster, for the most skillful canoeman.

Henry plunged into difficulties almost at once. On the first day, he ran his canoe onto a rock and broke her bow in. On the next, he was lost until ten o'clock in a fog. When he finally got under way again, one of his men, impatient at the delays, decided to sault a rapids instead of carrying over the short portage. Henry describes the tragic outcome of this gamble:

> One of my canoes, to avoid the trouble of making this portage, passed down near the N. shore with a full load . . . She had not gone many yards when, by some mismanagement of the foreman, the current bore down her bow full upon the shore, against a rock, upon which the fellow, taking advantage of his situation, jumped, whilst the current whirled the canoe around. The steersman, finding himself within reach of the shore, jumped upon the rock with one of the midmen; the other midman, not being sufficiently active, remained in the canoe, which was instantly carried out and lost to view amongst the high waves.
>
> At length she appeared and stood perpendicular for a moment, when she sank down again, and I then perceived the man riding upon a bale of dry goods in the midst of the waves. We made every exertion to get near him, and did not cease calling out to him to take courage and not let

go his hold; but alas! he sank under a heavy swell, and when the bale arose, the man appeared no more . . .

The canoe we found flat upon the water, broken in many places. However, we hauled her ashore, and afterward collected as many *pièces* as we could find. The loss amounted to five bales merchandise, two bales new tobacco, one bale canal tobacco, one bale kettles, one bale balls, one bale shot, one case guns.

After this disaster, Henry made twenty-seven more portages on the Rivière Winipic, either carrying over or saulting around them, without mishap. On the tenth day after leaving Rainy Lake House, he arrived at another great establishment of the North West Company's. This was Bas de la Rivière, or the Down River Fort.

Bas de la Rivière was on the site of old Fort Maurepas, built by Vérendrye, which had been occupied by traders since 1734. Alexander Henry the Elder had passed it in 1775, noting the large village of Cree. Now his nephew observed that many of these Indians, with three generations of white blood in their veins, were as fair as the French inhabitants of Montreal — and some of the girls prettier.

Like Rainy Lake House, Bas de la Rivière was both a supply depot and a trading post. To it each spring came the long boats of the Red and Assiniboine rivers, carrying as much as a ton of pemmican apiece for distribution to the fur brigades and the northern departments. It too was a big, solidly built, and properly cared-for establishment.

"This trading post has more the air of a large and well-cultivated farm than a fur trader's factory," wrote the Nor'-wester Gabriel Franchère. "A neat and elegant mansion, built on a slight eminence and surrounded by barns, stables, storehouses, etc., and by fields of barley, peas, oats and potatoes, reminded us of the civilized countries which we had left so long ago." And Nicholas Garry noted: "The post is placed in a very beautiful situation and is surrounded by cultivated lands where they grow potatoes, wheat and vegetables. At the moment there are fifty women and children living here at the expense of the Company. This is a sort of resting place for the Athabasca canoes."

For Henry, however, it was merely a place to dry out his rain-drenched packs, repair his canoes, purchase a boat, and push on. Next morning he entered Lac Winipic. To reach the head of this immense body of water and the mouth of the Red River of the North, he must now weather a long point of land extending northward into the lake. It took a bit of navigating, and many a trader had come to grief in attempting the six-league traverse. Alexander Henry the Elder was one of them.

"Next day," the elder Henry wrote in his famous book, "we encountered a severe gale, from the dangers of which we escaped by making the island called Buffalo's Head; but not without the loss of a canoe and four men." And the younger Henry must have remembered his uncle's telling of this calamity, and rather vividly too, as he worked out into the open water of the bay; for he himself was having certain difficulties:

We stood out with the intention of making the traverse; but had not gone above a mile when suddenly the wind rose to a gale from the N., followed by a high swell. Before we could reach shore we had several sand banks to pass over, where it was almost too shallow for the craft to swim. This occasioned a short, tumbling sea which dashed over us, and before we could land our canoes were half full of water and all of us wet to the skin. After much trouble we got everything on shore, though one of my canoes was split asunder from one gunnel to the other.

So the routine threat of disaster was once more averted; and Henry, having successfully rounded land's end, headed south for the Red River. The remaining six leagues were not all easy going; but with the help of bailing kettles and the protection of a high, rocky lee shore, his scattered canoes finally ran to safety.

And now, for the first time on this long and hazardous march, the journal of Alexander Henry the Younger blooms with those small observations of men and nature that help to set it apart from the prosaic diaries of all other traders:

Our disaster of yesterday being no encouragement to defy the elements, we dried our things and I went duck hunting. I shot several and observed the tracks of moose, red deer and bears.

The beach was covered with grasshoppers, which formed one continuous line as far as the eye could reach; in some places they lay six to nine inches deep, and in a state of putrefaction, which occasioned a horrid stench.

I shot a pelican, of which there are plenty here . . . We found an abundance of sand cherries, which were of an excellent flavor.

The brigade arrived at a marshy vastness over which clouds of wild fowl, then as now, rose continuously from the reeds and high grass; and it passed the River of Death. Here, some years ago, the Cree on their way to Hudson Bay had foolishly left their old people and children to summer during their absence. When they returned, it was plain enough who had fallen on the helpless camp — for only the Sioux could have wreaked such cruel and complete destruction. Only the Sioux, it was said, ate their enemies.

Pausing at this melancholy spot on his 1801 trip, Henry must have wondered anxiously how the people waiting for him at Pembina had fared while he was away. For that summer was an uneasy one throughout the *pays d'en haut*.

II

EVERYWHERE, now, the tribes were picking up the scarlet threads of old hates. The Plain Cree, the Blackfoot, the Crow, the Big Belly and the Assiniboine — and, of course, the Sioux — were on the prod again. The great "peace of the pox" was drawing to an ominous close.

As far back as the elder Henry's time, traders had occasionally run into trouble with the Indians over real or imagined wrongs. Some were plundered at the portages and driven, empty-handed, back to Canada. A few in lonely outposts were murdered. Eventually the braves began to attack the stronger forts; and in 1780 they formed a great conspiracy to pillage every post and kill every white in the Northwest.

But the smallpox struck first. The Saulteur and Sioux caught the disease at about the same time — some said from wearing the clothes of infected traders they had murdered. Others laid it to the plains tribes, who had fled in terror from the scourge to the woods and mountains. Whatever its origin, it had swept like a grass fire through the whole country, destroying entire clans and wiping out a full third of the Indian population before it ran its course.

This general calamity had saved the traders for a while. But now the war bands were gathering strength again. Ancient resentments were boiling up. And the traders watched anxiously as one depredation after another was reported from every quarter of the Northwest. Worst, perhaps, was the news from the Saskatchewan. There the Fall Indians had attacked Eagle Hills fort. When the Nor'westers repelled the assault, killing their chief l'Homme au Calumet, they turned to the neighboring Hudson's Bay Company post — and with better success. All the Hudson's Bay people were butchered. Even the women and children, normally carried off as captives, were tortured and killed in the most inhuman way.

As Henry entered the mouth of the Red River and arrived at the Forks — where the city of Winnipeg now stands — another disturbing rumor reached him. On the Assiniboine and the Qu'Appelle the bull boats of the pemmican posts had been harassed and some of the men killed. Troubled by these reports, he sent his canoes down the Red River while he himself, with two men, took to horse and hurried overland to Pembina. At sunset on August 22, 1801, he reached his Pembina River post. To his great relief, he found his people and fifty-five Saulteur all unharmed.

IV

Pembina

HENRY's new post stood where the Pembina joins the Red River, at almost the exact geographical center of the continental wilderness. On the east bank of the Red River, the forest belt ended; on the west side, the buffalo plains began. So the post was advantageously situated. It had plenty of wood for the fireplaces. It would never be without water. And it could depend on the plains, waving with high, rich grass, for an inexhaustible supply of meat.

Henry had picked this site with great care — far enough up the river to be near the beaver works, yet not so far up as to lay himself open to destruction by the Sioux. While he was at the Grand Portage, his second in command, Michel Langlois, had been busy with a gang of voyageurs, putting up the buildings and stockade of the new post. And here, in the spring of 1801, we find him settled in his headquarters and dispatching men to his outposts.

To Grandes Fourches, about seventy-five miles upriver, he sends John Cameron, a good man, with twenty-five packs of trade goods. Langlois with five men goes off to the Hair Hills, hauling his baggage in five small carts. Demarais and five voyageurs take canoes to Rivière aux Gratias, thirty miles downriver.

Henry wastes no time; he cannot afford to. Competitors are appearing from all quarters. Only two weeks after his own arrival, Thomas Miller, of the Hudson's Bay Company, shows up with eight Orkney men from Albany Factory, and begins to build within gunshot. Lower down the river, sixteen men of the XY Company start not one but two posts.

"None of them dare build above me," Henry remarks, "for fear of the Sioux." Yet, he does not take his rivals lightly. The struggle with the Hudson's Bay Company was everywhere becoming serious. Up to this time, the "North West Bullies" had got all the best of occasional clashes in the bush. But now the giant was bestirring himself. The "English" were thrusting deeper and deeper into the beaver lands. Their flag — the Union Jack with the letters H.B.C. on it, standing, some said, for "Here Before Christ" — was flying over posts on the Saskatchewan and the Assiniboine. Competition was growing bitter. Before long, on the prairies, at the Forks, at isolated posts, it would explode into open, bloody warfare.

Yet, you had to respect the English. You could almost be friendly with them. In a pinch, you could enclose your fort with theirs in a common stockade for defense against an even graver threat.

The XY people were another kettle of fish. The Nor'-westers regarded them as bungling interlopers — or, worse

yet, as renegades — and gave them the contemptuous tag of
"the Potties." They fought the Potties with glee, and watched
them starve — as seemed to be their habit — without pity.
Still, there was a lot of money behind the Potties; and with
Alexander Mackenzie at their head, they would have to be
reckoned with some day. So Henry took no chances. He had
a tower built, facing the XY forts, and set two men to keep
watch on the enemy.

His next concern was to finish the fort that Langlois was
building. It was not a very large fort. Compared with some
of the North West Company's great establishments — walled
towns, really, with brass cannon gleaming from the bastions —
it was but a mean and comfortless little post. Still, it provided
the essentials — including security against attack by as many,
Henry estimated, as 200 Sioux. It would serve.

When everything was finished — dwelling houses, built of
squared logs and properly plastered and whitewashed inside
and out; a storehouse 100 feet long and 20 wide; stables for
the horses; a shop or Indian Hall, where the trading would be
conducted — Henry ran the Union Jack up the flagpole and
gave his men a feast of rum and sugar to celebrate completion
of the work. Then, taking another look at the stockade Langlois had erected, he decided it was too flimsy. He ordered it
torn down and replaced by a stout new one of oak piquets,
with a heavy gate and two bastions. Later he added a blockhouse.

Henry dug a cellar under the shop, and in it placed his
stocks of high wine and gunpowder. He stowed his trade
goods and provisions in the store, and was ready for business.
To this post he gave the name of Pembina. For the next seven
years, it was to be his world.

2

DURING those seven years, Henry was preoccupied with every duty, care and worry — and there were hundreds of them — that fell to a trader's lot. But above all, the fierce and relentless scramble for beaver. Except for the specialized "pemmican posts" farther west, the success of any North West Company establishment was measured by the number of packs of beaver turned in to headquarters at the end of the season. Other animals — otter, marten, mink, fox, raccoon, bear, wolf, even muskrat — were valued for their pelts; but beaver was the real business of the posts, and everything else was incidental. In this competition Pembina could not hope to cope with the big posts in, for example, the rich Athabasca country. But there was still plenty of beaver in the nearby Hair Hills, and Henry omitted nothing short of arson and murder to secure a fair share of the precious pelts.

For the most part, he had to depend on his Indians. Next to the post was a village of Saulteur — a branch of the Chippewa — who hunted beaver for Henry year after year. Smaller bands of Indians turned in their hunts to the outposts manned by Langlois, Cameron, Demarais, and others. Sometimes a few roving Cree would show up at Pembina with a pack or two. And at regular intervals during the winter, Henry made long, hard, and sometimes dangerous trips to the camps of the beaver hunters, and snatched skins away before the English or the Potties could get them. These trips were called *dérouines*.

The hunters took to the beaver grounds in October. This was the month when the fur began to grow longer, denser and

richer in color. By the first of November, it was "prime" —
the skin thin, white and papery; the fur deep, silky, and almost
black. And from then until late in February, the sleepy
beaver, holed up in his snug underwater house, could expect
the terror to strike at any moment. All over the Northwest,
the beaver killers would be out with their traps and steel
"trenches," hacking through the thick frozen walls of his
house, cutting his dam, draining his pond, and slaying the be-
wildered little animal with axes as he fled from the violence of
men and dogs that had struck his quiet forest lake.

It was a hard and bloody business, but beaver must be had
for the fine hats of the *beau monde*, and the slaughter was
enormous. A party of two or three industrious hunters might
kill as many as two hundred in a single season; and we read in
Duncan McGillivray's Saskatchewan journal, "All the men
have returned from the meadows; they have killed in all about
2000 beaver." The annual returns from the posts of the North
West Company alone would be near 80,000 made beaver.

At Pembina the killing was on a rather modest scale. During
the best years of the post, when Henry had six or seven outposts contributing, the total returns were about 1800 skins.

Trading with the Indians for beaver was all done on credit.
Usually, the hunter was given an outfit of ammunition, weapons, clothing, and other necessities at the start of the season.
This was his debt, which he solemnly promised to pay off with
the returns of his hunt. It was reckoned in terms of beaver
skins or "*plus*," the universal currency of the *pays d'en haut*,
just as the "buck" was the coin of the American trading posts.

Thus, a large keg of liquor was worth 30 beaver skins or
"plews," as the Nor'westers, and after them the Americans,
spelled and pronounced it. A long gun was valued at 14 plews,

a three-point blanket at 6, an ax at 2, a fathom of Brazil tobacco at 3, a scalping knife at a single plew. It was not true, incidentally, that a trade gun was worth a pile of skins equal to its height — hence the unusually long barrels. Nor that these guns were so poorly made that they often burst at the first discharge — a common enough occurrence, certainly, but due less to faulty manufacture than to the Indians' optimistic overloading of their pieces. For all the trader's readiness to cheat, his goods were well made and of sound material.

3

LIKE most business with the Indians, trading called for a good deal of ceremony and palaver. When a band of hunters approached a prairie fort, it was customary for the chiefs to send a few young men ahead to announce its arrival. These heralds received some trifling presents and enough vermilion to paint the faces of the whole band. In full dress, the main body then rode up to the fort. Before the gate they pulled up their horses with a shout and fired off their guns. The traders replied by hoisting the flag and returning the salute.

The Indians were then admitted to the fort — but not before checking their weapons at the gate. In the Great Hall they were treated to a few drams of rum and a little tobacco. The pipe went round, while the chiefs related the news with great deliberation and ceremony. The rum cup also went round, and gradually the warriors shed their customary taciturnity. The Great Hall became a bedlam.

While their masters were observing these rites, the women were busy putting up the lodges outside the stockade. This

work completed, the whole band received a present of free
rum, "proportioned to the nation and the quality of their
chiefs." Drinks were on the house for twenty-four hours, in
which time the Indians usually succeeded in putting themselves completely under. When they had recovered from their
boisson, as the whites called these drinking bouts, the trading
began.

The giving of presents was a feature of trading that must
never be neglected. In addition to free liquor, the gifts might
consist of only a little tobacco and paint; or they might add
up to a list as long as the Nor'wester Larocque's, who once
passed out to the Crow: 2 large and 2 small axes, 8 ivory
combs, 10 wampum shells, 8 firesteels and flints, 4 cassettes, 6
masses of blue beads and a pound and a half of blue Canton
beads, 4 fathoms of Brazil tobacco, 2 pounds of vermilion, 8
dozen rings, 4 papers of colored glasses, 4 dozen awls, and
1000 rounds of ammunition.

Alexander Henry kept his generosity well within bounds.
He tells us that on one occasion:

> I gave out to the Indians their necessaries for debts to the
> amount of 20 skins each, and an assortment of small ar-
> ticles gratis — such as one scalper, two folders, and four
> flints apiece for the men, and to the women two awls, three
> needles, one skein of net thread, one fire steel, a little ver-
> milion and a fathom of tobacco.

The goods actually traded for pelts were more substantial.
They included guns, powder and balls, flints and firesteels,
point blankets, blue and scarlet cloth, Manchester goods
(striped cottons, dimities, janes, fustians, shawls, handker-
chiefs), nets, twine, thread, brass kettles, hunting and scalping
knives, silver crosses, beads, traps, axes, paint . . . in addition,

of course, to the indispensable rum and tobacco. When they ran out of goods *en dérouine,* traders were known to barter the buttons off their own coats.

4

WITH the onset of winter, trading would begin in earnest at Pembina. Every fall, Henry sent his hunters into the prairie to search for the Cree, the Assiniboine and the Saulteur and persuade them to come to his fort. He established flying posts in the Hair Hills — and suffered the bourgeois' usual frustrations and annoyances with his subalterns:

> I found it necessary to alter the arrangement of the people at the hills. None would remain under the command of Lagasse, nor do I think him a fit person to have property in charge. I therefore sent Hamel to take charge, desiring Lagasse to return to this place. I was also obliged to leave here two men who came with me to reinforce the mountain post.

Hardly less annoying were the Indians' drinking bouts; the killing and maiming that went with them; the incessant begging for liquor and presents; the offer of wives by grasping chiefs; and even threats by his own Indians and their wily old leader, Tabashaw:

> The Indians threatened to destroy us — Tabashaw at the head and Chamanau second in command. But I soon convinced them that it would prove a tough bone for them to gnaw. They then made a merit of necessity, and the ringleaders informed against the others; but I knew them too well to allow them to impose on me.

Almost as disturbing were the incessant rumors of war between the tribes. At one time Henry learned that the Saulteur were getting ready to attack the Sioux. Tobacco was passing — a preliminary to organized warfare. A Saulteur raiding party was gathering at the Bois Percé camp grounds. Demarais, in from his outpost in the Hair Hills, confirmed this: he himself had seen their tents, he told Henry. The Cree and Assiniboine were going to join them. And where was the rendezvous to be? At Demarais' post!

Henry could understand the old man's obvious anxiety. To permit a war party to gather at your fort was to ask for trouble, possibly pillage, even murder. Henry considered whom he might spare to reinforce poor Demarais in his lonely little post, at least until the danger was over. But he could think of no one. He shrugged: Demarais would have to take his chances alone. It was the way things went in the *pays d'en haut*. It was the business of trading.

5

PART of that business was an occasional trip to your outposts. One such visit "to see how Langlois was coming along with his Indians," almost finished Alexander Henry the Younger's career as a fur trader. On the first night out, his horse wandered off. Henry roused his two companions and sent them off across the frozen prairie in search of it:

> They were gone about an hour when they returned to tell me that they had seen him running full speed southward. They brought the twisted and broken cords with which he had been tied. This was a sad disappointment. I re-

solved to wait no longer, so I cut up the leather of my saddle, wrapped it upon my feet as best I could, and cut off the skirt of my capot to serve me as mitts. Wrapping our blankets around us, we set off at ten o'clock.

The men, including Henry himself, were already exhausted by three days of travel in the stabbing cold, with very little in their stomachs, and hardly any sleep. The journal continues:

> The weather was cruelly cold, with a strong wind. I killed a fat swan flying, and one of my men, being determined to eat it, took it up on his back. At two o'clock we crossed the Panbian river . . . One of my men complained of being knocked-up and wished me to stop for the night, but we were then some distance from the Red River and choking with thirst. I encouraged him to push on and throw away the swan, but he would not consent to part with it.

> Our shoes were entirely worn out, and we had no more leather to put under the soles. The short pointed grass annoyed us very much as we crawled along in great misery pain . . . It is not more than two inches high, about the thickness of an awl, and fully as sharp; it even pierces strong leather and socks, and when it pierces the skin the point breaks off and remains in the flesh.

At this point Henry began to wonder if they would ever make it to Langlois' post. But a terrible thirst, stronger than even their weariness, drove them on. It was after dark when they reached the Red River and plunged their faces into its icy water.

> We determined to go along the beach in search of the buildings. The walking was very ugly and tedious for persons whose feet were stuck full of this pointed grass . . .

After walking for hours, I imagined we were about opposite to where I had desired Langlois to build.

So they sat down and shouted hoarsely into the darkness.
Nobody answered. Henry began to suspect that perhaps
Langlois had been lured by the Indians to Rivière aux Gratias,
where they had wanted him to build his post. Well, in the
morning they would go on to the Rivière aux Gratias, he told
his men. When they protested that they could not go on without shoes, he answered that they would cut up their blankets
and make some. Without blankets, they would freeze, of
course; but they would probably perish anyhow, he reasoned,
unless they went on and found Langlois' post. They made
camp. Henry sat down on the riverbank and stared at the
turbid water.

The night was dark and cloudy, but I saw a small birch
canoe drifting near by; we hauled her up and emptied the
water, but found her in too bad a condition to be of any
service. With one of my men I began to look for a place
to sleep, whilst our fatigued companion lay stretched out
on the beach, declaring he did not care to live.

Suddenly he said in a faint voice that he heard some noise,
but was not certain whence it proceeded. We called again,
but no answer. I went a few paces up river when, looking
steadily across, I thought I saw a glimmer among the large
elms. I rubbed my eyes and took a second look, when I
was convinced it was really a light. I bellowed out lustily,
and was immediately answered by one of Langlois' men.

Henry was surrounded at once by every Canadian and Indian at the post, anxious to know how the bourgeois had
escaped the Sioux; for everyone, they supposed, had long since
been killed. Henry assured them that he was still alive —

although in rather poor shape at the moment. Then he inquired about the affairs of the post. They were, Langlois said, going tolerably well.

With that they left him in quiet, to pick the spiny grass blades out of his feet.

6

HENRY's woes continued to be complicated by the skulduggery of the Potties and the disloyalty of his own hunters. Pampered and encouraged by Crebassa, the XY trader, the Saulteur had become so insolent and demanding that he was never free from worry that they would leave him *en masse*. He summed up his troubles in his journal:

> Every man who had killed a few skins was considered a chief and treated accordingly. There was scarcely a common buck to be seen; all wore scarlet coats, had large kegs and flasks, and nothing was purchased by them but silverwork, strouds and blankets.

If Henry attempted to punish his hunters for their insolence, they fled to the Potties, who "were ready to approve their scoundrelly behavior and encourage them in mischief, even offering them protection." Each year the situation worsened, the Potties striving more and more to subvert Henry's Indians and get their pelts; and Henry, it is to be feared, became less and less scrupulous about how he struck back. He was not even above fighting with the Indian women — although with a certain hurt to his dignity — to obtain a few packs of beaver that the XY traders had already paid for:

> I went to the upper Tongue river to meet a band of Indians returning from hunting beaver, and fought several

battles with the women to get their furs from them. It was the most disagreeable dérouine I ever made; however, I got all they had, about a pack of good furs; but I was vexed at having been obliged to fight with the women.

Not infrequently violence broke out between him and his "neighbors." Once, having left Pierre Bonga in charge of the fort during a trip to his outposts, he returned to learn that the Potties had threatened to kill the Negro. Threats against his own life were so commonplace that he wrote them off in his journal with a few lines of comment:

Grande Gueule and myself had a serious dispute; he wanted to give his furs to the XY, which I prevented, at the risk of my life; he was advised by them to kill me.

When his Indians deserted to the XY camp and refused to pay up their debts, Henry resorted to the only law known in the *pays d'en haut*, the law of seizure by violence:

I took a mare from an XY Indian in payment of a debt. This affair came near being attended with serious consequences, as the fellow was a known villain and a chief of the XY making. I some time ago gave him a cruel beating, and bunged up his eyes so that he could not see for several days. He has ever since been bent on revenge, although he richly deserved the ill usage I gave him, having attempted to stab me with my own knife.

"Our men and the XY men quarreling and fighting," Henry wrote, almost parenthetically, on one occasion; a wearied acknowledgment of a situation that had long since become chronic. But some day they would carry things too far: stabbing a man with his own knife indeed! He was troubled and concerned about his men in the outposts, but he himself refused to be cowed. He strengthened his stockade, built a blockhouse of oak, and mounted a cohorn — a small hand mortar for throwing grenades and grapeshot — on his main bastion. After that, he could only wait and meet each separate threat resolutely but, if possible, without bloodshed.

> This would certainly have caused a critical situation, as those fellows are all so connected that to injure one is to injure the whole. Of this I was well aware, and always avoided pushing matters to extremities, at the same time not allowing myself to be imposed upon.

Tabashaw was still his greatest problem, and at the root of much of the trouble. He was a mean old Indian, without a doubt, and a menace to his own people, as well as to the whites:

> Indians drinking at the fort. Tabashaw stabbed a near relation of his own, Missistaygouine, in six different places in the breast and sides; every stab went up to the handle. The poor fellow lingered an hour and died.

Stirred up by their vindictive old chief, the Indians at all the outposts grew sullen and hostile, and at Pembina itself they threatened to attack openly:

> Indians very troublesome, threatening to level my fort to the ground, and Tabashaw breeding mischief. I had two narrow escapes from being stabbed by him, once in the hall, and soon afterward in the shop. I perceived they were bent on murdering some of us and then pillaging. I therefore desired all hands to keep on their guard and knock down the first Indian who should be insolent . . . I quarreled with Little Shell and dragged him out of the fort by the hair.

Next day, Tabashaw fired on Henry's people at the Rat River outpost. Soon afterwards, one of his men was shot in the thigh by an Indian bullet. Then Henry himself was twice fired at by Grande Gueule, both misses. And so went the war with the Potties and their Indian allies, a war that degraded the traders, debauched the natives, and promised the extermination of everyone at Pembina.

7

YET Henry always found time, somehow, to record in his journal the small events that formed the quiet background to all this strife and violence. Nothing was ever too trivial to escape his eye or arouse his curiosity, or too familiar to present some new facet of interest. Thus, the turns of the prairie year are always noted in the big book with the rawhide covers, as if each season were a fresh and vaguely marvelous experience. Winter comes to his first Red River post:

> No noise is heard but that of swans and geese screaming, as they fly on their way to warmer climates . . . Wolves are very numerous; they go in large droves, and keep up a terrible howling, day and night . . . The buffaloes are moving southward in one body . . . It is very cold; the tops of the trees and willows are covered with frimas . . .

The bucks, he observes, are lean and poor, having finished rutting, while the does are fat. With the first bite of cold, he is invaded by mice:

> We are plagued by great numbers of mice, which destroy almost everything but metals; our strouds and blankets are nearly all damaged, and they even carry off our beads. At night we see them running in droves over the floors; they are not shy in the least. They often wake us by scampering over our faces and playing on our beds . . .

Spring returns, and he puts down, like touches of gay color, the familiar signs of winter's retreat:

> Smoke is arising in every direction; this is caused by Indians returning from their hunts . . . Buffaloes are now mostly with calves of the spring . . . The raccoons are coming out of their winter quarters in the daytime, although they retire to their hollow trees at night . . . Fine warm weather. I made up my packs . . . Frogs begin to croak . . . Pigeons are flying north in great numbers . . . I also saw a swan.

He records the floods of spring — great masses of ice, driven by a raging crest, tumbling and tossing with thunderous reports. And their awesome aftermath, the thousands of dead buffalo:

> The river clear of ice, but drowned buffalo continue to drift by in entire herds . . . It is really astonishing what vast numbers have perished; they formed one continuous line in the current for two days and two nights.

Henry had a sharp eye for detail; he would not write, "The women gathered cranberries today," but, "Women collecting quantities of cranberries, which grow plentifully among the cypress and pine trees, where the soil is sandy and covered with light moss; they are of the small kind." And so, his account of the sometimes exceedingly strange world in which he lived is always explicit and circumstantial:

> At daybreak I was awakened by the bellowing of the buffaloes. I got up and was astonished when I climbed into the S. W. bastion. On my right the plains were black and appeared as if in motion, S. to N. Opposite the fort the ice was covered; and on my left, to the utmost extent of the reach below us, the river was covered with buffalo moving northward . . . I had seen almost incredible num-

bers of buffalo in the fall, but nothing in comparison with
what I now beheld . . . All hands soon attacked them with
a tremendous running fire, which put them to a quicker
pace, but had no effect in altering their course. The first
roads beaten in the snow were followed by those in the
rear.

The strange ways of these great animals fascinated him;
and his sense of wonder glows through such passages as this
one:

It is surprising how sagacious these animals are. When in
the least alarmed they will smell the track of even a single
person in the grass, and run away in a contrary direction.
I have seen large herds, walking very slowly to pasture, and
feeding as they went, come to a place where some person
had passed on foot, when they would instantly stop, smell
the ground, draw back a few paces, bellow, and tear up
the earth with their horns. Sometimes the whole herd
would range along the route, keeping up a terrible noise,
until one of them would be hardy enough to jump over,
when they would all follow.

Now and then he exhibits a rough sympathy for the dumb
sharers of his lonely life: his dying dog, the fine mount, of
which he is so proud; a buffalo calf bereft of its mother, that
follows him into the fort. And there is a wry Franciscan touch
in his concern for the winter comfort of his pet bear:

My tame bear making a hole, apparently desirous of taking
up his winter quarters. I got a place made for him, but he
did not like it; although snug and warm, he preferred making a place for himself.

There is a strange merging of his savage and civilized world
in the seasonal attraction of the fort dogs for the prairie
wolves:

We had a bitch in heat; she was very troublesome, and the
dogs made a terrible noise on her account, day and night.
I drove them all to the plains; a band of wolves got scent
of the bitch, and a furious battle ensued, in which one of
our dogs was torn to pieces. This often happens at this
season, when the wolves are copulating and our dogs get
among them. The female wolves prefer our dogs to their
own species, and daily come near the fort to entice the
dogs . . . Some of my men have amused themselves by
watching their motions in the act of copulating; rushing
upon them with an ax or club, when the dog, apprehend-
ing no danger, would remain quiet, and the wolf, unable to
run off, would be dispatched.

All through the Red River journal, like mortar between
building stones, thousands of terse notes cement together the
longer passages:

May 15th. Indians sober. I began to sow garden seed.
Joseph Cyr deserted under pretense of going to Portage la
Prairie. Men bringing home calves daily . . . *18th*. We
take plenty of sturgeon, Indians tormenting me for liquor
gratis . . . *20th*. Indians performing their grand medicine,
as usual in the spring . . . *21st*. A small canoe arrived
from Portage la Prairie, bringing nearly a bushel of potato
seed, some ammunition, tobacco, etc. Made the packs,
began the pemmican, and planted my potatoes. Mr.
Cameron arrived from Grandes Fourches . . .

Along with the routine of drunken brawls, trading, hunting,
dérouines, the incessant struggle with the Potties, and an occasional Indian scare — *"Aux armes! Aux armes! Voilà les gens
du large! Voilà les Sioux!* — the journal faithfully records
the placid flow of domestic life at Pembina:

Swarms of grasshoppers have destroyed the greater part of my kitchen garden — onions, cabbages, melons, cucumbers, carrots, parsnips and beets.

My hen began to lay again, all her chicks being now well grown. Men hoeing potatoes and corn.

Poires now ripening; raspberries ripe and in great abundance.

Extraordinary number of wild pigeons; I never saw so many before.

Engaged my men, settled their accounts, and gave them a treat of high wine; they were soon merry, then quarreled and fought. I saw five battles at the same moment, and soon after they all had bloody noses, bruised faces, black eyes, and torn clothes.

My hen having laid twelve eggs, and appearing inclined to set, I put them under her.

Two men in a small canoe arrived from Portage la Prairie with two kegs of grease and a cat for *les souris*.

Of my men, some are making wheels, others carts, others sawing boards and squaring timber; the smith is making nails, others sturgeon nets; some are smoking tongues; the most active and capable are gone with the Indians to hunt beaver and take care of the furs.

I gathered my cucumbers and made a nine-gallon keg of pickles, having plenty of vinegar from maple sap.

Out of 12 eggs my hen hatched 11 chickens.

But at times the uneventful drift of days is broken by small dramas of life and death, of fear and hatred and despair — even of a dark and pitiful kind of love — all of which Henry records with dutiful care:

Pierre Bonga's wife was delivered of a daughter — the first fruit of this fort and a very black one.

Oct. 6th. Two men returned with the body of Mrs. Cameron, who died yesterday at the Grand Passage. *9th.* We buried the corpse.

Charles Hesse cut an ugly gash in his woman's head with a cutlass this morning, through jealousy.

Lagasse arrived from Rivière aux Liards with news of Mr. Cameron's death; he expired on the 3rd. ist. at 7 P.M. As he was sitting on a stool, he fell on his face to the floor, and died instantly, without uttering one word . . . On the 8th. I dispatched three men with a train and six dogs for the corpse . . . 16th. Having got a coffin made, we buried Mr. Cameron alongside his deceased wife, attended by all the men, women and children of the fort. This was a melancholy day for all of us. He was a good-natured, inoffensive, zealous and sober young man.

My blacksmith's woman ran away with Charlo.

One of my men having beaten his woman, she went in the woods with a piece of rope and attempted to hang herself . . . Instances of this sort are not uncommon among the Saulteur women. An old woman belonging to Chamard, one of my men at Portage la Prairie, last winter in a fit of despair hung herself in the woods and was found the next day dead and stiff. This old woman had lost two grown daughters within a short time; she lamented them sadly, and one day, having quarreled with her old man and been beaten, she put an end to her troubles. I have known on this river several women who hanged themselves, having lost their husbands and been ill-used by their relations.

It is only rarely that the journal of Alexander Henry the Younger tells us anything about its author, and then inad-

vertently; but this short chronicle of a poor old Indian
woman's grief, we may suspect, is one of those times.

8

EXCEPT for John Cameron, Henry lost none of his men from
mortal illness; but death hung like a pack of wolves about
the Indian camp. Next to rum, tuberculosis was the chief
killer. It carried off one of Henry's ablest hunters and most
of his family:

> Charlo died early this morning. Since last August his two
> eldest daughters, two sons, their mother, and now their
> father have died. The complaint was a cough, which soon
> killed them. They were all in good health when I arrived
> at the Forks last summer.

The Canadians, however, fell victim to a remarkable variety
of complaints; and Henry's treatment of them was nothing if
not energetic. Here we have him doctoring one of his men
who was very ill with a colic:

> I gave him some essence of peppermint, but it did not cure
> him; soon after gave him some sweet oil, which he threw
> up; he was in great pain. I gave him a dose of jalap, which
> he soon threw up, and his pain increased. I then gave him
> an extraordinary dose of Glauber's salts, which after some
> time took its course, but did not appear to relieve him
> much.

The sick man, he reported next day, was finally relieved
by an emetic which "operated very well." No less strenuous
was his method of dealing with wounds:

> One of my men split his thumb with an ax in a shocking
> manner and, having neglected it, the wound was in a sad

condition. I washed it with sal ammoniac until it bled, when the poor fellow was dancing with pain and swore he would rather have it cut off.

And he had a specific for all the various kinds of dermatitis that a trader's diet brought on:

> Several men are plagued with a breaking out upon the skin, attended with intolerable itching. I gave them high wine and gunpowder to rub themselves with, which appeared to ease them and dry up the sores.

Pembina, like all other forts, was supplied with a medicine chest, a few basic surgical instruments, and a book of instructions; and with these Henry treated everything from chilblains to pneumonia. He had at his patients with Turlington's Balsam — the sovereign remedy of the fur trade — or opodeldoc; and sometimes, for good measure, he bled them — an operation, he says, that the Indian women enjoyed greatly. He also gave them vomits, and if the vomit didn't work, he gave them a purge. It was a rough and ready pharmaceutics, but it served — perhaps only because a French-Canadian voyageur was a hard man to kill.

Those who were seriously and chronically ill went down to the Grand Portage in the spring, to be treated by the Concern's doctor — in Henry's time a man in his early twenties named John McLoughlin, who was to become famous in American history as "the Father of Oregon." But until the communications were open, all at Pembina rested their simple trust in "Doctor Henry."

He was not the sort of man who would enjoy doctoring a lot of ailing Canadians and Indians. But there is no evidence in his journal that he ever shirked his duties as physician, surgeon, nurse, and — if it came to that — undertaker. On the contrary, he seems to have been a patient and resourceful man with the sick and injured.

> I passed a tedious day among the sick and lame . . . I have always some invalid in the fort.

A kind of wry compassion is mixed with irksomeness when he writes this of his little family.

V

Rum, Women and Rations

LIKE all traders' journals, that of Alexander Henry the Younger is a record of the systematic debauchery of the Indian tribes with alcohol. For the rum of the fur trade was not just something to barter — like blankets, guns and trinkets — for beaver. It was a deliberate means of reducing the natives to a state of groveling dependence. Whole tribes were encouraged to drink themselves to death. It was good for business.

This had not always been the case. In the French days, the Church had done her best to save the red heathen from her own children. She went so far as to excommunicate traders who sold rum to the Indians. But the traders found an easy way around the regulations: instead of selling rum, they simply gave it away. And when, under British rule, all restrictions were removed, the custom of giving rum as a present continued to be observed by both the Nor'westers and the Hudson's Bay Company. Free rum was everywhere a set preliminary to trading.

Traders' rum, incidentally, was not really rum at all. It was a concentrated form of alcohol, generally called high wine, which was carried in nine-gallon kegs and diluted with water just before drinking. The amount of dilution depended on the experience of the Indians. The tribes least accustomed to liquor were satisfied with a weak mixture; the more seasoned drinkers demanded something stronger. So three grades of rum were in common use. If you were a trader among the distant Blackfoot, you poured four or five quarts of high wine into a nine-gallon keg and filled it up with water to make "Blackfoot rum," the weakest of all. For the Cree and the Assiniboine, you used six quarts of high wine; for the Saulteur, veteran topers, eight or nine.

Whatever the mixture, it had a devastating effect on the Indians who drank it. As they themselves were aware, whole nations were rapidly foundering in the flood of traders' grog. Yet they were helpless to refrain from the deadly "frolics" that were steadily turning good warriors and hunters into sodden hangers-on about the posts. They were never able to take it or leave it alone.

Bored traders carefully reported each drinking bout, or *boisson*, in their journals, with an account of the dead and maimed. It was part of the business record. Thus Henry:

> Indians having asked for liquor, and promised to decamp and hunt well all summer, I gave them some. Grande Gueule stabbed Capot Rouge, Le Boeuf stabbed his young wife in the arm, Little Shell almost beat his old mother's

brains out with a club, and there was terrible fighting among them. I sowed garden seeds.

The orgies sometimes continued for days, while the traders waited patiently for the drinking to end and the trading to begin:

> Men and women have been drinking a match for three days and nights, during which it has been drink, fight — drink, fight — drink and fight again — guns, axes, and knives their weapons — very disagreeable.

If drinking led to fighting, fighting bred murder with such regularity that the traders hardly bothered to mention it:

> About ten days ago another Saulteur was murdered by his wife, who put the muzzle of his gun in his mouth and blew the back part of his head away. They were a young couple, with a boy about a year old; she had the handsomest face of all the women on this river, and he was a good, honest young fellow called La Biche. Murders among these people are so frequent that we pay little attention to them. Their only excuse for such outrages is that they are drunk.

In a hundred fort journals, the dreary record is the same. To some of the traders it was distasteful; to all, in a way, it was disturbing. For, if almost invariably the *boisson* led to mayhem, murder, rape and fires that burned down whole Indian camps, the traders themselves were not free from danger.

Few in Henry's time had forgotten Eagle Hills. At Eagle Hills Fort, on Battle River, a large band of drunken Cree had demanded liquor to prolong an already murderous drinking match. The terrified traders gave it to them — well-laced with laudanum. This was a common means of quieting troublesome Indians. Twenty drops in a glass of rum was usually effective as a Mickey Finn, although Henry tells of one stalwart buck who remained awake — and belligerent — after absorbing a hundred and twenty. This time, however, the Eagle Hills traders overdid it. Three of the Cree died. The others, suddenly sober, stabbed ten whites and half-breeds to death, then set out to massacre all the traders they could find.

Haunted by such chilling memories, few traders could write about the grim aftermaths of Indian frolics with anything like compassion. And Alexander Henry was the exception when he made this stark entry in his journal:

> L'Hiver stabbed Mishewashence to the heart three times and killed him instantly . . . We buried the murdered man, who left a widow and five helpless orphans, having no relations on the river. The behavior of the youngest was really piteous while we were burying the body; they called upon their deceased father not to leave them, but to return to their tent, and tried to prevent the men from covering the corpse with earth, screaming in a terrible manner; the mother was obliged to take them away.

But a Nor'wester's eyes were seldom dimmed by tears of pity; and Duncan McGillivray expressed a more typical viewpoint when he described the rum traffic in these cold and practical terms: "The love of rum is their first inducement to industry; they endure every hardship and fatigue to procure a skinful of this delicious beverage, and when a nation becomes addicted to drinking, there is a strong presumption that they will become excellent hunters." The Cree, he added, had just sold their lodges and most of their horses for a little firewater.

Of all the Nor'westers, only David Thompson saw anything immoral in the general policy of debasing the tribes with rum. He refused to give or sell liquor to the Indians, or even to serve it to his own men. For a few years, at least, he actually succeeded in keeping the nations of southern British Columbia, Washington and Idaho free from the deadly curse of the "delicious beverage."

As for the others, they contributed generously to the building fund of St. Gabriel's Street Church in Montreal. And they frowned on the Americans "who sell the Indians a spirit called whiskey, which is so poisonous as to produce paralytic affections and a long history of general disorders" — in the meantime, of course, flooding the *pays d'en haut* with prodigious quantities of their own benign mixture of high wine and pure spring water.

How prodigious the quantities really were is indicated by the statistics. In a single year, 60,000 gallons of high wine were sent into the *pays d'en haut* — the equivalent of half a million gallons of Blackfoot rum.

But not all of this vast consumption, it must be added, was accounted for by the Indians. The Canadians themselves relished a dram whenever they could get it. And when they could get it, incidentally, they behaved no better than the natives. None of the *boissons* described by Henry surpassed the bestiality and depravity of his own voyageurs' drinking matches.

"Of all the people in the world," Daniel Harmon summed it up, "I think the Canadians, when drunk, are the most disagreeable." Henry agreed with him: "My hunters and other men have been drinking and rioting since yesterday. They make more damned noise and trouble than a hundred Blackfeet."

The occasions for getting drunk, it is true, were not many in the *pays d'en haut*. Chief among them were the great holidays: Christmas, New Year's, Twelfth Night, St. Andrew's Day, and All Saints' Day. Each of these festivals was celebrated with an issue of rum, much visiting back and forth, and a dance in the evening that invariably wound up in a round of battles and such orgiastic rites as even Henry refrains from fully describing.

It was during a New Year's celebration on the Red River, incidentally, that Alexander Henry the Younger took to himself — somewhat to his subsequent bewilderment — the wife that was to stay with him and bear his children throughout his years in the Northwest.

2

IT WAS a rare Nor'wester who did not have an Indian or métis girl for a wife. Many of the Partners, like Henry himself, formed long-lasting liaisons with women of the country. As for the Canadian voyageurs, often half-breeds themselves, nothing could have been more natural than to shack up with a Cree or Saulteur girl and raise a family.

Had there been a priest handy, there is no reason to believe that many of these marriages *à la façon du pays* would not have been celebrated in proper form. But a priest was something that had not been seen in the Northwest for a long, long time. And so, all over the vast and empty reaches of the great fur land — in Hudson's Bay Company posts as well as in the Nor'wester's establishments — men simply bought themselves a woman to cook their rations, make and mend their gear, and keep their beds warm at night. Sometimes they paid less than a carrot of tobacco for her — never as much as a good team of dogs would fetch. Henry gives the going rate as one horse for one woman:

> Livernois exchanged his mare for a young wife, about eight years of age [the wife, not the mare]; it is common in the North West to give a horse for a woman.

On another occasion he notes, with obvious disgust:

> There are a few freemen about this place who have actually disposed of their women to the H. B. Co's people in barter for bear meat.

But they always paid something, the haughty bourgeois and the humble canoeman alike. The girls at the forts, particularly the daughters of the Canadians, were sold at a very early age — frequently as young as twelve or even ten years. A chief's daughter cost more than an ordinary buck's; a beauty brought a better price than a plain girl; and a sterile woman was valued above all.

The Nor'westers, it must be recorded, sometimes carried the custom of buying and selling women to the most sordid of levels. They bartered them solely for profit, entering the transactions in their account books, as they would a deal in furs. Thus, as early as 1778 we find that highly respected Irishman John Askin writing from Michilimackinac to the Clerk of the North West Company at Grand Portage: "I need two pretty slave girls from 9 to 16 years old. Please have the goodness to ask the gentlemen to procure two for me."

By Alexander Henry the Younger's time, the trade in girls was prevalent in the Northwest, to judge from this carefully grammatical entry in the journal of the great Archibald

Norman McLeod at Alexandria: "I gave the Chef de Canard's widow to the amount of 28 plus, and took the Slave woman, whom next fall I shall sell for a good price to one of the men."

But it was that professional reprobate James McKenzie, at Fort Chipewyan, far up on Lake Athabasca, who reveals the traffic in women in the most revolting detail. McKenzie took girls in payments for debts from his Indian hunters, and sold them to the highest bidders: "It may be a means of thickling some lecherous miser to part with some of his hoard," he wrote of one transaction. "I therefore kept the woman, to be disposed of in the season when the Peach River bucks look out for women in the month of May." When his Indians timidly protested, McKenzie threatened to cut off their heads.

Yet, even though they openly bought and paid for their women, the voyageurs and sometimes the bourgeois themselves were occasionally touched with something deep and even lasting at the sight of some dusky beauty or dark-eyed métis girl. There are times, indeed, when a note of all but unendurable longing creeps into the little love stories that now and then punctuate the sordid record of the traders' journals. Even the professionally cynical Henry — against whom, incidentally, there is no evidence of traffic in women — cannot conceal a kind of wondering sympathy when he writes:

> One of my men, who was much in debt, offered me his services as long as he could perform any duty on condition that I clothe him and allow him to take a woman he had fallen in love with; for himself he asked nothing but dressed leather to make a shirt, capot and trousers, all the year around, and a little tobacco. He is an able-bodied young man. This proposal did not surprise me, having seen several people as foolish as he, who would not hesitate

to sign an agreement of perpetual bondage on condition of being permitted to have a woman who had struck their fancy.

And there is the shorter, perhaps even more poignant entry, written with a true trader's attention to all the financial details:

> On the 12th, one of my men gave a mare that cost him G.H.V.P. currency equal to £16 13s. 4d. for one single touch at a Slave girl.

From such fleeting glimpses into the hearts of lonely men in the *pays d'en haut*, one perceives that the women of the tribes sometimes exercised a powerful fascination over even the most sophisticated of the bourgeois. Prosaic fort journals occasionally blossom with a little tribute to the charm of some native woman. And if a certain loss of perspective might be suspected in men so many years in the bush, we have such comments as this one by the highly cultivated Nicholas Garry, fresh up from Montreal: "At the Portage du Rat, we found a party of Indians . . . One of the women would have been beautiful in any country . . . She had a most handsome, intelligent countenance, and the finest black eyes, and a complexion that would have been considered as brunette and not darker anywhere."

Duncan Cameron, a seasoned Nor'wester in the Nipigon department, speaks of the Saulteur as being "very well featured, especially their women, some of whom would be real beauties if their complexion was fair." They all had excellent teeth, he added, and pretty black eyes, which they knew very well how to use on the traders. As for the métis, or half-breed, women at the trading posts — some of them far more French than Indian — even the great Sir John Franklin paused

to remark on their Gallic vivacity and provocative beauty
. . . and to add that they were all completely without morals.

That romantic Scotsman Alexander Ross gives us an enthusiastic — and perhaps overdrawn — picture of these fort
girls. They were, he says, "as fair as the generality of European ladies, the mixture of blood being so far removed from
the savage as hardly to leave any trace." Their lissome figures,
mischievous eyes, and remarkable gift for mimicry, he adds,
"combined to render them objects of no ordinary interest" —
especially when they were dressed in their gay holiday silks,
satins, and gold jewelry.

But it is from such realists as Alexander Henry that we get
what is, perhaps, a more valid picture of the women the
bourgeois married. In swift, oddly professional vignettes, his
journal gives us their ethnography, tribe by tribe. He shows
us the Cree women in their shifts of soft white doeskin ornamented with quill-work and long fringes, their faces heavily
vermilioned, their shiny black hair put up in large whorls
from which bunches of blue Spanish trade beads were suspended:

> Chastity does not seem to be a virtue among the Crees,
> who frequently make temporary exchange of wives among
> themselves . . . Polygamy is very common; the first wife
> is considered the mistress of the tent and rules the others,
> frequently with an iron rod, obliging them to perform all
> sorts of drudgery.

The Assiniboine women are lighter in color, with more
regular features. Their dress, customs, and manners are
similar to those of the Cree women:

> The Assiniboine often barter the persons of their women
> for a trifling recompense . . . They regard their wives in

the same light as all other savages in this country — that is, as mere slaves and drudges.

The women of the Blackfoot, Blood and Piegan, oddly enough, were sometimes fair-skinned and gray-eyed; but in most respects they seem not to have been very attractive:

> The women are a filthy set. Their dress consists of leather; their hair, never combed except with the fingers, is worn loose about the neck and always besmeared with red and lead-colored earth. This gives them a savage countenance, though the features of many of them would be agreeable, were they not so encrusted with earth . . . They are a most licentious people. Many of them have six or seven wives. The men, when inclined to treat a stranger with civility, always offer him the handsomest. At our establishments they are a nuisance in offering women, as they would bladders of grease, and often feel offended when their services are not accepted. Their women appear to be held in slavery, and stand in awe of their husbands.

Such were the women — women of another world and, indeed, of another age — from whom the Nor'westers, even the most cultured and fastidious, selected mates to share their loneliness and bear their children. For the most part they lack even a name in their husbands' journals. But it is not always so. Sometimes we come across one who stands out, living and real, among the museumlike figures. And occasionally, among the faceless drudges of the Indian camps, there is a woman whose beauty, or cleverness, or strength of character bound some white man to her with ties of extraordinary tenacity.

When this happened, the white man was faced with a problem, as his return to Canada drew near. For the common voyageur the difficulty was not so great: often he simply settled down at one of the Concern's posts, with his wife and brood. The number of voyageurs who made this decision was considerable. Henry tells us that in his time 1600 men, 400 women, and 600 children were drawing rations at the North West Company's establishments — a large part of them permanent residents.

If, on the other hand, the voyageur decided to return to civilization after many years in the bush, he had a choice to make: he could take his squaw and half-breed children with him — which he occasionally did; or, as was more often the case, he could sell or give them to another man.

With the bourgeois things were not quite so simple. He was sometimes a sensitive, or at least a responsible man; and the idea of abandoning the mother of his children to "the protection of some honest man," with provision for her support, of course, did not always square very well with his conscience. Besides, he was sometimes in love with his Indian or métis wife.

Such a one was Daniel Harmon, the young Vermonter, who had never slept in a tent before leaving Montreal. He took with him into the *pays d'en haut* not only the strict moral scruples of his Puritan forebears, but an almost pathological aversion to Indian women. He held out for nearly six years. Then, one night at South Branch Fort, high up on the Saskatchewan, he wrote out his capitulation to the inevitable.

"This day," he recorded in his journal, "a Canadian's daughter, a girl of about fourteen years of age, was offered to me; and after mature consideration concerning the step which I ought to take, I have finally concluded to accept her, as it is customary for all gentlemen who remain, for any length of time in this part of the world, to have a female companion with whom they can pass the time more socially and agree-ably than to live a lonely life, as they must do if single."

When, after nineteen years, Harmon's time in the North-west was up and he prepared to return to the United States, he decided — but not without a lot of soul searching — to take his wife and their little daughters, Sally and Polly, with him. Elisabeth — which was his wife's name, although Har-mon never bothers to tell us — bore him ten children in all; and they lived for many years in the little town of Coventry, Vermont, a respected and, as far as we know, a happy family.

William Conolly, a young Irishman who became a bour-geois of the North West Company, solved his problem neatly. Having early in his career married a Cree girl named Susanne, by whom he had six children, he simply sent her to a convent when the Church refused to recognize his Indian marriage, and wed a Miss Woolwich of L'Assomption.

John McDonnell took his métis wife, Magdeleine Poitras, back to Montreal with him and established her as the mistress of "Poplar Villa." A prosperous old gentleman, widely re-nowned for his piety, he was legally married to Magdeleine forty-six years after having taken her as his wife *à la façon du pays* on the Rivière Qu'Appelle.

David Thompson appears in Henry's journal with a young métis wife, Charlotte Small, the daughter of a fur trader and a Cree woman. He too brought his wife back to Canada, settling with her and their children at Terre Bonne. She died two months after his own death, their marriage having endured for fifty-eight years.

The great Sir Alexander Mackenzie, conforming to the pattern, took a chief's daughter to live with him in the North-west. His half-breed son Andrew became a Clerk in the service of the Concern. But there is no record of what became of the Indian girl who was the great explorer's wife before he married the celebrated beauty, Geddes Mackenzie, and became the Laird of Avoch.

As for Alexander Henry, he got himself "married" to a Saulteur girl after a riotous New Year's party at his first fort on the Red River. The final entry in his journal for January 1, 1801, is:

> Liard's daughter took possession of my room, and the devil himself could not have got her out.

Although he did not yet realize it, when Henry awoke on that chill, gray morning after the New Year's celebration, he had taken himself a wife. She was a chief's daughter, of course — no self-respecting bourgeois could settle for a girl of lesser social status. And she must have been a handful.

Henry, obviously baffled by the outcome of a little New Year's frivolity, was slow to accept the idea of its permanence. He urged his new roommate to return to her father. When she refused, he went out to hunt buffalo and think things over. On his return from an unsuccessful hunt, he noted heavily in his journal:

> I was vexed to find my room still occupied, and no sign of her budging.

The month passed with still no sign. The Indian women of the post amused themselves by sliding down the steep bank of the river, shrieking and laughing as they shot out onto the ice, sometimes plunging from their careening sleds into the deep snowbanks. And the new Mrs. Henry, it is a safe bet, was always among them; she was not the type of girl to miss any fun. Neither was she one who could be called predictable; and so, on January 30, Henry could at last write cheerfully:

> I got rid of my bed-fellow, who returned to her father with good grace. Fine weather.

Two days later, however, we find him reporting, with somewhat diminished buoyancy:

> The lady returned. A terrible snowstorm.

This sort of thing may have gone on for a considerable time; but in the end, "Her Ladyship," as Henry got into the habit of calling her, must have settled down and become a good and dependable wife. At least, we know that she became the permanent manager of his menage and several times the mother of his children. For in the roster of Fort Vermilion, almost ten years later, we find the occupants of Henry's apartment listed as, "Self . . . 1 man — 1 woman — 3 children."

Thus, we know that Henry, like most of his voyageurs, was a family man. But what, we may wonder, was the ultimate fate of that willful and unpredictable girl, the Liard's daughter, who settled down as his constant wife at last, and bore him children in the furthermost reaches of the *pays d'en haut?*

We do not know. The journal of Alexander Henry the Younger does not tell us.

3

ALTHOUGH the journal says nothing about it either, the first white woman ever to enter the Northwest may have been part of Henry's "family" at Pembina. She was Marie Gaboury, wife of one of his men, and — if we may believe the good Abbé Dugas, that gentle chronicler of voyageur tales — the first of her race on the Red River. Marie, according to legend, gave birth to a child at Pembina in 1807, and a year later went with her husband up the Saskatchewan in Henry's brigade. There she was a never-ending source of wonder to the Slave and Blackfoot squaws, and her breathtaking experiences became the folklore of both whites and Indians.

More substantial is the figure of "the Orkney girl," whose sensational appearance at Pembina is described in one of the more diverting passages of Henry's journal:

> This morning, one of Mr. Heney's Orkney lads, apparently indisposed, requested me to allow him to remain in my house for a short time. I was surprised at the fellow's demand; however, I told him to sit down and warm himself.
>
> I returned to my own room, where I had not been long before he sent one of my own people, requesting the favor of speaking with me. Accordingly, I stepped down to him, and was much surprised to find him extended on the hearth, uttering dreadful lamentations; he stretched out his hands toward me, and in piteous tones begged me to be kind to a poor, helpless, abandoned wretch, who was not of the sex I had supposed, but an unfortunate Orkney girl, pregnant and actually in childbirth.
>
> In saying this she opened her jacket and displayed a pair of beautiful, round, white breasts; she further informed me of the circumstances that had brought her to this state. The man who had debauched her in the Orkneys two years ago was wintering at Grandes Fourches.
>
> In about an hour she was safely delivered of a fine boy, and the same day she was conveyed home in my cariole, where she soon recovered.

This passage raises some doubt that Marie Gaboury, the Abbé Dugas notwithstanding, was actually the first white woman in the Northwest, and the first to give birth to an all-white child in the Red River country. The documentary evidence is on the side of the Orkney girl, who probably came to Pembina by way of James Bay and the Assiniboine.

It would be pleasant to add that she became the wife of the man she had followed to the New World, and that the little family became the earliest settlers in that remote part of what is now the United States. Probably nearer the truth, how-ever, was the report that she was sent home to the Orkneys and "became, with her daughter, public characters, and were known as vagrants, under the name of the Nor'westers."

4

MORE difficult than finding a wife in the *pays d'en haut* to cook one's rations was the problem of obtaining an adequate and dependable supply of food itself. It was one of Henry's problems at Pembina; it was one that extended right up to Headquarters. The vast organization of trading posts, supply systems, and communications known as the North West Com-pany existed, of course, for only one thing: beaver. But you couldn't eat beaver — or, at least, their pelts, or the hats into which they were finally made. And how to feed a thousand-odd men and their families in more than a hundred posts, and on their long wilderness journeys, was one of the Concern's biggest worries.

With the fur trader himself, it wasn't so much a question of how well he ate as of whether he ate at all. He was often on short rations, and the dread of famine hung over every post. Scattered through every trader's journal are such routine phrases as, "We were reduced to eating the parchment out of our windows," or "We dined on a pair of leather breeches," or "We were obliged to take the hair from the bear skins and roast the hide, which tastes like pork."

The eating of one's leather garments — sometimes broiled, sometimes boiled up into a glutinous broth — was so common in times of dire need, in fact, that it received no more than casual mention in the Nor'westers' journals. Thus, W. F. Wentzel, writing at his post on the Mackenzie River, said that he and twelve others lived for two months on nothing but dried beaver skins: "We destroyed in order to keep alive upward of three hundred beaver skins besides a few lynx and otter skins . . . We have a meal now and then; at intervals we are still two or three days without anything. All my men are dead of starvation, viz: Louis Le mai *dit* Poudrier and one of his children, François Pilon and William Henry, my hunter."

Other last resorts in the way of food were the old bones of animals or fish, which were cracked open and boiled; the spawn of fish, beaten up in warm water; and various herbs, low in food value, but capable of sustaining life, such as the often mentioned *choux-gras* of the prairie. Daniel Harmon tells of subsisting on rosebuds, "a kind of food neither very palatable nor nourishing . . . They are better than nothing, since they would just support life."

But the standard emergency ration of nature, mentioned by the very earliest missionaries and explorers, was a rock lichen called *tripe de roche*. It was necessary to close one's eyes while eating it, an early father remarks, but it filled the stomach, if nothing else. The elder Henry describes its preparation, "which is done by boiling it down into a mucilage, as thick as the white of an egg."

The distressing results of eating *tripe de roche* are vividly pictured by the free trader John Long: "Tripe de roche is a weed that grows to rocks, of a spongy nature and very unwholesome, causing violent pains in the bowels, and frequently occasions a flux. I am informed that traders in the Northwest have often experienced this disorder, and some of them in very severe weather have been compelled to eat it for fourteen days successively, which weakened them considerably. When the disorder does not terminate in a flux, it occasions violent vomiting, and sometimes spitting of blood, with acute spasms of the bowels."

Hardly the sort of dish one would care to serve often — yet it was not the last extremity of desperate men. For, as the elder Henry darkly hints, cannibalism was not unknown in the fur country. John Long, anything but a squeamish reporter, again tells of a starving voyageur who killed and ate not only a harmless Indian who had brought him food, but one of his two companions as well. Tricked into a confession of his guilt, he was summarily shot through the head by his bourgeois.

The food problem, at almost all times an acute one, was dealt with by the Nor'westers under two headings: the provisioning of the posts, and the provisioning of the fur brigades on the march.

The posts in the forest belt subsisted largely on fish. Often, indeed, the traders in the northern departments had no other food at all. Yet, eating nothing but fish the year around, without vegetables or even salt, they were healthier, Mackenzie avers, than the venison eaters of the west.

A prodigious amount of food was required to keep an active man going on an all-fish diet. In one house at Chipewyan, five men, a woman, and three children ate between them thirty-five whitefish, weighing between five and ten pounds apiece, every day. A large post would consume a thousand or more a week.

Fortunately, the lakes and streams of the Northwest were full of many kinds of fish, which were taken by both net and line in vast quantities. In the autumn, as many as 500 white-fish could be caught in a couple of hours with a scoop net from a canoe. Long mentions a catch of 18,000 pounds of whitefish netted through the ice in two months. Trout weighing up to 70 pounds were taken by the hundreds with both line and seine. Sturgeon of 150 pounds or more, Har-mon says, were sometimes driven onto sand bars and shot; "We have no trouble killing any number of them we please."

Among the kinds of fish mentioned by the Nor'westers were: whitefish, trout, sturgeon, pike, walleyed pike, carp, herring, sucker, fresh-water drum, smallmouthed bass, and bream. Of all these, the whitefish — fresh, frozen or dried — was considered the variety par excellence. "It is the only fish that sauce spoils," the Baron Lahontan maintained. Nicholas Garry was no less enthusiastic: "All I had heard of its excel-lent quality and taste fell far short of its real excellence. I should say it is the most delicate tasted fish I have ever eat." But Alexander Henry the Elder paid it perhaps the highest tribute of all: "Those who live on whitefish for months to-gether preserve their relish to the end. This cannot be said of trout."

With all this, many a gourmet will agree; still, a steady diet of even whitefish must have sated the heartiest appetite in

time. The voyageur was not one to complain much; but one
of his rare cries of anguish has come down to us in a trader's
journal: *"Toujours le poisson!"*

Better off were the posts in the buffalo country that subsisted on a fare of juicy steaks, roasts and tongues. As in the
case of fish, enormous quantities of meat were required to sustain a man who ate only flesh. The daily allowance of buffalo meat at Fort George was eight pounds a man. The
voyageurs who, between them, ate thirty-five whitefish a day
would have required forty rabbits to get the same amount of
nourishment. Two whole geese were no more than a meal
for a man in the northern posts.

The prairie posts were blessed with an almost inexhaustible supply of buffalo meat that delivered itself, so to speak,
to their very doors. Hunters sometimes killed entire herds
and returned with nothing but the tongues. In seasons of
lesser abundance, the whole carcass of the animal was utilized.
The hunters cut the meat up into twenty pieces — much
like our standard cuts of beef — for transportation to the post.
The choice cuts were the hump and back meat. The tongue
generally went to the hunter.

To the trader, settling down with his "family" for the long
prairie winter, the sight of tons of fat meat in his icehouse or
glacière must have been a comforting one. The size of his
store depended on his needs; but Duncan McGillivray gives
us an idea of what the average post required. In his *glacière*
were stacked 500 thighs and shoulders — the meat of 413
buffalo, weighing almost a quarter of a million pounds. Even
in the elder Henry's time, the beef reserves at some of the
posts were awe-inspiring. "At Fort des Prairies I remained
several days," he wrote, "hospitably entertained by my

friends, who covered their tables with the tongues and marrow of wild bulls. The quantity of provisions which I found collected here exceeded everything of which I had previously formed a notion. In one heap I saw fifty tons of beef, so fat that the men could scarcely find a sufficiency of lean."

While the meat of the buffalo made excellent steaks and roasts — although not so delicious as those of the moose — it was the fat cuts, especially the long *dépouilles* of back fat, that were most prized. "The Canadian voyageur's appetite for fat meat is insatiable," Franklin observed. And the bourgeois had no less a fondness for the grease and tallow that are mentioned so often — and almost as a delicacy — in their journals.

In this they were following a sound instinct. For, as Vilhjalmur Stefansson and other arctic explorers have often pointed out, a man could live long and well on meat alone — provided he got enough fat along with the lean. Without it — as the rabbit and fish eaters knew by experience — he was likely to become sick, and even to die, from fat starvation.

Hence, the North West Company took good care to satisfy the craving of its men for fat. Thousands of kegs of grease — really buffalo tallow — were put up at the "pemmican posts" for the northern departments. In one year at Pembina, Henry kegged up almost two tons of it, and another two tons in the form of pemmican. By the traders it was called "the bread of the *pays d'en haut*."

Henry, incidentally, has left us this list of provisions "destroyed" at his Pembina post in one winter by 17 men, 10 women, 14 children, and 45 dogs:

> 112 buffalo cows — 45,000 pounds
> 34 buffalo bulls — 18,000 pounds
> 3 red deer

      5 large black bears
      4 beavers
      3 swans
     12 outardes geese
     36 ducks
  1,150 fish of different kinds
    775 sturgeon
    410 pounds of grease
    140 pounds of bear meat
    325 bushels of potatoes and an assortment of kitchen
         vegetables

This adds up to about a ton of meat and fish apiece for every man, woman and child in the post; but more interesting, perhaps, is the inclusion of no small quantity of potatoes, and even kitchen vegetables, at the end of the list. Not every post was as fortunate as Pembina in this respect. Only the larger establishments were able to supplement their basic fish and meat diets with potatoes, cereals, and garden truck; but some of them did so on a rather large scale.

Like Bas de la Rivière, with its fields, barns, stables and storehouses, Rainy Lake also had its cultivated fields and domestic animals. And at Pembina, Alexander Henry himself did not do badly as a farmer. In the fall of one year he reported:

The men had gathered the following crops: 1000 bushels potatoes (produce of 21 bushels); 40 bushels turnips; 25 bushels carrots; 20 bushels beets; 20 bushels parsnips; 10 bushels cucumbers; 2 bushels melons; 5 bushels squashes; 10 bushels Indian corn; 200 large heads of cabbage; 300 small and Savoy cabbages. All these vegetables are exclusive of what have been eaten and destroyed since my arrival.

The virgin prairie soil produced not only abundantly, but spectacularly for Farmer Henry:

> I measured an onion, 22 inches in circumference; a carrot 18 inches long and, at the thick end, 14 inches in circumference; a turnip with its leaves weighed 25 pounds, and the leaves alone weighed 15 pounds.

The North West Company's post at Fond du Lac, on the St. Louis River, kept two horses, a cow, a bull, and a few pigs. The fort at Leech Lake had a garden that produced a thousand bushels of potatoes, thirty of oats, cabbages, carrots, beets, beans, turnips, pumpkins and Indian corn. The Concern had also brought horses to the post, "even cats and hens."

And how, one might wonder, did the Concern succeed in transporting horses, cows, bulls and other livestock through a roadless wilderness, traversible by only canoe and dog sledge, to forts a thousand miles or more from any civilized settlement? Were they brought out in the Company's small schooners, such as the *Otter* and the *Beaver*, to the Grand Portage, and thence over the winter ice to the Interior posts? Were they even carried while young and small, perhaps, in the great *canots du maître?* Or, had they already been brought to the *pays d'en haut* by the French, in the earliest days of the fur trade? Peter Pond, writing of his trip up the Fox River, in what is now Wisconsin, says: "I ort to have Menshand that the french at ye Villeg whare we Incampt Rase fine black Cattel & Horses with Sum swine."

It is something to speculate about — like so many of the Nor'westers' doings!

In addition to his garden and livestock, there were other ways a trader could vary his diet of straight meat, or fish, or a combination of both. He could, for instance, buy certain

items of food from the Indians. Among these, wild rice —
or, as the traders often called it, wild oats — was perhaps the
most important. Rainy Lake was the great source of supply.
Growing in the water to a height of more than eight feet, the
rice was harvested by the Indians, who drove their canoes
through the rice beds and beat out the grain. In ordinary
seasons, Harmon tells us, the North West Company bought
from 1200 to 1500 bushels of wild rice from the natives; "and
it constitutes a principle article of food at the posts in this
vicinity."

Maple sugar, also bought from the Indians, was more than
a luxury on the trader's table: it was often an important staple,
and sometimes all he had to eat for long periods of time. It
was made from the sap of the true and bastard maples, and
even a certain variety of birch. The work of gathering the
sap and boiling it down was left mostly to the women. In the
spring the whole tribe went to the sugar bush, where the men
cut wood for the fires and hunted game for food, while the
squaws gathered and boiled the sap. The elder Henry describes one sugar-making expedition that produced 1600
pounds of sugar, besides 36 gallons of syrup — not counting
300 pounds consumed on the ground. During the whole
month in the bush, he tells us, sugar was the principal food.
He knew Indians, he adds, who lived wholly on sugar and —
understandably enough — grew fat.

Game was bought from the Indians, or procured by the
trader's gun: venison, moose, bear, antelope, as well as ducks,
geese, swans, and occasionally their eggs. By the voyageurs,
if not always by the bourgeois, dogs were frequently purchased for food. A small dog, of a species specially bred for
eating, was regarded as a great delicacy by the Canadians.

The Nor'wester, whose Indian wife cooked for him, soon accustomed himself to the eating habits of the natives; and he could speak with equanimity, if not enthusiasm, of a meal of "five Indian dogs, bear, beaver, mountain cat, and raccoon, boiled in bear's grease and mixed with huckleberries."

In the delicatessen department, so to speak, the Nor'wester had little to choose from, although certain luxury items did appear on his table now and then. He highly esteemed the tail of the beaver, the tongue of the buffalo, and the snout of the moose; and from the Indians he learned to relish the sweet and highly nutritious marrow in roasted buffalo bones.

Most important of his luxuries, perhaps, was the flour he had brought all the weary miles from the Grand Portage. Sometimes he made with it a kind of thick flour-and-pemmican soup called rubbaboo. More often, he fashioned *galettes*, small unleavened cakes, which he baked in the ashes. When he had chicken or gull eggs, he made up a pudding of some sort, or "fritters," which were probably an approximation of our flapjacks. It can also be assumed that, without yeast, he made sourdough bread whenever his cabin was warm enough to promote its rising. And at the Grand Portage and some of the big Interior posts, he baked proper loaves of bread: there were ovens, for instance, at Rainy Lake House. On the great fete days, flour and a little sugar always accompanied rum as a special treat.

As for fruit, the Nor'wester had none except what he could find growing wild. But these he must have enjoyed greatly; for he always has time — especially Alexander Henry — to pause in his journal and tell us: "We found an abundance of sand cherries, which were of an excellent flavor," or, "Red raspberries are now ripe and very good . . . the panbian is fine and large, and of a beautiful red, but requires the frost to ripen it." He seems, indeed, to have had not only great quantities, but also many varieties of wild fruits and berries to eat fresh or dried, in his pemmican, or with his meat and fish.

In addition to his regular winter provisions, each Partner was allowed certain luxuries: six pounds of tea, four of coffee, four of chocolate. Clerks received a lesser allowance, each according to his rank. The Partners also took biscuits with them, which were invariably so crumbled at the end of the trip that they had to be eaten with a spoon.

Now and then a gourmet among them brought along a hamper of wine; and we have Duncan Cameron writing: "Invited my neighbor to dine with me and gave him good Madeira to drink" . . . and adding ruefully that his neighbor seemed to prefer rum. Alexander Henry once concocted a cordial of Jamaica rum, wild cherries and a few pounds of sugar.

Salt, when he could get it, was used by the trader as a condiment and sometimes to preserve meat, although freezing and drying usually served the latter purpose. At every post, no effort was spared to obtain a supply from some nearby salt pit or saline spring.

And so the Nor'wester and his voyageurs maintained their defenses against starvation, and sometimes even feasted on plenty. But what, one wonders, of the children, so numerous at every post? What did their Indian mothers feed them? For a long time, of course, they were nursed at the breast — perhaps for two or three years, as was the custom with the tribes. But when the child was weaned, at last, his diet was one that Dr. Spock himself might have approved. As described by John Long, it included a pap made of Indian corn and milk, if it could be obtained; wild rice, pounded fine, boiled and mixed with maple sugar; and the broth of meat or fish. Another kind of pap, he adds, was made of a root called *toquo*, which was also baked into a kind of zwieback for the infants of the posts.

5

THE Nor'wester on the march was faced with an entirely different problem of food supply. There was remarkably little game along the Northwest Road, and not much else that could be bought from the Indians en route. Once the plains were gained, hunters were sent out to shoot buffalo; but the brigades that continued on to the northern posts could not live off the land; they had to carry their rations with them in already overloaded canoes.

The answer to this problem was lyed corn, wild rice and pemmican. The corn, grown by the Ottawa and Saulteur around Sault Ste. Marie, was processed at Detroit by boiling it in lye water, which removed the outer husk. It was then washed and dried, and was ready for use. One quart of lyed corn — called hominy by the Americans — was boiled for two hours over a moderate fire in a gallon of water. Soon after it came to a boil, two ounces of melted suet were added. This caused the corn to split open and form "a pretty thick pudding." Alexander Mackenzie maintained that, with a little salt, it was a wholesome, palatable, easily digestible dish. A quart of it, he said, would keep a canoeman going for twenty-four hours.

Mackenzie also observed that lyed corn was about the

cheapest food the Concern could give its men, a voyageur's daily allowance costing only tenpence. And the elder Henry wryly commented that, since it was fare that nobody but a French-Canadian would put up with, the monopoly of the fur trade was probably in the North West Company's hands forever!

Indian corn and grease — possibly supplemented by a few fish, game birds, eggs, and Indian dogs along the way — took the brigades as far as Rainy Lake. Here wild rice replaced the corn as far as Lac Winipic. After that, pemmican sustained the western brigades until they reached the buffalo plains and fresh meat; but the northern canoes had to depend on pemmican all the way to their wintering stations. The provisioning of Alexander Henry's canoes, from Lake Superior to the Saskatchewan, would be typical:

> At 4 P.M. I arrived at Fort Vermilion, having been two months on my voyage from Fort William, with a brigade of 11 canoes, loaded with 28 pieces each, and manned by five men and one woman. Our expenditure of provisions for each canoe during the voyage was: two bags of corn, 1½ bushels each, and 15 pounds of grease, to Lac la Pluie; two bags of wild rice, 1½ bushels each, and 10 pounds of grease to Bas de la Rivière Winipic; four bags of pemmican of 90 pounds each to serve until we came among the buffalo — generally near the Monte, or at farthest the Elbow of the Saskatchewan.

This, in a few words, was the formula that made possible the long voyages of the fur brigades, which must often be accomplished with hairbreadth precision between the spring thaw and the fall freeze-up. The North West Company's network of hundreds of canoe routes and more than a hundred forts, scattered over half the continent, could never have functioned without corn, rice and pemmican. And of the three, pemmican was perhaps the most important.

The Nor'westers got the idea, as they did so many, from the Indians. Or perhaps it should be said that Peter Pond did, since he, before anyone else, realized the logistical importance of pemmican and made a systematic use of it. Where the elder Henry and the Frobishers had failed in early attempts to reach the rich Athabasca country, Pond succeeded; and the key to his success is found in his own words: "Provisions, not only for the winter season but for the course of the next summer, must be provided, which is dry'd meat, pounded to a powder and mixed with buffaloes greese, which preserves it in warm seasons." In other words, pemmican.

Almost every trader, from Peter Pond down, described pemmican, and how it was manufactured; but none so well as David Thompson. It was made, he explained, of the lean and fleshy parts of the buffalo, dried, smoked, and pounded fine. In that state, it was called beat meat. To it was added the fat of the buffalo. There were two kinds: that from the inside of the animal, called "hard fat" or grease; and that which lay along the backbone in large flakes and, when melted, resembled butter in softness and sweetness.

The best pemmican, Thompson tells us, was made from twenty pounds each of soft and hard fat, slowly melted together and well mixed with fifty pounds of beat meat. It was stored in bags made of buffalo hide, with the hair on the outside, called *taureaux*. When they could be obtained, dried berries, and sometimes maple sugar, were mixed with the pemmican. "On the great Plains," Thompson wrote, "there is a shrub bearing a very sweet berry of dark blue color, much sought after. Great quantities are dried by the Natives; in this state the berries are as sweet as the best currants, and as much as possible mixed to make Pemmican."

Properly made and stored, the ninety-pound bags of pemmican would keep for years. Post masters took great pride in the quality of the product they turned out. But sometimes, through nobody's fault, it went sour, and great quantities had to be thrown to the post dogs. Often, as in the case of dried meat, mold formed; but that, the traders cheerfully agreed, only improved the flavor.

Pemmican could be hacked off the piece and eaten in its natural state; or it could be boiled up with corn or rice to make a highly nourishing and not unpalatable kind of stew. Whereas a daily allowance of eight pounds of fresh meat was required to sustain a man, two pounds, or even a pound and a half of pemmican would do. A better emergency ration for men in a cold climate has never been developed.

So vital was pemmican indeed to the North West Company's system of communications that a highly specialized organization was set up to make and distribute it. On the prairies were built the famous "pemmican posts" — Fort Alexandria, Fort George, Fort Vermilion, Fort de la Montée — whose principal business was not pelts but provisions, chiefly pemmican, for the canoe brigades and the hungry posts in the forest belt. Archibald Norman McLeod gives us a glimpse of the activities at Alexandria: "I got the last Pounded meat we have made into Pimican, viz. 30 bags of 90 lb., so that we now have 62 bags of that Species of provisions of the above weight. I likewise got nine kegs filled with grease, or Tallow rather, each keg nett 70 lb."

Looking into his storehouse in January, Duncan McGillivray noted that he had 8900 pounds of pounded meat, with enough fat to make it up into pemmican — sufficient, he added, to "answer the expectations of the Gentn. of the Northern Posts, who depend on us for this necessary article." In April, he made his pounded meat and grease into two hundred bags of pemmican.

For one year, 1807-1808, Alexander Henry listed the returns from his four Lower Red River posts as only 60 packs of furs, but 334 bags of pemmican and 48 kegs of grease; a striking statistical sidelight on the importance of beat meat and grease in the economy of the North West Company.

Getting the huge production of pemmican from the prairie posts to where it was needed was a major problem in logistics; and the Nor'westers solved it with their usual flair for organization. Besides the posts that specialized in making pemmican, certain others — principally Cumberland House and Fort Bas de la Rivière — were established at strategic spots to distribute it. To Cumberland House, at the juncture of the Saskatchewan and the waterways leading to Athabasca, the pemmican posts sent hundreds of *taureaux* in skin canoes and roughly built boats. And there the vast store of shaggy buffalo-hide bags was rationed out to the Great Northern brigades for the posts in the forest — Fort Chipewyan, Fort de l'Isle, Fort Resolution, Fort Providence — where the supply of pemmican made of deer and bear meat was both scanty and uncertain. The pemmican from the Red River and Assiniboine posts was distributed from Bas de la Rivière. And later on, Fort Esperance on the Qu'Appelle became the North West Company's chief depot for rushing emergency supplies to posts in distress.

Wherever he was stationed, and however long the march he must make to his wintering grounds, the Nor'wester could usually depend on his supply of pemmican to see him to journey's end and, if necessary, through a winter's scarcity of game and fish. It was his staff of life in a way that bread never was in more civilized parts of the world. It was often his last defense against the forces of famine that hung, like wolves on the trail of a wounded caribou, about every trading post. And he never spoke of it with anything but respect.

VI

Blood on the Prairie

PEMBINA was even lonelier than most posts. Far off the main routes of the fur trade, it was never visited by canoes on their way to or from other departments. And so, month after month, Henry saw no one, talked with no one but his own people — and his Indians, whose surly demands could hardly be called conversation.

Now and then he visited his neighbor, Mr. Miller, the Hudson's Bay Company factor, and had a glass with him. Occasionally he had the company of his cousin William Henry, and a few others — some of whom, like Edward Harrison, who "could neither walk, run, or ride with dogs," Henry considered distinguished chiefly for their stupidity. He did some reading, for at one point he speaks of the destruction of his "library" by fire. But all in all, the intellectual climate at Pembina was not very stimulating.

For amusement, the white traders had little except the usual holiday celebrations, dances and drinking matches — and, even for a Nor'wester, Henry seems to have been a formidable bottle man. The Indians were more resourceful. When the frost bit down four feet into the prairie, and the smoke rolled into the fort from the chimneys, and the air was blue with the peculiar haze of extreme cold, little trapping or hunting could be done; and then Henry's Saulteur amused themselves in their own Indian ways:

> This is delightful weather for the Indian women to play their favorite game of *coullion* on the ice; they generally keep it up till dark, whilst the men are at their game of *platter*, and others beat the drum to their wabbano songs.

For sport, the voyageurs went raccoon hunting, smoking the little animals out of hollow trees. They routed sleeping bears from their winter quarters with specially trained dogs. And they seined sturgeon, huge fish weighing up to 150 pounds, most of which, meat eaters themselves, they gave to the Indians.

As for the bourgeois, their sport was buffalo running. In later times, the vicinity of Pembina was the center of the great annual buffalo hunt in which five or six hundred settlers from Lord Selkirk's Red River settlement took part. From their sprawling tent camp on the prairie, the hunters rode at full speed into the panic-stricken herds, killing as many as a thousand animals in a single day. "In the evening," Alexander Ross records on one occasion, "no less than 1375 buffalo tongues were brought into camp."

In Henry's time, the buffalo around Pembina were probably even more numerous:

The ravages of the buffalo at this place are astonishing. The beach, once a soft black mud into which a man could sink knee-deep, is now made hard as pavement by the numerous herds coming to drink. The willows are entirely trampled and torn to pieces; even the bark of the smaller trees is rubbed off in many places. The grass on the bank of the river is entirely worn away. Numerous paths, some of which are a foot deep in the hard turf, come from the plains to the brink of the river, and the vast quantity of dung gives the place the appearance of a cattle yard.

Henry and his men had fine sport killing the great animals as they came down to the river for water:

We amused ourselves by lying in wait close under the bank for the buffaloes that came to drink. When the poor brutes came within ten yards of us, on a sudden we would fire a volley of 25 guns at them, killing and wounding many, of which we took only the tongues.

But the sport was not always so tame — or so one-sided — as Henry discovered when he undertook to chase a buffalo bull alone:

Just as I came up to him at full speed and prepared to fire, my horse suddenly stopped . . . As I was not prepared for this, I was pitched over his head, and fell within a few yards of the bull's nose; but fortunately for me, he paid more attention to my horse than to me. The grass was long, and I lay quiet . . . I discharged both barrels of my double gun at him; he turned and made one plunge toward me, but had not time to repeat it before he fell, with his nose not more than three paces off.

In November the sport of buffalo running turned into hard, dirty, dangerous work in which the whole post took part. Now buffalo were killed in vast numbers for meat from which to make the pemmican. They were killed on the prairie, in the woods to which they retreated from the cold, and on the open plains again when the weather moderated. They were shot from the bastions of the fort. One even wandered into the stockade and was roped by a man. It was a busy season at Pembina:

> People continually *en dérouine* to Indians' tents; arrivals and departured to the different outposts, and men hauling home meat from the hunters' tents. Buffalo near the fort; I killed two bulls with one ball. Hunters running buffalo, with which the plains are covered; at the fort heard them fire, and saw the cows fall; they killed 23. The beasts were bellowing all night.

The meat road to the fort became a hard-beaten highway from the plains, where the hunters were settling down to a methodical slaughter:

> Buffalo passing northward in as great numbers as I ever saw them . . . My men go daily for meat to the hunters' tent, three miles distant, with 15 or 20 horse travailles, and return with 30 cows; in this manner our winter stock is being rapidly completed.

With March it was all over. Fresh meat would no longer stay frozen, and much of what was in the *glacière* spoiled, causing a terrible stench in the post. Besides, the cows — ugly now with great bald patches on their hides — were scrawny and lean from a winter of foraging in the snow. The hunters came in from their tent, and the women took over at the grease kettles and pounding skins. When their job was finished, a hundred or more square, flat bags of pemmican would be stacked in the hangard, awaiting delivery to Bas de la Rivière.

2

TWICE a year, and no more, the world touched Pembina. In the spring by canoe, and again in early winter by dog sledge, two men arrived with the express. In their rawhide pouches — which sometimes had to be thawed out before they could be opened — they brought letters, reports, and periodicals from "below." Henry received his mail, turned over his own letters and dispatches to be carried back to Headquarters or Montreal, and the express was off again. Nothing was more important to the Nor'westers than this fast and astonishingly dependable system of communication.

In Montreal, the Agents of the Concern must know at the earliest possible date how many furs had been gathered at each post in the *pays d'en haut*. They must be told what supplies were on hand, and what were needed. They must be apprised of the number of men required for the winter's operations, of new posts built and old ones abandoned, trouble with the Indians, fights with rivals. They must be kept informed about deaths and defections, expectations (usually very depressing) for the coming season. They must have, in short, "every kind of information and remarks regarding the state of the Country."

The Wintering Partners, on the other hand, had to be kept informed about the plans and decisions made at Grand Portage, and later at Kaministiquia. And they had to have regular mail from "home," even though — as was often the case — their only address was, "Wherever he may be found." To supply these needs, an elaborate system of expresses reaching from Montreal westward to the Grand Portage, northward to Great Slave Lake, across the mountains to the Pacific Coast, and for thousands of miles into every corner of the trackless fur country, had been organized.

Two expresses left the northern departments each year, passed through the whole country, collecting and distributing mail, and hurried on to the Grand Portage or Sault Ste. Marie. The winter express left Athabasca early in January on snow-shoes and dog sledge, traveling in subzero weather and con-stantly in peril of Indian attack. With luck, it arrived at Headquarters early in April. The summer express, traveling by light canoe, left as soon as the ice went out, hurrying ahead of the fur brigades, with advance reports on the winter outfits. Sometimes, to get the important facts to the Agents even more quickly, a digest of the mail was made at Head-quarters and sent ahead by sledge or canoe to meet the Agents on their way up from Montreal.

Extraordinary measures, indeed, were taken to speed up the delivery of the dispatches, including some almost incredible feats of canoe and dog-sledge travel. The dogs could make 40 miles a day or more, the canoes as much as a hundred. One trip from Lake Superior to Athabasca, 3000 miles, was per-formed in 74 days. James Keith, a Clerk on the Columbia River, left Fort George in August with dispatches for the East, crossed the Rockies, delivered his packet at Kaministi-quia, and was back on the Pacific in November. A voyageur, Jean Baptiste Lajimonière, made the winter trip from the Forks to Quebec — a distance of 1800 miles — in only 36 days.

Although journeys like these were usually emergency runs, the regular expresses were held to a schedule that allowed for no duck hunting or berry picking along the way. With fixed dates for arrivals and departures, mail was carried not only from Headquarters to the Interior posts, but between the posts themselves. Chipewyan could correspond with Vermilion, Pembina with Bas de la Rivière; and we find the bourgeois doing a good deal of writing back and forth among themselves. Thus Hugh Faries at Rainy Lake copies the letters from Montreal and sends them along to the mail-starved upper posts; and Harmon complains because heavy snows have delayed the express from Athabasca.

At Pembina, Henry probably received newspapers and periodicals as well as Company and personal mail, for he mentions the destruction of newspapers and pamphlets when his "library" was damaged by fire. The Montreal *Gazette* and even *The Times* of London were sent to the larger posts; and we hear of traders reading a fresh copy of *The Times* every morning — each exactly one year old.

"Spot news" was conveyed by letter or special printed bulletins; and in that way, no doubt, Henry kept roughly in touch with what was going on in Canada and the world at large. In 1804, for example, he received news of Simon McTavish's sudden death, and of the swift coalition of the North West Company and the XY Company — now that "The Premier" and Alexander Mackenzie could quarrel no more.

To Pembina the expresses brought news that Napoleon Bonaparte had crowned himself Emperor; and soon afterwards that he had been defeated by Lord Nelson in a great naval battle at Trafalgar. Closer to home was the report that a party of Americans under two captains, Lewis and Clark, had wintered with the Mandan on their way to the Pacific. This, to the Nor'westers, was disturbing information; but it was soon followed by the reassuring news that Simon Fraser had been sent west of the Rockies, and that David Thompson was on his way to establish a North West Company fort on the coast in opposition to the Americans.

Thus, at long intervals and often so late that new events had nullified the old, word from "below" — from Canada, and the bustling new nation to the south, and from overseas, trickled into Pembina. And more and more disturbing with each arrival of the express, came reports of trouble with the Indians throughout the Northwest.

3

AT PEMBINA itself Henry was having his own worries. When he built a blockhouse to strengthen his fort, he explained to his Saulteur that it was for defense against the Sioux. But what he really feared was the Saulteur themselves. Pampered and encouraged by the XY people, they had become so insolent and demanding that Henry expected bloodshed at any moment. As they became more numerous around his posts, they grew increasingly arrogant. Playing the Nor'westers against the Potties and the English, they succeeded in wheedling vast quantities of free liquor out of everybody; and they soon learned that a show of hostility was helpful. Often enough, indeed, they succeeded in sowing panic among Henry's people:

> On returning to the fort, I found the men alarmed; all the women and children had fled to the woods. They had been informed by an old woman that the Indians were preparing to attack the fort; but after a great bustle, everything quieted down.

Besides this constant threat of violence, perhaps all-out assault, by his own Saulteur, there was always the old fear of the Sioux. The mounted Indians of the plains were increasingly on the prod, attacking fur brigades on the western rivers, murdering defenseless traders and their families in lonely little outposts, making an occasional pass at strong forts, and incessantly harassing the Saulteur. Terror of them kept Henry's own hunters out of the beaver hills, even drove the buffalo runners in from the plains; and Pembina itself was never free from the dread of their sudden appearance on the prairie across the river.

The Saulteur, indeed, had plenty to be worried about. Little by little, in spreading across what is now the state of Minnesota, they had pushed the Sioux out of their ancient forest home. There had been a great deal of bloody fighting, naturally, and the usual atrocities. Sioux children had been sold into slavery in Montreal. If now the Sioux were out for vengeance of a particularly cruel and savage brand, who indeed were the Saulteur to complain?

Henry, however, was more concerned about the safety of his own people. From the flying posts, reports were continually coming in of threats and insults to his men; of narrow escapes from pillage and murder in the Hair Hills. Henry remembered his first Red River post, and how the squaws had frantically dug holes along the riverbanks, in which to hide their children from the Sioux. Now things were almost as bad at Pembina. The flare-ups of terror had been groundless, of course — so far. But there was no denying the danger; and each new rumor contributed to the rawness of nerves that kept the whole establishment in a constant state of jumpiness.

From this atmosphere of unrelieved tension and apprehension, Henry was happy to escape for a few months each year, when he made his usual trip to the summer Rendezvous.

4

THE Nor'westers no longer held their great annual meetings at the Grand Portage. As soon as they had made certain that the Portage was in United States territory, they prudently moved their headquarters thirty miles eastward, to the mouth of the Kaministiquia River. Here, on a site that had been occupied by the French from Duluth's time to the end of their regime, they built the New Fort. Thunder Bay, on which it stood, had got its name from the incredible electric storms that played over it in the hot summer months. It seemed an appropriate situation, somehow, for the headquarters of the turbulent Nor'westers.

To Alexander Henry, as to every Nor'wester who first laid eyes on it, the New Fort must have been almost awesome. Nothing like it had ever been seen in the *pays d'en haut* before; and one could compare it, indeed, only with the great stone fort the English had been forty years building on the Bay.

Inside its fifteen-foot stockades, protected by bastions and heavy gates, innumerable solidly built structures — including three elegant buildings with long porticoes and balconies — were ranged around a spacious parade. Brass cannon gleamed in the sun; the Union Jack flew from a tall flagpole in the center of the square.

Where the river Kaministiquia emptied into Thunder Bay,

a wharf ran the whole length of the fort; and here the Concern's sailing vessels unloaded merchandise from Sault Ste. Marie and took on furs from the Interior. All around the fort, land was cleared and green with growing barley, oats and peas. Across the river, a little village of log cabins housed the families of voyageurs too old to take their places in a north canoe and too proud to return to their native districts on the St. Lawrence.

At this great establishment the Nor'westers now held their annual Rendezvous, ate and drank their Gargantuan meals, dressed and danced to the pipes and fiddles with the "daughters of the country," just as they had at the Grand Portage. But in far more luxurious style.

The new dining hall, a noble apartment sixty feet long, could seat two hundred guests. A finely executed bust of Simon McTavish graced it, together with portraits of the various Partners. A full-length picture of Nelson and a painting of the Battle of the Nile hung on one of the walls. On another was placed David Thompson's Great Map of the West. In such surroundings, rubbing elbows with gentlemen who gathered at Kaministiquia from all corners of the world, a bush-weary Winterer could feel himself a part of civilized society for a few short weeks.

Henry made several trips to Kaministiquia while he was master of the Lower Red River department. A naturally gregarious man, he treasured these brief intervals when he could escape the cares and tedium of Pembina, and could meet and talk and drink with his friends from Canada and the other posts.

Not only at the New Fort, but at the way stations along the route to Kaministiquia — Rainy Lake, Bas de la Rivière, the

Forks — scores of brigades commanded by the bourgeois of the Concern were constantly coming and going. At these points Henry could satisfy his need for being with others of his own rank, his hunger for intelligent conversation; and we can almost see a Nor'wester's pride and sense of identity with a great organization in such journal entries as this one, made at Bas de la Rivière:

> Early our two brigades arrived, the 18 craft abreast, all singing and keeping time with their paddles and oars; the canoes being heavy loaded and having only three men apiece, made it easy to keep in chorus with the boats.

And yet, it seemed that he could never get back quickly enough to his isolated post on the prairie. He boasted at times, in his laconic way, of the record trip his brigade had made from Kaministiquia to the Forks. In July of 1805 he completed the trip in twenty-one days, and expressed the belief that, with a lading as heavy as his, it was impossible to perform the voyage in less time. "But I almost wished that I had not been so expeditious," he added, when he learned what had happened at Pembina during his absence.

5

WHAT had happened was what he and his people had feared and dreaded from their first days on the Red River — what they had never ceased to fear and dread during all the years since the women had dug holes in the riverbank and hid away their children. The Sioux had struck at last.

They had struck as the Sioux always did — which is to say, with the last ounce of ferocity — and there is little that could be added to Alexander Henry's own stark account of the massacre:

Here I received the unwelcome news that the Sioux had fallen upon a small camp of my Indians at Tongue River, not many miles from the fort, on the 3rd of July, and had killed and taken prisoners 14 persons — men, women, and children.

My beau-père was the first man that fell. He had climbed a tree to see if the buffalo were at hand. He had no sooner reached the top than two Sioux fired at the same moment, and both balls passed through his body. He had only time to call out to his family, who were in the tent about 100 paces from him: "Save yourselves! The Sioux are killing us!" He then fell dead, his body breaking several branches of the tree as it dropped.

The noise brought the Indians out of the tent, when, perceiving their danger, the women and children instantly ran through the plains toward an island of wood on Tongue River, about a mile distant. The men took their arms and made off, keeping in the rear of the women and children, whom they urged on.

The main war party of the Sioux arrived in a few moments and opened fire:

The men, by expert manoeuvres and incessant fire, prevented the enemy from closing in on them, while the women and children continued to fly, and the men followed. They were within 200 paces of the wood, and some of the most active had actually entered it, when the enemy surrounded and fell upon them.

Only one man survived this onslaught, Grande Gueule, who escaped in the woods. Two others were killed instantly. One, Little Chief, stood his ground alone and bought time with his life for the women and children.

He waited deliberately until the enemy came very near, when he fired at the one who appeared to be the chief.

and knocked the Sioux from his horse. Three young girls and a boy were taken prisoner; the remainder were all murdered and mutilated in a horrible manner.

Several of the women and children found safety in the thick willows, where the Sioux horsemen could not follow; but Henry's own mother-in-law and her brood were not so fortunate:

> This woman, having two young children that could not walk fast enough, had taken one of them on her back, and had prevailed upon her sister-in-law to carry the other. But when they got near the woods and the enemy rushed upon them with hideous yells and war whoops, the young woman was so frightened that she threw down the child, and soon overtook the mother; who, observing that the child was missing, and hearing its screams, kissed her little daughter, saying with tears streaming from her eyes: "Take courage, my daughter. Try to reach the woods — and if you do, go to your eldest sister, who will be kind to you. I must turn back and recover your sister — take courage, run fast, my daughter!"

> Poor woman! She actually did recover her child, and was running off with both children, when she was felled by a blow on the head with a war club. She recovered instantly, drew her knife and plunged it into the neck of her murderer; but others coming up, she was dispatched. Thus my belle-mère ended her days.

Next day, Henry's people ventured out from the fort to the place of the massacre. Horrible as it was, the scene was not an unfamiliar one along the hostile frontiers of the fur trade:

> My beau-père's head was severed from his body even with his shoulders, his right arm and left foot were cut

off, his right leg from the knee stripped of the skin, and all carried off.

In the plains lay the bodies of the women and children, within a few yards of each other, and the remains of Little Chief, who had fought so bravely, lay near his wife and children. The enemy had raised his scalp, cut the flesh from the bone, and taken away the skull for a water dish; his limbs were severed from his body, and only the trunk remained, with the belly and breast ripped up and thrown over his face . . . [Little Chief's wife] was also butchered in a shocking manner and her children were dismembered and thrown in different directions . . .

When Henry arrived at Pembina, a war party of Saulteur, Cree and Assiniboine was forming to pursue the marauders. He gave them a nine-gallon keg of gunpowder and a hundred musket balls. "Here, take these, and with them revenge the death of my beau-père and his family," he said.

After many delays, three hundred mounted men finally took the war road. They wasted three months in a timid, bickering foray into Sioux territory, carefully avoiding contact with the enemy. At last they straggled back to their base without having fired a gun.

6

ONE of the Indians who left Pembina in this fatuous pursuit of the Sioux killers was really an American named John Tanner.

Tanner was the son of a Virginia clergyman. At the age of nine, he was captured by the Shawnee while gathering walnuts on his father's farm in Kentucky. Sold to the Ottawa, he was adopted by Netnokwa, a stouthearted, strong-willed, hard-drinking old woman who was really chief of the band — and as good a mother to Tanner as ever a man had.

Repaying Netnokwa with a simple and complete loyalty, young Tanner became the most steadfast of her sons. He also grew up to be as "wild" an Indian as any of his new relatives. He forgot his English speech, forgot even his name. As "The Falcon," a Saulteur brave, he married an Indian wife and raised an Indian family. He went where his band went — eventually as far as the Red River.

We know that Tanner was roaming the region around Pembina while Henry was there; he was, in fact, one of the very "Indians" with whom Henry traded. Yet the Nor'-wester, who must have known him well, has nothing what-ever to say about the Falcon. He could sometimes be strangely silent.

Tanner, however, refers to Henry in a book that, years later, he wrote about his captivity and adventures. The words of his *Narrative*, for example, almost repeat those of Henry's journal when he says: "Mr. H., the trader at Pem-binah, gave the Ojibbeways a ten-gallon keg of powder, and 100 balls, to pursue the party that had killed the chief, his father-in-law."

Tanner also had a good deal to say about the white traders — little of it good. He tells us exactly how the Indians were robbed of their pelts by every kind of trickery and violence; how he saw Netnokwa cheated of her whole winter's catch of furs and left destitute and starving to face a cruel winter with her little family; how he himself, time after time, had to defend his own winter's work at the risk of a beating, or even death. The picture he leaves us of the white trader — as seen through Indian eyes — is not a pretty one. And yet it can be noted that the Falcon's ghastly tale of cupidity and inhuman brutality never once speaks with anything but respect of "Mr. H., the trader at Pembinah."

7

BY THE spring of 1806, Pembina was definitely in the final stages of a steady decline. Everything, it seemed to Henry, was going wrong. His Indians, more troublesome than ever, brought in fewer and fewer skins and demanded more and more liquor. The Sioux kept his buffalo runners in such a state of alarm that they would not venture into the plains. Some sort of epidemic was killing off the beaver. Crebassa, the rascally XY trader, continued to stir up the Saulteur against Henry, even after the coalition. On top of everything else, incredible numbers of mosquitoes made everyone, man and beast, miserable.

About the only good news that Henry was able to report was the death of "our great chief Tabashaw" at the hands of the Sioux. Almost the only cheerful note in the journal was the curiously Pepysian entry:

> Played with J. McKenzie of the H. B. Co. with drum, fife, etc. and drank out of a ten-gallon keg of brandy.

And it was this low level of existence at Pembina, perhaps, that induced Henry, in the summer of 1806, to undertake an excursion to the Mandan.

Even before he had entered the Northwest, of course, he had heard about these remarkable "blond Indians" on the Missouri. They were talked of everywhere. With their fair complexions, light hair, and blue or gray eyes, they were not Indians at all, some said. They were a lost tribe of Israel. Or they were descendants of a band of Welsh colonists who had come to America before Columbus — as witness their ancient fortifications, the peculiar blue beads they made by a secret process, and their skin canoes, exactly like Welsh coracles.

Ever since Vérendrye's time, traders had ventured among them — the Nor'westers, Hudson's Bay people, free men, and lately the Americans. All had come back with fascinating reports on "the white-bearded Sioux," and even more fascinating stories about their women — whose moral conduct, no worse or better than usual in the tribes, was distinguished by a certain picturesqueness of its own.

Firsthand accounts of the Mandan, and their near relations the Big Belly, tended to become highly colored as they were passed on from one trader to another; but there is no doubt about their special attraction for bourgeois and voyageur alike. And the sober David Thompson reduced it all to the simplest terms, perhaps, when he wrote: "The curse of the Mandans is an almost total want of chastity: this, the men knew, and I found it was almost their sole motive for their journey thereto. The goods they bought, they sold at 50 to 60 per cent above what they cost; and reserving enough to pay their debts and buy some corn, they spent the rest on Women."

It is not very clear from his journal what Alexander Henry the Younger's motive was in visiting the Mandan, but it certainly was not a desire to trade. Perhaps he, like so many others, merely wanted to see the strange sights and sample the exotic experiences that were the topic of so much camp fire conversation in the Northwest. He was fed up with life at Pembina. He wanted a holiday.

And so, immediately after his return from Kaministiquia in July of 1806, he began preparations for his journey. Three days later he was on his way to the fabulous lands of the Mandan.

VII

The Blond Indians

HENRY left Pembina with two Canadians and immediately ran into heavy going. The spring rains had turned the prairie into a sea of gumbo mud, into which their horses sank up to their bellies. Occasionally it was necessary to swim swollen streams. Three times they were forced to flounder through "abominably ugly muskegs."

But all this was nothing compared to the scourge of mosquitoes that drove both horses and riders mad. In the voyageur's scale of woes, the torment inflicted by these savage insects outranked cold, hunger, and the grinding toil of forced marches. Henry makes it all very vivid:

> Our horses, which had little rest last night, were almost ungovernable, tearing up the grass, throwing their fore-feet over their heads to drive away the insects, and biting their sides until our legs were in danger of their teeth.

The poor tortured, enraged beasts often attempted to throw themselves down and roll in the water.

Having fought and floundered their way to Portage la Prairie, they arrived to hear nothing but bad news. Famine gripped the whole country south of Lake Manitoba. Of the two horses Henry had sent ahead for his journey, one was too sick to travel, the other too lame. He himself was "unwell all day with a fever." Yet, he was determined to go ahead, even if it had to be on foot. And so, weak and scarcely able to sit his "cruel beast," he set out again for Rivière la Souris, a hundred miles up the Assiniboine, and arrived there on the evening of the second day.

At Souris both the Nor'westers and the Hudson's Bay Company had posts. Assiniboine House, the North West Company's fort, was in charge of François Antoine Larocque. Larocque was a remarkable man, even among Nor'westers. Well read, studious, fluent in both French and English, he was also famous for his great energy and courage. Few had ventured farther into Sioux country. Except for Vérendrye, he was the first white man who had ever penetrated the lands of the Crow. And, of most interest to Henry, he had twice visited the Mandan. The first time was with Lewis and Clark, the second on an expedition of his own that took him almost to the Rockies.

But Larocque seemed little inclined to talk about his journeys. To Henry's disgust, he held forth, instead, on a system of double-entry bookkeeping he had invented for his post. He evaded Henry's urgent questions: What was the best route to the Mandan country — and the safest? How could horses be obtained? Where could a guide be found?

At length Henry began to suspect that Larocque, hungry

for company, was deliberately making it difficult for him to leave this lonely post. He went to bed that night, weak and ill, with none of his questions answered.

Next day, still very unwell, he went ahead with his preparations for leaving Assiniboine House. The place depressed him. All the Indians were away. There was no trade. The fort was starving. "Everything here," he wrote in his journal, "bore the aspect of distress and desolation." All he wanted was to get away:

> I prepared for my journey, notwithstanding many obstacles that were laid in my way to deter me. I was determined to push on, even should I be obliged to go with only two men and a sketch of the route I had with me.

That very day, however, things looked up. First and most important, he hired a guide. An old Irishman named Hugh McCracken offered his services. He was a former artilleryman, who had once lived in the Mandan villages for several months, and in 1797 had guided David Thompson to them. Thompson had reported his "old soldier" subsequently killed by the Sioux; but here he was, very much alive, and ready to show Henry the way to the Missouri!

With a guide engaged, Henry felt a good deal better. But not for long. Another obstacle — this one seemingly insurmountable — now confronted him:

> I could not get a horse to carry my baggage for love or money; neither had my guide a horse himself, nor could he procure him one for a long time. I had almost given up hope—

But now his luck changed with a rush. Charles Chaboillez, master of Fort Dauphin, showed up at Assiniboine House, on his way to Rivière Qu'Appelle. With him were his young

Clerk Alan McDonald, several voyageurs, and — most important of all to Henry — a string of sound horses. Chaboillez listened to Henry's troubles and proposed a neat and unexpected solution: he would go along on the Mandan trip, together with McDonald, a couple of the voyageurs, and all the horses necessary. They shook hands on it, drank a dram to bind the bargain, and began making plans. Early next morning they were off for the Missouri:

> *July 14th.* Early all hands were alert, preparing for our departure. Our party consisted of seven persons and eight horses . . . We provided ourselves with a few articles for the Missourie Indians, such as ammunition, tobacco, knives, beads, etc.; half a bag of pemmican and three pieces of dried meat formed all our stock of provisions.
>
> We had each 50 pounds' weight, which with ourselves, our arms, blankets, and a little ammunition for present use, formed a heavy burden for our horses. The eighth horse carried my tent and some baggage, including a compass and a spyglass.

At eight o'clock the expedition mounted up, bade Larocque good-by, and started out at a slow trot on a west-southwest course toward the country of the Mandan.

2

STRIKING through a series of high, barren hills, over which herds of antelope raced in every direction, they came to the Rivière la Souris late in the afternoon and made camp at old Fort de la Frenier, long since abandoned. The weather was extremely hot, the mosquitoes intolerable.

Saddling up at three the next morning, they followed the

Souris, passing several Assiniboine camps; and Henry, with a flash of the sensitivity that sometimes lights up the rude pages of his journal, observed:

> These people are remarkable for choosing the most delightful spots to pitch their tents, commonly on elevated places where there is no wood to interrupt the view. They would be a happy people, were it not for their continual wars and frequent quarrels among themselves, which generally end in bloodshed. The common causes of these quarrels are women and horses.

Avoiding its great windings, they followed the river southward to the northern border of what is now the state of North Dakota. The plains were alive with buffalo, just beginning the rutting season; they tore up the ground as they thundered across the prairie, and filled the night with a terrible bellowing. Antelope observed them curiously.

> We saw a number of cabbrie . . . some almost as large as fallow deer, and others much smaller, red and white spotted; the latter had young, and did not appear so shy as those we had seen before. The young ones, sighting us, would run up to within a few yards, while the dams would come on behind them with more caution, until their curiosity was satisfied.

While he wrote this charming passage, Henry was suffering from painful boils, caused by the extreme heat and the friction of his leather breeches. "The horse I rode was a cruel beast, with the worst trot I ever saw; both blisters burst soon, and I was in great pain."

Crossing a level plain in the great loop of the Souris, they passed the spot where Lewis and Clark's "Old Menard" had been murdered by the Assiniboine. They reached a wood and, having had enough of steaks flavored with the smoke of buffalo-dung fires, they decided to camp and cook supper. There would be no more wood, McCracken assured them, until they reached the Missouri.

They were now at the edge of the great Mandan Plain — the *Coteau du Missouri* — a succession of hills and valleys covered with huge round boulders. Breaking camp the next morning, they continued over this strange plain until they came to a long lake with a cluster of trees at one end. McCracken stared at it with puzzlement in his blue scout's eyes. They were off course, he told Henry. He had never seen a wooded lake in this plain. He had never even heard of one.

This was not good news. They were now in the country of the Sioux, the natural enemies of all neighboring tribes — and so, by association, of all who had dealings with them. A halt was called to talk the situation over.

A voyageur who had once been to the Missouri ventured to contradict the guide. The lake, he said, was one called the Dog's Den, where the Sioux had captured and tortured a couple of Americans a few years before. McCracken, on the other hand, maintained that it could not be the Dog's Den — they were far to the west of the Dog's Den. It would be best, he said, to cross the lake and shape a course due south. Sooner or later, they would strike the Missouri. In the end, Henry accepted his guide's judgment.

They found a narrow strait in the lake and forded it. The water, although perfectly clear, was loaded with alkali; and the horses, after drying out, were incrusted with white crystals. They left this lake behind and rode toward a range of blue hills on the southern horizon:

We continued on our S. course until five o'clock, when, ascending a range of very high hills running E. and W., we could discern through the spyglass the high red banks of the Missouri, about six leagues distant.

So they had all but reached the great river on which the Mandan had built their five towns. But at what point? It was a critical question; for the Pawnee — who hated the whites as heartily as the Sioux — had also built on the Missouri. Were Henry and his party about to blunder into the hostile Pawnee village? He describes the situation with somewhat less than his usual aplomb:

> Our situation was perplexing, and it remained with me to determine what course we should pursue. I was at a loss. If we were below the Mandanes, and persisted in following the river downwards, we should fall in with the Pawnees or the Titons, both of which nations we supposed to be at war with the Mandanes, and would have no mercy on us.

> On the other hand, if we were above the villages and kept on westward, as some of our party were inclined to do, we might travel to the south branch of the Saskatchewan without finding anybody except some war party, who would soon end our troubles by knocking us in the head.

While Henry was pondering this dilemma, a couple of buffalo bulls, lashing at flies with their tails, and from a distance looking for all the world like Indians whipping their ponies, threw the voyageurs into a panic. Henry laughed at their fears, but he himself was not altogether easy in his mind. He decided to camp for the night.

They made their pitch on a high hill, entrenching their camp and fortifying it with baggage, saddles and large stones. Below them stretched the infinite darkness of the Mandan Plain. The night passed in anxious waiting for daybreak; but dawn, spreading slowly over the vast prairie sky, did little to restore the courage of the expedition:

> At daybreak it was very cold, and our fingers were benumbed in saddling. Sullen silence reigned. I must confess my mind was not at ease, my people being so far from agreement as to our situation.
>
> Three of them had already been to the Mandanes, one of them no later than last year. It was those very fellows who insisted that we were too low down. The western course we had kept since leaving Rivière la Souris establishment persuaded me that our guide was right, and that we must be above the village; but having so many voices against me, I did not wish to insist upon it.

In the end, he settled the dispute by telling McCracken to make up his mind and lead the way. The old Irishman gave the bourgeois a kind of military salute, swung into his saddle, and without a word started eastward. There were some muttered protests, but all followed him.

Around nine o'clock McCracken pulled up and pointed to the horizon. Faint but distinct, about five leagues away, some high hills called the Snake's Den broke the flatness of the *Coteau du Missouri*. No argument now — everyone knew that landmark. They were going to hit the Missouri near the Mandan villages. McCracken had been right all along.

At noon they sighted the river itself, and soon descended the high banks to the water's edge. On the beach they saw many tracks of the natives and a great quantity of old corn cobs. After having washed the horses and themselves in the Missouri, they saddled up and rode easily down the river, under the stupendous bank of the Snake's Den, a 300-foot precipice of red earth.

3

Not far from the Snake's Den stood the summer village of the Big Belly, mentioned by Lewis and Clark. It was deserted now, about thirty earth-and-timber lodges in a field of weeds. The clearing was full of wild fruit — pears, red cherries, raspberries and gooseberries — on which the men feasted.

Late in the afternoon they arrived opposite a village on the other side of the river. They hallooed to the Indians to come and ferry them over, but no one paid any attention to their shouts. So the party kept on, floundering through a wood in deep mud, and emerging at last into sunny fields of corn, beans, squashes and sunflowers.

Near these fields they saw a sight that plunged Henry's volatile Canadians into deep melancholy: great numbers of corpses exposed on stages about eight feet above the ground — a Mandan burial place.

Hurriedly leaving this grisly village of the dead, they soon met a Mandan, armed with a gun and standing guard over a large number of women and children hoeing corn. He had been observing them for some time, apparently; for he showed no surprise, but came up and shook hands in a most friendly manner. After speaking with him in the sign language, Mc-Cracken reported that Black Cat, grand chief of the Mandan, would welcome them at the next village. By the time they reached this village, called Rooptahee, the chief and his braves were waiting for them outside the stockade.

Black Cat was an imposing figure in his beautiful shirt of white doeskin, strung with scalplocks, beads and ermine. He greeted Henry and Chaboillez gravely and bade them all welcome to his nation's capital:

> The chief then conducted us to one of his huts, which was appropriated for the reception of strangers. He keeps one of his wives in the house we entered, to wait on his guests, cook, bring water, and even serve as bed-fellow when required.

Buffalo hides were spread before the fire for the travelers to sit on, and large dishes of corn, beans and boiled meat brought in. As soon as the white men had eaten and smoked a pipe, the Indians crowded around, eager to trade. When Henry told them he had merely come to visit them and see their country, they took him for a liar:

> They could not comprehend why we should have come so far out of mere curiosity, and said that all white people who came there did so with a view to trade. They suspected that we had goods which we wished to take over the river to the other villages, and were anxious to prevent it. They plagued us until dark, when they retired disappointed.

Thus Henry's first day in Rooptahee ended on a somewhat sour note. The atmosphere of the place became noticeably chilly; and Henry, in fact, seems to have been left pretty much alone in a suddenly hostile village. He took a walk in the evening, and the acerbity of his mood is reflected in his comments on what he saw:

> Toward evening, having gone down to the river-side, I observed their custom of washing themselves in the Missourie. Both men and women make it a rule to go down to the river and wash every morning and evening.

Modesty in the female sex appears to be a virtue unknown. The women wear a kind of leather shift which reaches down to the calves of the legs; this they slip off at some distance from the shore and walk deliberately into the water, entirely naked, in the presence of men, both old and young, who pay no attention to them.

Some few are modest enough to conceal with one hand what should not be exposed to public view, but even this is done so carelessly as seldom to answer the purpose — a flea or louse, of which they have a good store, will make them raise the hand to the part attacked, leaving their nudities exposed.

George Catlin, the American artist who spent some time among the Mandan, saw the scene through more romantic eyes: "To this spot they repair by hundreds, every morning at sunrise, where, on a beautiful beach, they can be seen running and glistening in the sun, whilst they are playing their innocent gambols and leaping into the stream." Armed sentinels, Catlin adds, were stationed "to protect and guard this sacred ground from the approach of men or boys from any direction."

After recording his own dim view of the Mandan's bathing habits, Henry turned in for the night; but not before mentioning still another annoyance:

This evening we were plagued for some time by young women, who came in and wanted to lie with us; but as we did not care to accept their kind offers, they retired very much displeased, and muttering something we could not understand.

He got to sleep finally, but only to be awakened by what he accurately describes as "some extraordinary noise in the village."

The Mandan had a reputation among the traders for some strange and peculiar sexual customs. Thompson, for example, describes a "detestable ceremony" during which, for three days, both men and women wandered about the village "as if in great distress, seeking for persons they cannot find." On the third day, both sexes, weeping with dry eyes, formed lines opposite each other. "In a few minutes, several women advance to the men, each of them takes the man she chooses by the hand, he rises and goes with her to where she pleases, and they lie down together. And thus until none remains, which finishes this abominable ceremony."

When Henry went to the door of his hut to investigate the "extraordinary noise" that had broken his sleep, he beheld a scarcely less remarkable scene:

> I saw about 25 persons of both sexes, entirely naked, going about the village, singing and dancing. At times they withdrew in couples, but soon rejoined their companions in dance and song. During this short separation from the rest, they appeared to be very closely engaged, and notwithstanding the night was dark I could perceive them occupied in enjoying each other with as little ceremony as if it had been only the common calls of nature.

> This affair continued for about two hours, during which they made the tour of the village several times. What was the meaning of this ceremony I could not learn; but certainly there could be no performance more lascivious than the one I witnessed.

The Mandan, as the traders said, certainly were a peculiar people!

4

EVEN their appearance was singular. Every trader literate enough to record his impressions has left us his own description of the strange "blond Indians" of the Missouri. But none with more explicitness than Henry:

> What struck me as extraordinary among these people was several children about ten years of age, whose hair was perfectly gray, and who thus resembled aged persons; those I saw were all girls. These people in general have not such strong coarse hair as other natives of North America; they have it much finer, rather inclining to a dark brown, and I observed some whose hair was almost fair. I saw one Big Belly with yellow hair; which I believe could scarcely proceed from any connection with the whites from our quarter, as it is not more than 30 years since they first saw any of us, and this man was at least 40 years old. Their eyes are not that jet black which is common to other Indians, but, like their hair, is inclined to a dark brown; some few are dark gray.

Catlin said that a visitor to the Mandan was likely to exclaim, "These are not Indians!" He wrote: "There are a great many of these people whose complexions appear as light as half breeds; and amongst the women particularly, there are many whose skins are almost white, with the most pleasing symmetry and proportion of features, with hazel, with grey, and with blue eyes." Especially among the women, every shade and color of hair was to be found — except auburn. There were no redheads among the Mandan. But "there is yet one strange and unaccountable peculiarity which can probably be seen nowhere else on earth . . . There are many, of both sexes, and of every age from infancy to manhood, with hair of a bright, silvery grey, and in some instances almost perfectly white."

These "platinum blondes" of the Missouri, according to Catlin, displayed their tresses in "an almost incredible profusion, which spreads over their shoulder and falls as low as the knee." They also followed — with what must have been an especially bizarre effect — the universal custom of tracing the part in their hair with vermilion.

The dress of the Mandan consisted of a tunic or shirt made of two deer or mountain-sheep skins; leggings of the same material; and buckskin moccasins. The skins, as white as Canton crepe, were often beautifully ornamented with beads, colored porcupine quills, and the scalplocks of enemies. To this basic habit — surprisingly uniform among all the tribes of the Northwest — was added a vast variety of headdresses, ornamented robes, necklaces, bracelets, and other adornments, often of exquisite workmanship.

Most splendid of all were certain characters to be found in every Indian community, but blossoming with uncommon luxuriance along the Missouri. "These gay and tinselled bucks," Catlin wrote, "may be seen on a pleasant day in all their plumes, astride of their pied or dappled ponies, with a fan in the right hand, made of a turkey's tail . . . parading through and lounging about the village for an hour or so, when they will cautiously bend their course to the suburbs of the town, where they will sit or recline upon their horses, overlooking the beautiful games where the braves and young aspirants are contending in manly and athletic amusements; — when they are fatigued with this severe effort, they wend their way back again, lift off their fine white saddle of doe-skin, which is wadded with buffalo's hair, turn out their pony, take a little refreshment, smoke a pipe, fan themselves to sleep, and doze away the rest of the day."

Among the "neat and sometimes splendid" Mandan, Henry, in an old corduroy jacket, greasy leather breeches, and a battered felt hat, must have cut a poor figure indeed. And this, perhaps, explains the polite but indifferent reception they gave him. The Mandan, like all other Indians, were inclined to judge a man — and particularly a white man — by what he wore.

Everything was soon set to rights, however, by Jean Baptiste La France, a Hudson's Bay trader who was living with the Mandan. Hearing of Henry's arrival, he came to visit the Nor'westers:

> He informed Black Cat, our kind host, who his guests were, and told him that our visit was from mere curiosity. The chief instantly retired to his family hut and brought out his flag, which was soon flying over the hut in which we were accommodated. This flag was given to him in 1804-05 by Captains Lewis and Clark, who also gave him a silver medal.

And so, clothed with a new dignity and importance, Henry and his party settled down under the Stars and Stripes to enjoy their holiday on the Missouri.

5

NEXT morning, they were ferried in round skin boats to the Great Village of the Mandan — refusing, on the way over, to fire a salute to a big American flag flying from one of the huts at the waterside. They were greeted by Big Man, a chief who wore a medal displaying the profile of President Thomas Jefferson. Big Man took them to his hut and gave Henry his own bed.

Very pleasantly indeed were they treated by the whole village. The only jarring note was a Canadian named Jussaume — the same Jussaume who later accompanied Big Man to Washington as Lewis and Clark's interpreter. He was a familiar type in the fur country — the renegade; and Henry's brief sketch of him would do equally well for all of his kind:

> This man has resided among the Indians for upward of 15 years, speaks their language tolerably well, and has a wife and family who dress like natives. He retains the outward appearance of a Christian, but his principles, as far as I could observe, are much worse than those of the Mandanes; he is possessed of every superstition natural to those people, nor is he different in every mean, dirty trick they have acquired from intercourse with the set of scoundrels who visit these parts — some to trade, others to screen themselves from justice.

Enjoying the villagers' hospitality and a palatable fare of pounded peas and parched corn, Henry took time to describe the remarkable Mandan capital. The Mandan were the first settled, agricultural Indians he had ever seen — something between the pueblo people of the Spanish west and the nomadic hunters of the woods and plains. And their principal village of Matootanha lived up to all the tales Henry had heard of it.

From a distance, it looked like a cluster of several hundred molehills, circling a central plaza of about four acres in extent, some close together, so that a man could scarcely walk between them, others twenty or thirty feet apart. But what molehills! A Mandan's circular hut was ninety feet in diameter. Stoutly built of logs and beams, thatched with willow withes to a thickness of six inches, then covered with a foot of earth, it not only kept out the bitter prairie cold, but served as a strong fortress against the raiding Sioux and Pawnee. In times of peace, the Mandan lounged and sunned themselves on the roof — never neglecting, however, to take in the horses and bar the door with a heavy piece of timber at night.

Inside, thirty or forty men, women and children lived in orderly and sociable comfort. The master of the hut occupied a couch, covered with buffalo skins, near the door:

> Upon this a Mandane sits all day, receives his friends, smokes and chats the time away with the greatest dignity; he sometimes passes the whole night there, when he is not inclined to lie with any of his wives.

Beyond the master's couch extended a row of beds, one for each of his wives, with the favorite's nearest his own; and after them, the children's. At the end of the room, like an altar in a church, stood his medicine stage, adorned with his arms, shield, scalps, and all that he treasured most. The rest of the space — except for a mortar and pestle — was vacant during the day, but occupied by the horses at night. A large clear area around the central fire was the "family room." More than one family seldom lived in a single house.

In front of each hut, long stages were erected for drying corn, sliced squashes, beans and meat. "When the harvest is over," Henry wrote in his journal, "this must certainly have a pretty effect." The whole appearance of a Mandan village, indeed, was one of order, security, plenty, and a general level of civilization that Henry had observed in no other tribe he had ever visited.

6

HENRY and his party tarried for only one day in Matootanha
— like any tourists, they were eager to get on and see other
sights — but it was a day filled with bustle and stir:

> Soon after our arrival a great uproar was occasioned by the
> unexpected arrival of six Pawnees from their own village
> about 60 leagues below on the same river. They had been
> sent in an embassy to treat for peace.

Henry learned that the Pawnee, once the Mandan's closest
friends, had become their bitterest enemies. Only that spring,
they had joined the Sioux in raiding a Mandan village. In
reprisal, the Mandan and their relatives the Big Belly had
sworn to exterminate the Pawnee. And now, inexplicably,
the Pawnee were suing for peace. What to do?

A messenger was instantly dispatched to the Big Belly villages up river with the news of the Pawnee's arrival. In the
meantime, the emissaries were hospitably entertained and plied
with beans, corn and dried meat. Later on, no doubt, they
would be knocked on the head, Henry thought. But strict
inter-tribal usage, he learned, made it perfectly safe for
emissaries to ride into a fiercely hostile village for negotiation.
Even the Sioux ran no risk.

Soon about thirty Big Belly raced into Matootanha on
horseback, and the palaver began. It was conducted entirely
in the extraordinary language of signs, gestures, and grunts
that was the common tongue of all the prairie tribes. It
ended, at last, on a startlingly modern note: The Mandan demanded a "summit conference." They were tired of dealing

with emissaries; if the Pawnee really wanted peace, let them send their great war chief Red Tail to settle matters. The six Pawnee cheerfully agreed to depart next morning with this message, and the village settled down to the quiet routines of an agricultural community. But not for long:

Toward evening there was a whooping and howling among the young men, who were standing upon their huts. This was to announce [the arrival of] a hunting party . . . The party consisted of 100 mounted men, each loaded with about half a buffalo; but some had more than others, according to the strength of the horse, which the owner always rides, no matter how heavily his beast is loaded.

Henry is amused by the Mandan's method of dividing up the spoils of the hunt:

The women whose husbands or sons have not been hunting enter the huts of those who have secured meat; the mistress gives them a share and they walk away with it. It often happens that so many of her acquaintances and friends thus drop in that not a mouthful remains for her own family. When this happens, she goes in turn to the huts of her friends who have been hunting, and comes away with a load. It is customary for them to go to as many huts as they think proper, and bring away more or less, according to the degree of intimacy that exists between the families, particularly among the women; for they are not without the little jealousies, domestic broils, and tales of scandal, like those of civilized nations.

Impatient to see what sights awaited them up the river, Henry and his companions left Matootanha on horseback after a crowded one day's stay in that friendly and turbulent village.

7

THE beginning of their journey was an enchanting jaunt over a smooth and level plain, through plantations of corn, beans, squashes and sunflowers, where the women and children worked and chattered in the early morning sunshine. They came to a small village of a peaceful but valorous tribe called the Soulier, visited with its people, then continued along the riverbank on a delightful, hard, dry road:

> Upon each side were pleasant cultivated spots, some of which stretched up the rising ground on our left, whilst on our right they ran nearly to the Missourie. In these fields were many women and children at work, who all appeared industrious. Upon the road were passing and repassing every moment natives, afoot and on horseback, curious to examine and stare at us. Many horses were feeding in every direction beyond the plantation. The whole view was agreeable, and had more the appearance of a country inhabited by a civilized nation than by a set of savages.

Less than a mile beyond this idyllic scene, however, everything suddenly changed. They had reached the lands of the Big Belly. The first Big Belly village they came to was only a small one, but it gave a foretaste of trials ahead:

> The children and even the youth collected and followed us in crowds, laughing and making sport of us, to the great entertainment of the men, who were seated upon their huts enjoying the cool morning air, and by their significant smiles seemed to applaud such proceedings. The dogs also assailed us from every quarter and were very troublesome. We, therefore, made no stop at this village.

A mile farther on, they entered the Great Village of the Big Belly, which consisted of about 130 huts. Here they received a correct but cool welcome. No derisive children tagged after them, and no dogs snapped at their heels; but neither did anyone pay them any attention. They were simply taken to a large hut — a sort of boarding house for white traders, apparently — and left to themselves.

At this point, it would seem, Alexander Henry formed an opinion of the Big Belly that only intensified as he remained among them:

> They do not appear to be of such sociable and affable disposition as their neighbors; they are proud and haughty, and think there is no race on earth equal to themselves; they despise other nations. Were it not that they must have traders to bring them arms and ammunition . . . a white man would stand a poor chance for his life among this set of savages . . . Upon the whole, they appeared to me to be a fierce and savage set of scoundrels, still more loose and licentious than the Mandanes.

After this warm-up, Henry goes on to attribute to his hosts a long list of astonishing sexual practices, unnatural lusts, and filthy personal habits; and, for good measure, comments with heavily underscored disgust on the Big Belly women. It is a fair question, however, whether his appraisal was not merely a sour reaction to the apathetic, even disdainful reception he had received. Another Nor'wester, who happened to be in the same Big Belly village when Henry arrived, suggests as much.

Charles McKenzie and James Caldwell were in the hut to which the Big Belly so unceremoniously conducted Henry and his men. Hearing his name called by a familiar voice,

McKenzie rushed to the door, dressed as he was, in Indian clothes. The greeting he received from Henry and his party could hardly have been called cordial.

"Their first salutation," McKenzie wrote in his own *Missouri Journal*, "was a reproach to my dress." But McKenzie could be caustic himself. "Their appearance," he noted, "was not to their credit, nor the interest of the company . . . Mr. Chaboillez had on a *capot* which had once been white, a good pair of leather breeches, and a weather beaten hat, with a stout black beard of nine days' growth. Mr. Henry differed only in the *capot*, as he had on a corduroy jacket! . . . It was most galling to me, who understood some of the Indian language, to hear them despised and the American captains, whom they had despised until then, praised."

It is not hard to understand McKenzie's obvious distress. He and the other traders had labored to implant in the minds of the haughty Big Belly one simple but vital idea: the traders themselves were only humble, helpless men; but back of each one of them stood the shadowy figures of the great Chiefs of the Whites, the bourgeois in the north, who were all-knowing, all-powerful, and must never be offended. And now Henry and Chaboillez had shown up in old corduroy jackets, dirty capotes, and battered hats to shatter this carefully developed image of the awesome Chiefs of the Whites. What must the Big Belly have thought? McKenzie knew well enough. "They, indeed, could scarcely believe Messrs. Chaboillez and Henry to be those whom we called our Chiefs," he wrote. "They asked me, who made them chiefs? What made them superior to other white men?"

McKenzie did his best to pick up the pieces of the shattered image and put them together again. But it is easy to sense his conviction that, after Henry's visit to the Big Belly, things would never be the same. Henry, on the other hand, had his own views about his hosts, and took little pains to conceal them. "Mr. Henry avowed his disappointment and did not disguise his detestation of the Indians," McKenzie also wrote. "He kept at a distance from the crowd and smoked his pipe alone."

Even the Americans, however, who had spent the previous winter under Lewis and Clark among the Big Belly, had fared no better in winning the respect of those arrogant Indians. For all their flag hoisting and medal giving, they had succeeded — in British eyes, at least — in gaining nothing but disdain. The Big Belly even refused to accept the presents offered by the Americans. According to Henry:

> They were disgusted at the high-sounding language the American captains bestowed on themselves and their own nation, wishing to impress the Indians with the idea that they were great warriors, and a powerful people, who, if exasperated, could crush all the nations of the earth.

> This manner of proceeding did not agree with these haughty savages, who have too high an opinion of themselves to entertain the idea of acknowledging any race to be their superiors.

"If the United States ever attempted to reduce the Big Bellies by force," Henry adds darkly, "they will meet with more resistance than they may be now aware of."

8

A COUPLE of days in the Big Belly village was about all that Henry could take. The food, consisting largely of putrid meat, was uneatable. The sanitary habits of the villagers were nauseating. Their fickle bargaining customs were enough to drive a trader to distraction. Their savage dogs were a constant menace. Not even their women were tolerable:

> We took our lodgings for the night in LeBorgne's hut, with several women whose husbands were absent, and who would have had no objections to our filling the vacancy, especially as they observed we had some articles they fancied. But I believe most of us were already too much disgusted with them . . . to wish to become more intimately acquainted.

So, after viewing the bones of three hundred Sioux who had fallen in a great battle with the Big Belly, Henry and his men set off for the lower Mandan village, where the food was good, no dogs barked, and the girls were fascinating.

Here they spent a day watching the Mandan race their horses, shoot at marks with their strong bone-and-sinew bows, and perform warlike manoeuvres with spear and ax on horseback. There is a pleasant holiday atmosphere about the journal at this point; and it is difficult to reconcile the "mild, sociable, and affable people" described by Henry with the atrociously inhuman practices to which they were addicted. The journal describes one of them in this shocking, if matter-of-fact passage:

> When a young man has attained the age of 20 years, he generally, in the depth of winter, performs his penance by setting out entirely naked and alone, with only two or three pairs of shoes, the iron barb of an arrow, and no means of making a fire.
>
> In this condition he repairs to a certain high hill, a day's journey from the village. On this hill he must remain as

many days as his strength will permit, during which time he neither eats, drinks, nor sleeps, but passes the time in dancing, bawling, howling and lamenting. Here also he amputates a finger with the iron barb brought for that purpose. Some have been known to be absent for seven days in the severest weather.

After several days — more or fewer — the penitent makes his appearance, coming at full speed, and as there is someone continually upon the huts, information is instantly spread of his return. He is met by a particular friend, who has kept account of the number of days he has been absent, and for every day has prepared a bull's head, to which has been fastened 1½ fathoms of cord.

The other end of this is then affixed to an incision in the penitent's back or shoulders, by pinching up a fold of skin and flesh, through which is thrust the barb of an arrow; as many days as he has been absent, so many must be the incisions and the number of heads must also tally with them.

He must then walk around the village, howling and bawling, with all those bulls' heads trailing on the ground . . . So many days as he has been absent, so many times must he walk around the village, never ceasing to utter lamentations. Some have been known to fall senseless during this painful ordeal; but even then, they only allow themselves a few moments to recover and proceed again . . . Some never recover, and others languish for months before they get well.

More spectacular, and perhaps unsurpassed for sheer horror in the whole literature of self-immolation, are the ghastly rites depicted by Catlin, an actual eye-witness, in both words and pictures. The ceremonies took place in the grand medicine lodge on the fourth day of the Mandan religious ritual. The first three days had been occupied with dances and spectacles in preparation for the climactic event. The young candidates for self-torture had already undergone four days of abstinence from food, drink and sleep.

After these preliminaries, two men stationed themselves near the middle of the lodge, one armed with a scalping knife, the other with a handful of wooden splints. While the chiefs looked on, the hollow-eyed young men stepped forward to receive the final torment. Through incisions in their shoulders and breasts, made with serrated knives to produce maximum pain, the splints were thrust. Cords dangling from the roof of the lodge were then fastened to the skewers, and the victims were hoisted until their feet were off the ground. Similar splints were then thrust through the flesh of each arm, thigh and calf. Catlin, with a somewhat sadistic relish, it would seem, supplies the details:

"Each one was then instantly raised with the cords, until the weight of the body was suspended by them, and then, while the blood was streaming down their limbs, the bystanders hung upon the splints and in many instances, the skull of a buffalo with the horns on it, was attached to each lower arm and each lower leg, for the purpose, probably, of preventing by their great weight the struggling which might otherwise take place to their disadvantage whilst hung up.

"When these things were all adjusted, each one was raised higher by the cords, until these weights all swung clear from the ground, leaving his feet, in most cases, some six or eight feet above the ground. In this plight they at once became appalling and frightful to look at — the flesh, to support the weight of their bodies, with the additional weights which were attached to them, was raised six or eight inches by the skewers;

and their heads sunk forward on their breasts, or thrown backwards, in a much more frightful condition, according to the way in which they were hung up."

The first stages of these tortures, according to Catlin, were borne with "pleasant smiles." But as the medicine men began to twirl the victim and all his weights in mid-air, he broke out "in the most lamentable and heart-rending cries that the human spirit is capable of." After fifteen minutes or so, his voice and strength gave out. When not the slightest sign of struggling could be detected, he was at last lowered to the ground and left to lie for six or eight minutes. As soon as he had recovered, he presented himself to a medicine man, made a short speech to the Great Spirit, and had his little finger chopped off with a blow of the hatchet.

Catlin devotes a good many lurid pages to the Mandan ceremonies, and embellishes them with a few sketches made on the spot. He also supplies a paragraph or two of appropriate moralizing: "My heart sickened with disgust for so abominable and ignorant a custom, and still I stand ready with all my heart to excuse and forgive them for adhering so strictly to an ancient celebration, founded in superstition and mysteries, of which they know not the origin." But Henry, ordinarily so detailed, has only a page and a half of comment — and that singularly terse, even hurried. Perhaps, for once, the meat was too strong for his robust Nor'wester's stomach.

9

THE Mandan villages seem to have been in an almost constant state of uproar. The day after Henry's return to Matootanha, a temporary calm was broken by the arrival — at breakneck speed, as usual — of two messengers. They had come straight from Le Borgne, the supreme chief of both the Big Belly and the Mandan. Le Borgne was at a Cheyenne village, where he was negotiating a peace treaty. He had been successful in his mission, the messengers announced; and now everyone was summoned to the Cheyenne camp for the great treaty ceremony.

The village was at once seized by a spasm of preparation, "women and children uncovering caches and filling bags, repairing saddles, making and mending shoes and smocks, cleaning and rubbing the leather with white earth." Part of this feverish activity, Henry learned, was the Mandan women's eagerness to trade corn and beans for the Cheyenne's dressed leather robes, trimmed with porcupine quills and feathers, which seemed to be high fashion along the Missouri.

Henry was happy to receive an invitation from Le Borgne's brother to accompany him to the Cheyenne camp. This would give him an opportunity to meet the great chief, whose fame had spread throughout the Northwest and, indeed, to the eastern seaboard. But, as usual, there was a small fly in the ointment:

> My landlord was so obliging as to insist on my accepting the services of his young wife on my journey, for which purpose he had provided her with a horse and other accessories. I did not in the least relish this proposal, and signified as much to him; but he was determined to send her along, and I could only hope to give her the slip in the crowd. As she was not ready to start at the same time we did, I had a favorable opportunity of avoiding her.

And so, saved by a common feminine failing, Henry set out alone with his companions. At one o'clock they came to a hill, the top of which was completely covered with men, women, children and horses. Here an old chief called Chokecherry took command as generalissimo, and all moved southward, the men in the van, the women bringing up the rear. Henry's own description of the cavalcade is a compact and vivid picture of the American Plains Indian in one of his finer moments:

> The men's horses were light, and all the young men wore their finest habiliments and war dresses. Many had scalps suspended from the bits of their Spanish bridles, or dangling at their horses' breasts, or attached to the handles of their spears and battle-axes; all were armed with guns, spears, battle-axes, and bows and arrows. The party mustered 500 men and 300 women, all mounted.

> Soon after getting into motion, the young men formed themselves into parties of 10 to 30 abreast and proceeded at a slow, regular pace, singing their war songs, accompanied with a number of rattles; this, with the continual neighing and snorting of the horses, which in a manner kept time with their songs, made an imposing, warlike spectacle.

As the party rode into the hill country, old Chokecherry ordered the women to place themselves in the center of the column, with strong parties of men in the van, the rear, and on both flanks. "This precaution was taken lest an enemy might cut off some of the women, who were always straggling behind." At night, camp was made beside a pond of stagnant water.

At eleven o'clock next day a halt was called for the purpose of dressing, painting, and preparing for a grand arrival at the Cheyenne camp. This took a couple of hours:

> At one o'clock, all were decked to the best advantage,

to make them look more savage and ferocious than they naturally were . . . Orders then given to mount and proceed were instantly obeyed, everyone admiring his own ferocious appearance, and careful to keep in the nicest order, without disarranging his dress or daubing. No more races were run; nothing but singing was heard. The young fellows appeared as stiff and proud of their persons as courtiers going to make formal appearance at a grand levee, and scarcely deigned to look at one of us otherwise than with contempt.

By midafternoon, having come up with no Cheyenne, the party grew suspicious of treachery. The chiefs ordered the column to occupy a high hill, while they conferred. Perhaps the Cheyenne had been joined by the Sioux and, stronger now, had forgotten their peaceful promises. Perhaps they had killed Le Borgne and the other chiefs who had gone to their camp in peace. Since they knew there were women in the Mandan's party, perhaps they had laid an ambuscade to fall on it.

The chiefs decided to play it safe. They deployed their men defensively on the hilltop, then sent a scouting party ahead. After some time, the scouts appeared on a distant hill and waved the party on. The Cheyenne camp was but a short distance away. The column, pausing only to freshen up, organized for its grand approach:

In the front was Le Borgne's brother, attended by Two Crows on his left, holding out the stem, and a war chief on his right, supporting an American flag on a long pole. These three men advanced ten paces; 40 Big Bellies immediately followed and formed abreast, singing and shaking their rattles. To the right and left of these, and somewhat in the rear, two parties of 30 men each filed off, singing in the same manner. In the rear of those, again, but in the middle line, was formed another party of 40 young men, also singing.

The center of these four squads was a vacant place, into which we were desired to form abreast, in company with some of the most respectable old men. The four squads kept perfect order, closing and extending their ranks as the very rugged ground required. Behind them and us came small parties of tens, twenties and thirties, singing and shouting at intervals. The women brought up the rear.

Presently, a small band of Cheyenne riding beautiful, spirited horses dashed up to greet them. About a mile farther on, a large party of horsemen advanced abreast. Out of this band galloped the great chief of the Cheyenne on a black stallion. Riding up to the flag, he folded it in his arms, then embraced the war chiefs, and after that shook hands with Henry and his companions. This part of the ceremony over, all the Cheyenne rode headlong into the Mandan and Big Belly ranks, each adopting an erstwhile foe as comrade by embracing him — at a gallop!

Thus, protesting brotherly love at every step, the former enemies swept toward the Cheyenne camp. Suddenly, on a pleasant, level plain, the white leather tents of the Cheyenne — more than two hundred of them — circled in beautiful symmetry. A young man, riding at breakneck speed, dashed through the ranks in search of the white men:

Desiring us to follow him, he wheeled about and rode off. We were not slow to follow him. We entered the camp and rode on to the further end after our conductor, who stopped at a large tent, before the door of which a flag was flying.

This was Le Borgne's tent. In a few moments the great chief himself came out to receive them.

10

EVERY white trader who ever visited the Missouri Indians agreed on one thing: Le Borgne was a great man. Most were impelled by the forcefulness of his personality to insert a short "profile" of the famous leader into their journals; but none has left us so vivid a picture of him as Alexander Henry the Younger's:

> Le Borgne himself came out to receive us and, having shaken us very kindly by the hand, desired us to enter, whilst his women unsaddled our horses and took in our baggage. He appeared highly pleased to see us, and instantly ordered his women to prepare something to eat.
>
> This man is upward of six feet high, and stout in proportion, but not in the least inclined to corpulency; he has lost the sight of his right eye, a thick white coat entirely covering the sight; but the penetrating look from his left eye, the great size of his aquiline nose, and the width of his mouth, make ample amends for that single deficiency, and give him the aspect of a fierce, savage brute.
>
> His countenance fully denotes his character, which is that of a brave, enterprising warrior. This man is the great chief of the Big Bellies, and indeed is the principal man of the five villages; whatever he says is law.
>
> On many occasions he has displayed his personal bravery in civic quarrels, and in disturbances between his own tribe and the Mandans, in every one of which he has gained the advantage and succeeded in his own plans, not always without the death of his adversary, which no individual dares avenge. He is the oldest of five brothers, and appears to be about 45 years of age.

Outside, a pandemonium of friendship had struck the Cheyenne camp. The chiefs on both sides galloped through and around the tent circles, haranguing their men and ordering everyone to observe the new order of love and brotherhood. But inside Le Borgne's tent all was serene:

> During all these performances Le Borgne never once looked out of his tent, but sat unconcernedly smoking and talking with us. His manners appeared pleasant; in conversation a perpetual smile played upon his countenance; when matters did not please him, he still smiled, but it was then a ghastly grin.

To this official portrait of a great man, Henry then adds a few informal touches:

> To his women he is a mere brute; he uses them more like slaves than wives. They appear to be in continual dread of him, and not without cause, as he has butchered some of them with his own hands and with the greatest composure imaginable . . . Although he is not of a jealous disposition, he does not approve of his women disposing of their persons without his knowledge.

> He has often been guilty of debauching young women, both maidens and wives. Some he has kept for his own use, and others he has returned to their friends or husbands when tired of their company; and still none have dared to avenge the affront. When any female strikes his fancy, he makes no ceremony, but uses her as if she were his own.

Henry passed a pleasant hour or so with Le Borgne, learning many interesting things from him about the roving western tribes — the Cheyenne, the Pawnee, and the Arapahoe — who traded with the Spaniards. Outside, nothing was heard but singing throughout the camp, and the voices of the women bartering their corn for the beautiful leather robes and smocks of the Cheyenne, as if at a country fair.

Then, just as the sun was going down, the peace was shattered by an extraordinary commotion. The uproar, it turned out, had been caused by the arrival of a dozen Assiniboine, inveterate enemies of the Cheyenne, who, for some reason hard to fathom, had followed the Big Belly and Mandan into the camp and now claimed their protection. The Cheyenne were all for exterminating the lot; and the Mandan and Big Belly were, to say the least, very embarrassed. But Le Borgne, acting on some obscure impulse of Indian chivalry, swore to defend them to the death. And this, it soon appeared, he might have to do:

> The Schians soon surrounded them and wished to strike some of the Assiniboines; but Le Borgne, who was by this time joined by many of his own people, kept them at bay by flourishing his battleax. He desired them to desist; saying that if any of them were imprudent enough to hurt an Assiniboine whilst under his protection, he might advance and make the attempt, but the event would show who would be the most pitiful.

Le Borgne finally herded the Assiniboine safely into his own tent; and things simmered down to a point where some of the Cheyenne even dropped in for a friendly pipe. But no one, including Henry, was deceived by this surface placidity. The uneasy peace was soon broken again, in fact, by a rumor that the Cheyenne had stolen some of the Mandan's horses:

> This alleged insult added fuel to the flames; our great man got up in a rage and went out to inquire into the affair, declaring that if the report proved true, he would instantly spread death and destruction through the camp.

While everyone was preparing for a showdown, Le Borgne returned with the news that it had all been a mistake; his own men had taken the horses to round up some strays.

The situation, if less tense, was still anything but harmonious next day. Le Borgne, however, had committed himself to the adoption of a Cheyenne son; and so the ceremony took place as scheduled. It was a long, tedious ceremony, involving a great deal of smoking and palaver, with an obvious lack of enthusiasm on both sides:

> Le Borgne, who sat in the tent during all this part of the ceremony wrapped up in an American flag, said not a word, but cast many a sardonic grin at his adopted son. At its conclusion he arose, wrapped the flag around his adopted son, giving into his hands the three cords which tied the three horses at the door.

The adopted son showed his own disrelish for the whole proceedings by instantly handing the cords to his wife. After that, the forms of the ceremony were continued, but mutual animosities finally got the upper hand, and the Cheyenne chiefs walked out of the meeting.

> It was about 3 p. m. when affairs thus assumed a gloomy aspect; harangues were made through the camp by both parties, evidently not of a very amiable nature; frequent menaces were made by our party, and the other as often retorted. The adopted son sullenly went to his own tent; horses were collected on both sides; everybody was surly and gloomy.

Early next morning, Le Borgne ordered his people to break camp and prepare for departure. It was a withdrawal, actually, under pressure from the Cheyenne, who rode boldly into the ranks of the Mandan and Big Belly, hurling insults and offering battle:

We really expected every moment to see some of them strike a fatal blow, and thus precipitate the conflict, as they certainly pushed our party to the last extremity. I could not help admiring the conduct of our commander-in-chief, Le Borgne; in all this tumult he said very little, and appeared quite unconcerned; but I observed he was always on his guard, and that no Schian personally insulted him.

Reaching the hill from which they had first sighted the Cheyenne camp, Le Borgne decided to form up in battle array and call the Cheyenne's bluff:

The women with the pack horses were placed in the center, and a large body of men were stationed around them as a guard. Le Borgne, accompanied by a large party, well armed, with guns loaded and fresh primed, and balls in their mouths, returned to the Schians, who awaited their approach. We remained in suspense for some time, observing the motions of Le Borgne and his party, whom we every moment expected to see engaged in battle; but after a short conference with the enemy, they returned, having, they said, frightened the Schians back to camp.

As they rode homeward, Le Borgne explained to Henry why they had not given battle. "My son," the great chief said, "we had too many women and children with us to commence hostilities ourselves. They would all have been destroyed. But had we been attacked, we would not have flinched."

11

ARRIVING back at the great Mandan village of Matootanha, Henry settled accounts with his host and set out on his return journey with a stock of the Mandan's emergency ration:

parched corn pounded into flour, mixed with a little fat, and made up into balls about the size of a hen's egg. Crossing the river, they took the same road by which they had come, until they met McKenzie and Caldwell, who were also returning to the Assiniboine. Together, they started toward the country of the Sioux.

Their party now consisted of ten men and twenty-five horses, a cavalcade that looked strong from a distance. Its real strength, however, was slight. They had but three guns and a pair of pistols among them. Nevertheless, as soon as they came to the heights of the Snake's Den — from which they had first sighted the Missouri on the outward trip — they set their course due north, a short but dangerous route on the Sioux frontiers.

The march home was over soggy prairie, with many river crossings; but by pushing steadily ahead, often through the darkness, Henry arrived at Assiniboine House at eleven-thirty o'clock on the night of August ninth — just ten days after leaving the Missouri.

He must have felt right at home; for here he found "a troublesome set of Indians, all drinking." Assiniboine House was, in fact, a miserable post; but it offered some, at least, of civilization's amenities:

> A wash, a shave, a change of linen was very acceptable, as I had worn the same shirt since leaving Pembina river, and it was not entirely free from vermin, notwithstanding daily efforts to destroy them. I went to sleep in clean blankets on a soft feather bed, and only those who have experienced like hardships can form any idea of my delightful repose.

But not even such luxury could keep Henry for more than a day at Assiniboine House. With one man, he left for Pembina by the shortest route, through the Hair Hills. After two weeks of harrowing travel over flooded plains and swollen rivers, he arrived safely at his Red River post:

> I proceeded to my headquarters, where I found all hands had arrived [from Kaministiquia], and the Indians camped at the fort anxiously awaiting me to have a drinking match.

Thus, on a familiar note, ended Alexander Henry's pleasure jaunt to the lands of the Mandan.

12

THINGS went badly at Pembina after his return. The post, already in an exhausted state as far as beaver was concerned, received its "death blow," as Henry termed it, at Portage la Prairie:

> The main cause of this was an unfortunate quarrel which took place last spring, when some were killed and others wounded, among them one of our principal men, whose head was split open with an ax.

At about the same time, some of Henry's hunters were attacked by a war party of Sioux, and a Canadian killed. But this, as it turned out, was but a curtain-raiser to an attack on Pembina itself.

With the aid of his cohorn, loaded with a pound of powder and thirty musket balls, Henry repelled that assault with the loss of only one dog killed by Sioux bullets. It was, however, a decidedly disagreeable affair, and it did nothing to lessen his distaste for a rapidly deteriorating situation.

Even the harvest failed in the fall of 1807, and fire blackened the country for miles around. The Indians did very little hunting and much drinking. Bad coughs and colds attacked every man, woman and child at Pembina. The Sioux continued to terrorize the buffalo and beaver hunters. And, to top it all off, the spring of 1808 brought the worst grasshopper plague ever experienced in that part of the country:

> Swarms of grasshoppers have destroyed the greater part of the vegetables in my kitchen garden — onions, cabbages, melons, cucumbers, carrots, parsnips, and beets. They have also attacked the potatoes and corn, but these were strong enough at the root to sprout again . . . The swarms appear about the 15th of June, generally in clouds from the S., and spread destruction; the very trees are stripped of their leaves. Grasshoppers pass northward until millions are drowned in Lac Winipic and cause a horrid stench.

All in all, it was a very depressing year — and, with the beaver kill reduced by half, hardly a profitable one. But good news was on the way. It arrived at the end of a sweltering August day with three young Indians who had come, in the remarkable time of ten days, from Lac la Pluie:

> They brought me a packet from the mountain, Fort William, and Montreal . . . The main motive of the express was to forward a statement of the arrangement of the department by our council at Fort William, wherein I was appointed to Lower Fort des Prairies.

Nothing could have been more welcome to Henry than this appointment. Now, at last, he would be free from the intolerable ennui of Pembina, and master of a post, far up the Saskatchewan and within sight of the Rockies, that any Nor'-wester would have been happy to command. For the eyes of every man in the great, sprawling, ever-expanding Concern were now turned toward the Shining Mountains — and beyond them, to the Columbia.

VIII

The Saskatchewan

HENRY lost no time in leaving Pembina. Within a week he was at the entrance of Lac Winipic, on his way to Lower Fort des Prairies, commonly called Fort Vermilion. Here he bade adieu to the Saulteur — and not without a tinge of regret. He had spent a long time among these people, after all, and he had married one of their women. And now he could not leave without a few good words for them in his journal:

> I have experienced every trouble, danger, and inconvenience which attends the management of affairs among that turbulent nation. I have been frequently fired at by them and have had several narrow escapes for my life. But I am happy to say they never pillaged me of the value of a needle.

Interpolating a short homily on the evils of the fur trade, no matter where conducted, he then concludes hopefully:

"But let us now proceed on our voyage to other nations, who may treat us more leniently."

The start of the voyage was not, however, very auspicious. Immediately after entering Lac Winipic, his brigade lost itself in the narrow, rush-choked channels; then spent a perilous night buffeted about by the wind in utter darkness. They lost themselves again. They were windbound. Terrible squalls, with thunder and lightning, blew Henry's tent down and soaked everyone to the skin. After five days of this, the brigade was forced to land on a spit of land appropriately named Pointe Maligne; and here Henry encountered the great Nor'wester-geographer David Thompson, also beaten into temporary submission by the elements:

> At sunrise, the wind having abated, we with great diffi-
> culty loaded our canoes and embarked, hoisted sail, and
> kept along the shore; but the wind increased to such a
> gale that we could scarcely carry two feet of sail. At
> Pointe au Canot Casse we discovered a sail ahead, which,
> on approaching Pointe Maligne, put ashore. On coming
> up with it, we found it to be Mr. D. Thompson, bound
> for the Columbia via the Saskatchewan river.

They camped together, and while they waited for the wind to die down, Henry and Thompson had much to talk about.

2

DAVID Thompson, at this time thirty-eight years old, was a short, powerfully built man, brown as a Cree, with his long black hair chopped off in a square bang above his eyebrows. His face was deeply lined and weathered, his dark eyes full of animation, his bearing tinged with a kind of somber dignity. Neatly dressed in a sober suit of fustian, he looked more like a schoolteacher than a fur trader.

Thompson had been reared in the Grey Coat School, an English orphanage at Westminster, where he was taught a little mathematics. At the age of fourteen, the school bound him out to the Hudson's Bay Company, and the lad began his apprenticeship on the bleak shores of the Bay. After serving a few years as clerk, storekeeper and hunter at Forts York and Churchill, he went inland on the Company's business. By 1786, he had followed the Saskatchewan farther west than any white man had yet ventured.

During the next two years Thompson, then nineteen, began making the endless series of astronomical observations that add up to an almost incredible feat of geodetic surveying, and form the basis for his reputation as the greatest land geographer the world has ever known.

It is almost impossible, indeed, to follow David Thompson's vast peregrinations from then on. He went everywhere, and wherever he went, he took his observations and made his notes for the Great Map he had always in mind — with little help or encouragement, however, from the Honorable Company. On his great exploration to Lake Athabasca, for example, he was forced to make his own canoe and start on a long and hazardous expedition without a guide, and without equipment except a fish net, a few rounds of ammunition, a sextant and a compass!

Not long after this — and quite understandably, perhaps — Thompson left the Hudson's Bay Company, walked seventy-five miles through the bush to the nearest North West Company post, and signed up with the Nor'westers. "This day," he wrote in his journal, "left the service of the Hudson's Bay Company, and entered that of the Merchants from Canada. May God Almighty prosper me."

The difference between the stuffy Gentlemen on the Bay and the free-wheeling Nor'westers is well illustrated by Thompson's first assignment. He was not to be encumbered with trading responsibilities at all. His sole job was (1) to determine the 49th parallel of latitude — the new boundary between the United States and Canada, (2) to visit the Mandan, (3) to search for fossil bones of large animals, and (4) to fix the positions of the North West Company's trading posts. During his first year, he made a tremendous 4000-mile swing through totally unsurveyed territory, touching at points far up on the Assiniboine, the Mandan villages, the headwaters of the Mississippi, the site of present-day Duluth, Sault Ste. Marie, and the Grand Portage — a one-man survey that has never, perhaps, been equaled.

This vast wilderness loop was merely a warm-up, however, for the surveys that followed; and by the winter of 1799, Thompson was busy at Fort George on the first stages of his Great Map of the West. With him was his wife, Charlotte Small, the half-breed daughter of Patrick Small, master of the North West Company's fort at Isle à la Crosse. Charlotte was fourteen when she married Thompson. At the time of her husband's meeting with Henry on Lac Winipic, she had borne him three children and was awaiting a fourth at a post called Boggy Hall on the Saskatchewan. Wherever Thompson went, Charlotte went. When his longest and most perilous expedition took him over the Rocky Mountains to the Columbia River, in 1806-07, she and the children were with him.

By that time the great geographer was also employing his

unusual talents as a trader. He built Kootenay House on the Columbia and, all the while checking his latitudes and longitudes, opened trading relations with the Flathead and Kootenay, in what are now the states of Idaho and Montana. As a trader, his methods were unorthodox in two respects: he refused to give or sell rum to his Indian customers, and he browbeat his voyageurs into attending divine service — conducted by himself in fantastic French — every Sunday. He was much respected by the Indians, who called him Koo-Koo-Sint.

Now he was hurrying back to the Columbia, to build more forts and pick up his trade with the Kootenay. But he had other, bigger things in mind. He wanted to take his brigade all the way down the Columbia to the sea, where the Americans were building. If the Piegan would let him! The Piegan had threatened to kill him. They did not like his supplying their enemies, the Kootenay, with guns. He would have to find a way around the Piegan . . .

As he listened to this modest, far-ranging man unfolding his epic plans, the restlessness so apparent in his journal of late must have gripped Henry. For a long time now he had chafed under the dull routine of Pembina; he had been irked beyond endurance by the petty squabbles and drunken quarrels that marked the slow passage of time at that lonely prairie post. "Now, by God," he could say to himself, "I'll see what it's like out there." For his new post, high up on the Saskatchewan, would put him within striking distance of many of the places Thompson had mentioned: the headwaters of that great river, the beautiful Kootenay Plain, the snow-capped Shining Mountains themselves . . .

Thompson and his men had penetrated those mountains in every direction, at all seasons, and by every mode of transportation — canoe, dog sledge, horse, afoot. They knew the enormous, mysterious, fearful peaks as intimately as he himself knew the plains. They were the advance guard of all that colorful company of trappers, hunters and Indian fighters who, a full generation later, would begin to penetrate the unknown regions of the West. They were the first of the Mountain Men.

And Alexander Henry the Younger, listening to David Thompson on the stormy shore of Lac Winipic, must have longed mightily — like any Nor'wester — to see what they had seen.

3

WHEN the wind died down, they joined their brigades and continued northward together. A new storm blew up. They fought their way under double-reefed sail, or with no sail at all, around the Detour, a point of land extending for twenty-five miles into the lake, and arrived in a driving rain at the mouth of the mighty Saskatchewan. At this point, Henry had come some three hundred miles up Lac Winipic, battling every inch of the way over one of the largest and most treacherous stretches of water in the Northwest. He still had more than six hundred miles to go by canoe and horse before he reached his new post.

The Saskatchewan, one of the world's great streams, was to British America what the Missouri had become to the United States. Without a single obstacle to navigation, it provided a freeway for almost a thousand miles from Cumberland House to its sources on the Continental Divide. It gave access, by a vast chain of lakes, northward to Athabasca; and eastward to

Hudson Bay. It was the six-lane highway of the fur trade to every quarter of the continent — but getting into it was no easy matter!

Henry and Thompson portaged around the Grand Rapids at its mouth. The men cursed the logs the Hudson's Bay people from York Factory had laid from one end of the carry to the other, as rollers for their big boats. *Sacrés!* and *lâches!* shattered the darkness as one voyageur after another stumbled and sprawled over them. Thunder, lightning and rain all night. Then a plague of mosquitoes.

At daybreak the brigades were off again, under a canopy of pelicans lumbering through the gray air above the marshes. Sometimes they hoisted sail and scudded before a fine breeze; sometimes they towed and poled laboriously; sometimes they battled gales in which "we expected every moment our canoes would be swamped." They lost themselves in a mazy channel of the river, frequently running aground on mud banks, paddling and dragging their craft until the men were "bushed." At night, unable to find dry land on which to pitch a tent, they slept in their canoes among the rushes. If there was any kind of hardship and trouble that wasn't a voyageur's lot, they wondered what it was. But even the marshes of the Saskatchewan come to an end at last, and finally they reached the main channel and the first dry land they had seen for days.

They had now come to the Pas, which may be found on modern maps near the western border of Manitoba. At this place the French had built Fort Paskoyac in the old days, and Henry could see traces of it from his canoe. Here his uncle, the elder Henry, had paused with the two Frobishers in 1775. It was a deserted spot now, with only one Indian family living in a rotting leather tent.

Two days of uphill work against the strong current brought them to Cumberland House, one of the most important points, from the standpoint of the fur trade, on the whole North American continent. The Hudson's Bay Company, the North West Company, and the XY Company all had establishments in the vicinity; and they were all known as "Cumberland House."

The North West Company's post was the focal point of an immense network of canoe routes radiating in every direction of the compass to the outermost limits of the fur country. It was literally true that a canoe could start from here and, with no portage of more than a day's length, could go to the Arctic Ocean, Hudson Bay, the Gulf of St. Lawrence, or to the Gulf of Mexico; and with hardly greater trouble, to the Pacific Ocean.

Because of this strategic location, the North West Company had made Cumberland House a provisioning depot for its northern brigades. It was also a convenient place for the traders bound for Kaministiquia or Rainy Lake to leave their wives and children until they returned: fish were plentiful here, and living cheap. In other respects, however, it was a post of minor importance to the Nor'westers, since the English monopolized the trade in the vicinity. So, after "settling" his people for the winter, Henry hurried after his brigade, without even stopping the night at Cumberland House.

The river soon became broad and strong. Now the paddle was laid aside for the setting pole and towing line; and so it would be all the way to the Rockies. Travel was a dream on this great, smooth-running river — at least for the bourgeois — and Henry describes his satisfaction in "taking a comfortable nap without any noise to disturb me; the canoe glided as if under easy sail."

In the deep cut of the river there was little to see except the sky overhead, often cloud-piled and, viewed from the bottom of a kind of canyon, abnormally blue. Ahead, the great stream seemed to stretch away on a perfectly straight course, so vast were its bends. The current continued to grow stronger.

On the last day of August, they camped on the site of old Fort St. Louis, built almost sixty years before by the French. Sometimes the rusted rim of a carriage wheel, or a broken plowshare could be found in the high grass of the prairie on which the post stood; and the old road to the plains could still be seen, winding up a valley. Smoking his pipe in the dusk, as his men made camp, Henry must have almost felt the presence of the Commandant de la Corne and his men, who so long ago had come so far from the little towns along the St. Lawrence to build this forgotten post. One could never, it seemed, quite leave the French behind!

Now they passed the ruins of old Fort Nipeween and arrived at the Forks, where the Saskatchewan divided into two streams, one running from the southwest, the other from the northwest. Henry continued up the higher fork. The course of the river grew more devious, the current faster, with rapids frequent and often dangerous. The labor of poling and tracking became man-killing; but there was nothing, apparently, that a Canadian could not live through:

> The track along the beach has become very bad for the men at the line; the bank comes in close to the water's edge at many places, which are obstructed by heaps of earth and wood daily sliding from the upper part of the shore . . . At such places cold springs issue and form miry rivulets, into which the men sink knee-deep. The exertion they are obliged to make keeps them in a perspiration, and with their blood thus boiling, as it were, they throw themselves upon their bellies at those springs and take enor-

mous draughts of ice-cold water; but I never saw that this had any bad effect upon them.

While the canoemen toiled at the towing lines and the long, steel-spiked setting poles — swinging them in rhythm as regular and almost as graceful as that of paddling — the women ran along the high banks gathering fruit and berries for the crews. "This," Henry wrote, "alleviates the labor and revives the spirits of the men."

On the shore, as the canoes swept up the broad, strongly-flowing stream, the memento of an obscure tragedy caught his eye:

> At this spot about two feet of rope hung from a tree, where a woman, in a fit of despair at ill usage from her Canadian husband, had determined to put an end to her troubles by hanging herself; but she was discovered and cut down before it was too late.

They arrived at the Great Plains. Even the small clumps of hemlock and brushwood had disappeared now, and except for an occasional willow island in the river, not a tree was to be seen from horizon to horizon. Paths were worn deep in the sand at the buffalo crossings; a herd was seen swimming in the river. The Indians of the plains, Cree and Assiniboine, began to show up and plague Henry for liquor and tobacco. These Indians, knowing nothing about canoes, tossed whatever they had — dried meat, berries, bladders of fat — into the already heavily-loaded craft, and almost sank them.

They arrived at the Montée. This was the place where a direct road ran between the north and south branches of the Saskatchewan. It was a good road, much used by the Indians, and only one day's journey across the plains. But the Montée was also the place where the bourgeois abandoned the plodding canoes and took to horse. Two men from upriver were waiting for Henry with mounts.

After the long, cramped days in the canoe, he found it pleasant to ride with his hunter across the open plains, against a west wind that seemed to carry the smell of mountain snows. At night he rejoined his brigade — which long ago had left Thompson's behind — and a strong camp was made. They were now in uncertain Indian country, so each night every man was issued ten musket balls and enough powder to fire them.

A general uneasiness turned into genuine alarm when, at a sharp bend of the Saskatchewan called the Elbow, a white stranger dashed into camp with news that the Cree had gathered at Battle River for the purpose of stopping Henry and preventing him from supplying the Slave with arms and ammunition. A couple of days later, while hunting buffalo, Henry was certain that the showdown had come:

> We suddenly perceived a large body of horsemen from above, coming directly toward us. We halted, and determined to sell our lives as dearly as possible; any attempt to save ourselves by flight would have been in vain. From the halooing and whooping they made, urging their horses at full speed, we had reason to suppose they were badly inclined and would consequently give us no quarter.

This threat, however, turned out to be only a hunting party with Henry's own hunter at their head. That night, nevertheless, Henry took care to check up on the Indian camp. He was taking no chances in this definitely hostile territory. It was in this vicinity, he remembered, that the Cree had massacred the traders at Eagle Hills Fort; next day, in fact, they passed the ruins of that ill-fated post.

As they approached Battle River, the Saskatchewan's largest tributary, the terrain became rougher and covered with poplar-clad hummocks and well-wooded valleys. It was not bad beaver country. Battle River itself was extremely rich in furs; but it was hard to persuade the hunters to venture into this domain of the blood-thirsty Slave and Assiniboine.

Those Indians who visited Henry's camps — and they were a great many now — brought nothing to trade but dried berries and bear meat. Henry gave them a little rum and tobacco, and pushed on impatiently, "heartily tired of such a set of beggars." While the brigade poled its way up the river, he hunted buffalo along the banks, always keeping the canoes in sight.

On September 13, 1808, he crossed the Red Deer River, "nooned" at La Plante's River to refresh the horses, and fell upon a well-beaten Indian track that led through small plains and hummocks of poplars and willows to the end of his long journey:

> At sunset we sighted Fort Vermilion, in a long flat bottom of meadow, directly opposite the entrance of Vermilion River, which falls in on the S. A large camp of Slaves began to whoop and haloo as we came down the hills and appeared rejoiced to see us. We passed the H. B. C. fort and entered our own, where we were warmly welcomed.

On the following day David Thompson rode in, and on the next Henry's own brigade arrived, decked out in their gaudiest feathers and finery, firing off guns, and shouting the wild, final notes of their paddle song as they swept up to the fort.

Four months of grinding travel lay between them and their starting point; but that night they held a dance that lasted until daybreak. Henry's Hudson's Bay Company neighbors joined the party, and "all was mirth — our men as smart and active as if they had rested for a month."

IX

Vermilion

FORT VERMILION was one of several posts high up the Saskat-chewan — Forts Vermilion, George, Augustus — known col-lectively as Fort des Prairies. It was already an old post, and by no means a small one. Within its stout stockade on the north bank of the river, at the foot of "a superb hill," ten houses and three tents sheltered a hundred and thirty persons — thirty-six men, twenty-seven Indian women, and their sixty-seven children.

Vermilion was a rendezvous for the Cree, Assiniboine, Blackfoot and Slave tribes, among whom were some of the most implacably hostile Indians ever encountered by the whites. Of Assiniboine alone, Henry reckoned 880 tents, rep-resenting 2000 men armed with 1100 guns. He considered them a people of uneven quality:

> They are rather timorous, and nothing but their numbers causes them to be dreaded . . . They are the most expert and dextrous nation of the plains in constructing pounds and driving buffalo into them . . . Their principal occupation is making pounded meat and grease . . . They are excellent riders and notorious horse thieves, even among themselves, perpetually embroiled on account of horses and women . . . They often barter the persons of their women for a trifling recompense . . .

The Slave Indians — among whom he includes the Blackfoot, Blood and Piegan — totaled about 650 tents and 1400 warriors. Henry describes them as a tall, well-proportioned people, given to bizarre decoration of their bodies, famous thieves, extremely licentious, wealthy in horses, much afflicted with venereal disease, and cruel beyond imagination:

> They are great warriors, and so easily prey on their enemies that many of the old men have killed with their own hands, during their younger days, 15 to 20 men. Women and children are never reckoned, and he is considered but a moderate warrior who has killed only 10 men . . . Like all other savages, they are excessively cruel to their enemies. I have heard instances that chilled my blood with horror.

Even fiercer in their hatred of the whites, if possible, were the Fall and Rapid Indians, once very numerous, but now decimated by smallpox. They were a more industrious people than the Slave, Henry wrote, and brought in a good trade of dried provisions, beaver pelts, bear and buffalo skins. This, however, did not interfere with their very active hostility:

> They are an audacious, turbulent race, and have repeatedly attempted to massacre us. The first attack was on old Fort Brule in 1793, when they pillaged the H.B.C. fort on the

South Branch, which they destroyed, massacred the people, and pillaged everything they could find, leaving the place in ashes. At the same time they attempted to destroy the N. W. Co. fort.

The Nor'westers repelled the latter attack with the loss of a chief and some dead and wounded in the Indians' ranks. "Since that time," Henry concludes dryly, "they have been more peaceable."

The Cree, a numerous people inhabiting the country northwest of the Saulteur lands as far as the Peace River, he finds stupid, lazy, cowardly, and much addicted to horse stealing:

> They are generally found in large camps winter and summer, idle throughout the year. Buffalo is their only object. Although passionately fond of liquor and tobacco, they will not resort to the woods, where they can procure furs to purchase those articles.

No trait, of course, could be more exasperating to a fur trader; but the tattooed and overdressed Cree had plenty of other dubious characteristics:

> Chastity does not seem to be a virtue among the Crees, who frequently make temporary exchange of their wives . . . Venereal disease is common and appears to be a principal cause of death . . . They are a useless set of fellows — a nuisance both to us and to their neighbors.

For the Sarcee, a small tribe of but 150 warriors, Henry appears to have had considerable respect:

> They affect to despise the Slaves for their brutish and dastardly manners, and though comparatively few in numbers, frequently set them at defiance.

Such were the wild, dangerous, unpredictable people surrounding Henry's new post on the Saskatchewan; such were his customers for the liquor, arms, ammunition and gewgaws he had brought from Canada. Within a few days he had set up shop and was bartering with the Blackfoot for meat. David Thompson and his men departed for the Columbia. Henry settled down for the long winter's trade:

> I have taken up my quarters for the winter at this post, where I expect to be visited by numerous tribes from the S. — Blackfeet, Sarcees, Fall Indians, Blood Indians, and Assiniboines — and on the N. by about 100 tents of Crees.

But what actually happened at Fort Vermilion during the winter of 1808, we do not know.

2

ALEXANDER Henry, who could write pages about a trivial incident, could also cover a whole season's activities at a busy post with a single sentence: "Here I passed the winter, during which nothing occurred but the routine of the trade."

Yet that was the winter, we know from other sources, that John McDonald of Garth made one of his spectacular appearances at Vermilion — this time to rescue David Thompson from the Blackfoot. It was also the year that Garth, returning to his post on the Qu'Appelle, had his boats attacked by hostiles — an event that shook the whole Northwest.

Among the victims of that massacre was Marguerite Trottier, daughter of one of Henry's hunters, and, according to the Abbé Dugas, a métis of great beauty. In Garth's stark account of the tragedy, she was "ravished, then scalped and left for dead on the shore; she managed to crawl on board and hide herself under the covering . . ." Miraculously, she recovered, became a Christian, married a Canadian of good family, and lived to be almost a hundred!

Oddly enough, Henry makes no reference to events as dramatic and as close to him as these. He closes his journal for the year 1808 with the flat statement that "nothing occurred," and with that the record of his doings is a blank until the summer of the following year. From the minutes of the 1809 Rendezvous, however, we know that he was at Fort William in the spring. There, incidentally, he received a severe reprimand from the Partners for his old habit of racing his canoe.

When, in the fall of 1809, we join Henry again, he is back at Fort Vermilion.

3

THREE hundred tents of Blackfoot were waiting patiently for his return with the trade goods and liquor — particularly, of course, the liquor. The Indians were not in a very good humor. Most of them had just returned from war on the Upper Missouri, without having had any success, however, in finding either Indians or Americans to plunder:

So they were deprived of their usual spoils in scalps and horses of the former, and missed a supply of beaver and merchandise from the latter, from whom they took considerable booty last year on an excursion of this kind.

Their lack of success deprived Henry of a certain amount of trade — at the expense of the Americans, naturally — but he seems to have been almost resigned to the loss, so disagreeable had trade with the Blackfoot become:

At present our neighbors [the Hudson's Bay Company] trade with about two-thirds of the Blackfeet, and I would willingly give up the whole of them. Last year, it is true, we got some beaver from them; but this was the spoils of war, they having fallen on a party of Americans on the Missourie, stripped them of everything, and brought off a quantity of skins.

Doing business with the plains Indians, Henry had discovered, was quite different from dealing with the rum-sodden and thoroughly debased woods tribes. The northern posts had little to fear from the miserable Cree, for example, who must disperse and hunt in small bands in order to get a living from their desolate forests. Exactly the opposite had to be said of the prairie posts. There a trader must be prepared to put up not only with the annoying and frequently dangerous drinking bouts, family feuds, and personal quarrels that kept every post in a turmoil; but he must also cope with incessant intertribal wars that, besides disrupting the trade, always threatened to involve the trader himself in the Indians' bloody hostilities.

This situation was aggravated by the fact that the plains Indians required little of the traders. Innumerable herds of prairie animals provided not only an inexhaustible food supply, but clothing and tents as well; and guns and ammunition were not needed to kill buffalo in great numbers. Aside from woolen blankets and strouds — much warmer and more comfortable than rain-soaked deerskin garments — the plains tribes desired so little from the whites, indeed, that they found it hardly worth while to spend long, toilsome days in search of beaver and other pelts for trading. A little beat meat, grease and dried berries brought them enough in trade to satisfy their modest wants — and left plenty of time for more interesting pursuits.

Among these, of course, war ranked first. The tribes frequenting Fort Vermilion were continuously raiding each other for horses or women; and it was the misfortune of Henry and his people to be drawn into their unending wars:

> The frequent disturbances between the Slaves and Crees cause a certain jealousy, which they often wish to revenge on us, saying that we are more partial to one tribe than to the other . . . That affair of last summer, when the Piegans were murdered, has exasperated the Slave tribes, and they all appear determined to be revenged, either on the Crees or ourselves, although they know we are innocent.

So tight did the situation become, in fact, that Henry went to the extraordinary expedient of building a separate Indian house, store and shop outside the main post. By this means, the Indians could be kept at a safe distance from the strongly stockaded fort while trading. Under the swivel gun on the bastion, they were less inclined to throw their weight around.

These unusual security measures were backed up by a policy of unflinching firmness in all dealings with the natives. The slightest show of softness, every trader knew, was tantamount to signing his own death warrant. Justice, therefore, was swift — when an Indian was in the dock — and likely to be so severe as to give even such a hard-bitten bourgeois as Alexander Henry certain qualms.

4

PUNISHMENT for crimes and misdemeanors in the *pays d'en haut* was dealt out on different levels, usually with the bourgeois as judge, jury, and often executioner. When the offense was a major one committed by a trader or voyageur against a white man, the culprit was sent down to Montreal for trial. There was a certain mystery about such a proceeding that impressed the Indians even more, perhaps, than immediate execution. Thus, when a voyageur at La Pointe, having conceived a passion for a trader's wife, murdered not only her but the trader and his children as well, the Indians in the vicinity long maintained that the murderer was taken to Montreal and torn to pieces by horses.

In those infrequent cases of voyageurs mutinying, the ringleaders were shipped down to Montreal to stand trial for breach of contract. Their followers were taken care of on the spot.

For ordinary transgressions, such as stealing from the common store, the voyageur received a flogging, or perhaps a forthright thrashing at the hands of the bourgeois himself. Only the most flagrant offenses appear to have been punished severely; and then it was the Indian who felt most heavily the hand of bourgeois justice. He took his punishment in swift, violent, and often revolting forms — particularly, of course, if his offense was against the person of a white man.

Thus, when a voyageur was killed by an Indian at the Lac Coutereille post, Jean Baptiste Cadot — that college-educated drunkard who, with Alexander Henry, had been made a Partner at the 1801 Rendezvous — forced the Indians to turn the slayer over to him. He was delivered to Cadot at Fond du Lac. Then, "in order that the Ojibways might learn the proper respect for the lives of white men," the bourgeois had him stabbed to death in the presence of "a vast concourse of his people."

Nor was murder the only offense for which the Indian paid with his life at the hands of his white judges. Stealing was also a capital crime, if the whim of the bourgeois so decided. The Nor'wester John Clarke, for example, made a great show of hanging one of his Indians for the theft of a silver goblet. In that case, however, the Indians retaliated; they massacred a wintering party of nine Nor'westers.

It was not often that the natives struck back; but when they did, the retribution was ghastly enough to give the traders bad dreams for a long time. And it is not hard to detect a note of uneasiness in his journal when Henry recounts the punishment of a Cree lad for horse stealing at Vermilion. The Cree was guilty, sure enough — his companion informed on him; and justice must be served. The Hudson's Bay Company factor, indeed, was all for finishing him off without ado:

> Mr. Longmore was intoxicated, and insisted upon killing the Indian; he came over, armed *capapee*, and I had some trouble to prevent murder.

What followed, however, was not much better than murder. After a pompous and farcical "trial," the young Cree was locked up for the night. On the cold, wintry morning of October 11 — ice was already forming along the edges of the Saskatchewan — he paid for his indiscretion at the hands of a large and hung-over firing squad:

> At nine o'clock he was conducted down to the river below the H. B. house, and shot by a discharge of 15 guns — much against my own inclination, I must confess. I had various reasons for not wishing him to be executed, corporal punishment being all I desired; but my neighbors insisted on killing him . . .

The Assiniboine, looking back darkly and muttering threats, left Vermilion immediately after the execution for their camp on Battle River. But they were back again in four days:

Indians came back to trade horses for liquor, and those camped here sold both horses and tents for liquor. Some took rum on debt. They were coming and going all day, trading and begging liquor. These fellows are great drunkards; they part with everything for rum.

So firewater washed out the thirst for vengeance, and the post settled down to the fall work of repairing the houses and stockades, mudding the chimneys, and cutting hay for the horses. By the middle of October all was finished, and everyone was "entered and settled for the winter."

5

BUT the winter of 1809-10 turned out to be such an unpleasant one that Henry suddenly decided to abandon Fort Vermilion altogether.

The hostility of the Indians increased daily. Late in the fall, Henry received word that the Cree and Assiniboine had declared formal war on the traders. He sent word of the uprising to James Hughes, the Partner in charge of Fort Augustus upriver; then became too sick with a sore throat to care much what happened.

Recovering, he took up the business of his post, with always a wary eye on his sinister customers. They did not, as he expected, launch an assault in force; instead, they opened a kind of war of nerves. Hardly a day passed that the chief of one of the bands did not make some threat or ugly gesture. At times these displays of hostility came close to open violence:

My people had a narrow escape this morning from being murdered by a party of 16 thieves who met them at Plante's river. They said the thieves had been watching for several days near the fort, and had been up as far as Moose creek, but could find no horses; also that they had watched two days near the fort, to shoot me, as they really wanted my scalp; but that, having been disappointed about both my scalp and my horses, they must absolutely have Clement's scalp.

Clement talked himself out of that one, somehow; and the Cree bandits, after pillaging everybody, left with a promise to shoot Henry on sight. This sort of thing, kept up all winter long, was naturally wearing on the nerves. But even worse was the horse stealing. Good running and hunting horses were costly and hard to come by at Vermilion, and the Indians, of course, stole the traders' best. On what a scale is suggested by almost daily entries in the journal:

> Found that five more horses were stolen . . . 32 horses were stolen during the night N. of the fort . . . Men searching for their horses . . . 18 Assiniboines went up to Fort Augustus to steal all the horses they could find . . . Two H. B. men arrived from Fort Augustus with the news that 65 horses have been stolen by the Assiniboines . . .

A great deal of time was wasted in moving the horse herds about for greater safety, and in rounding up stolen animals. Meanwhile, the trade had to be carried on, and meat killed and hauled: by February, 550 buffalo thighs and 380 shoulders had been laid away in the icehouse.

During this trying time, Henry never neglected his journal. We read that two men from the Columbia arrived; Henry quarreled with Longmore, the Hudson's Bay Company factor; he made a trip upriver to Fort Augustus (modern Edmonton); his hen laid her first egg; the fort dogs began to kill colts and he was forced to shoot several; and . . .

Put tongues to thaw and perused Gass' Journal Across the Rocky Mountains.

Henry, we may be sure, read Sergeant Patrick Gass' *Journal* of the Lewis and Clark Expedition with more than casual interest. He himself was planning a trip to the West — a look, at least, at the other side of the mountains. But the troubles with the Indians, tying him down to Vermilion, had forced him to put it off.

The troubles increased as the winter wore on, and by the middle of February had become so intolerable that Henry suddenly decided to evacuate Vermilion:

> Mr. Hughes and myself determined to abandon both Fort Vermilion and Fort Augustus, and to build at Terre Blanche. The latter, being a more central place, will answer the same purpose as the two present establishments and save the expense of one of them; it will also draw all the Slaves to trade at one place, where we can better defend ourselves.

Two days later, he and Hughes were off to choose a site for the new post. Longmore went with them. On the way, they decided to build their posts close together and surround them with a common stockade — so deep was their fear of the Slave!

Having selected a spot about halfway to Fort Augustus, Henry returned to Vermilion and sent a building party up-river to clear ground for the new post. His journal picks up the thread of day-to-day life:

> Three men arrived from Fort Augustus, where our people had fought a running battle with the Assiniboines.

> Desrosiers and Sansregret arrived from the South Branch with a packet from the E. containing intelligence of the

death at Eagle Lake of Mr. Aneas McDonnell, who was murdered by one of the H. B. men.

J. Durand's wife ill of an abortion. The wife of Francois Deschamps, Jr. was delivered of a boy, and an hour afterward was running about the fort.

March 25th. According to my calculation, this is Easter. Weather clear and cold; no sign of spring; snow dry even on the very top of the banks, where it lies in piles, and not a speck of ground is to be seen in any direction.

The post's primary function, the making of pemmican, was hindered by the extraordinary cold. The grease, hardening instantly, did not penetrate the mix properly. So Henry began to make pemmican in the house, turning out 135 bags of it in two days. Not until the middle of April did the weather become mild enough to allow the drying of meat on the roofs of the houses. But from this time on, his journal takes on the tempo of springtime activities at a big pemmican post:

> Made up 19 bags of pemmican with cherries. We made up the rest of our pemmican today — 97 bags; in all 292 bags.

> We began to make our packs, erect our press, and fill the kegs with grease: 84 kegs filled and 12 packs made.

> Making packs again, and women smoking dressed skins; 63 finished.

Simultaneously, the work at Terre Blanche was being pushed by both Henry and his Hudson's Bay Company neighbors; and "our work here has gone well, considering the backward and stormy spring." At 10 o'clock on the morning of May 31, 1810, Henry and his family, and all the remaining people at the post, abandoned Fort Vermilion, "leaving our icehouse open, containing about 400 limbs of buffalo, still frozen."

We formed a cavalcade of 44 horses, 60 dogs, 12 men, 6 women, and 1 blind man . . . We made frequent stops to rest our lean, weak horses. One of our dogs that remained behind overtook us, with a fresh wound in his side, apparently from an arrow . . . We stopped near Fort George and kept watch during the night.

Henry's hen, he does not forget to mention, "was molested on leaving Fort Vermilion, when she had been sitting two days on 13 eggs."

On June 3 the emigrants arrived at Terre Blanche. Henry found the new post destitute of meat, with but thirty-eight bags of pemmican to feed 138 men, women and children of the North West Company and 85 of the Hudson's Bay Company.

6

At Terre Blanche House there was a continuous coming and going of canoes from far-off places — Slave Lake, Athabasca, Kaministiquia, the Rocky Mountains, the Columbia. The big rush was on to the Pacific. Thompson was building his posts on the upper Columbia and scouting the Coast for the Nor'-westers. John Jacob Astor was at Fort Astoria for the Americans. And now the Hudson's Bay Company was probing the great wilderness void beyond the mountains — where the beaver, incidentally, were said to be as thick as buffalo chips at a river crossing.

The Great Company's canoes — an expedition of seventeen men, including four Indians — passed through Terre Blanche under command of one Joseph Howse. It was not Howse's first trip to the Rockies. In 1808 rumors of David Thompson's epic jaunts had penetrated to the board room of the Hudson's Bay Company in London, and the directors had instructed John McNab at York Factory to find out just how far west Thompson had got. McNab, for want of an experienced mountain man, had given the job to his young clerk, Howse.

Howse reached the mountains, but ventured no farther. He soon cleared out of the battleground of the Piegan and Flathead, and turned in a report based largely on hearsay. But now he was back again, this time with a much larger force and two canoes laden with trade goods. Henry's sharp eyes did not neglect to note their contents: "They embarked four rolls of tobacco, two kegs of high wine, powder, several bags of balls, a bag of shot, pemmican, etc." Next day, he saw Howse follow the canoes by land.

Henry did not record his emotions as he watched the Hudson's Bay party grow small across the prairie. But they were not, we can be certain, a saintly resignation to his own small and troubled life of a trader at Terre Blanche.

7

Two days later David Thompson and his family arrived from the Columbia in a light canoe. The great explorer seemed to bring with him some of the glacial freshness of the high places from which he had just descended. He had traveled very fast, arriving at Terre Blanche only four days after launching his canoe on the Saskatchewan, just below the Continental Divide. "The snow," he reported, "was four feet deep in the pass." By "the pass" he meant the short mountain portage that connected the headwaters of the Saskatchewan with Blaeberry Creek and the Columbia. Thompson had discovered it three years ago, and had continuously made use of it ever since; but the geographies, a hundred and fifty years later, were to label it Howse Pass — for the Hudson's Bay clerk who, as yet, had not even seen it!

Thompson said that he had kept no proper winter quarters west of the mountains that year. He had traded at Salish House, at Kootenay House, at Kullyspell House — he had wintered "all over the mountains." And wherever he went, he had traded, built posts, made observations, sought new routes. He had been almost constantly on the move, probing the country and amassing endless columns of data for his Great Map of the West.

During all these wanderings, Thompson had managed to maintain an uneasy friendship with the Indians. The Kootenay, on the west side of the Rockies, were hospitable; and he had even risked wintering among them with Charlotte and the children. But their enemies, the Piegan, who lived in the Saskatchewan Valley on the east side of the mountains, were less well disposed. To protect himself against them, Thompson had built Kootenay House in lovely Windemere Valley — the first trading post erected on the Columbia.

But neither Kootenay House nor the respect most of the tribes had for him could solve the Piegan problem. Incensed by the killing of two of their tribe by Captain Clark, of the Lewis and Clark expedition, the Piegan had transferred their hatred of Americans to all whites — including even Thompson. And now they had blocked his way across the mountains, and threatened to kill him if he tried to get to the Kootenay.

There was only one thing to do, Thompson told Henry:

he must go around the Piegan. They were plains Indians, with a superstitious fear of the woods. If he could find a new forest road over the mountains, he would be safe from them. He thought there was such a route — perhaps from the Athabasca River, far to the north, over what is now called Athabasca Pass. In the fall, he said, he would attempt to find it.

That would be a heartbreaking winter trip, Henry knew, and one full of unknown perils; but he had no doubt that Thompson would undertake it. He was forty years old — longer than most men lasted in the fur trade — and had no business attempting it. But Henry said nothing to dissuade him: he well knew that nothing could stop this indomitable man.

8

AFTER a five days' visit, Thompson was off with his family, and Terre Blanche House settled back into the troubled routine of a Saskatchewan post:

> I have finished hauling home meat with the cart horses; my share for the summer is 30 animals.

> Women drying meat; men working at the Indian house . . . Men finished the chimnies . . . Three men worked at the fort gate.

> Piche and other lads came in from my hunter's tents on a visit. Piche made the wife of one of my men desert, and she is lurking in the woods near the fort.

> Letendre and family arrived, bringing upward of 100 beaver skins . . . Furs on hand today: 292 beaver, 208 swans, 70 martins, 24 dressed skins, 12 muskrats, 3 grissly

bears; four black do.; 2 cubs; 5 loup-cerviers, 4 prime otters; 4 common do.; 1 fox; 1 wolverine, 1 mink, 1 buffalo robe.

The women bring in great quantities of poires, raspberries and strawberries.

Found one of my chickens dead this morning, and discovered that the cock had killed it . . . I must make a separate coop for him; he is really a brute, tormenting the sitting hens and killing the chickens.

We had a dance this evening, when all got three drams apiece; 15 quarts of high wine were drunk.

Pigeons passing from N. to S. in immense flocks, particularly in the morning and evening . . . The frost last night froze all our potato-tops, and this morning's sun has leveled them to the ground.

To Henry's usual annoyances during the ensuing summer were added two special ones: fights and threats of fights between the various Indian tribes surrounding Terre Blanche; and a plague of free trappers, who were convinced that fortunes in beaver lay just beyond the mountains:

Troubled with those mongrel freeman and Indians all day . . . they make more mischief than the most savage Blackfeet of the plains . . . Still pestered with those vagabonds all day, but prevailed upon some of them to give up the idea of the Columbia . . . where they will be even a greater nuisance to us than they are here.

Canoes from above and below continued to arrive — while Henry took tea with Mr. Hallett, the new Hudson's Bay Company factor, and his men were "doing very little but amusing themselves chatting with the new arrivals." The idleness and tedium must have become too much for him at last.

For almost immediately after the arrival of the brigade from Kaministiquia — eleven canoes laden with liquor and trade goods for the new season — he left Terre Blanche for Rocky Mountain House, the North West Company's uppermost post on the Saskatchewan. It was his plan to winter there.

9

HENRY's journal gives no warning of the long leap up the river. One comes suddenly on the entry for September 24: "At four o'clock I sent off three canoes for the Rocky Mountains; the fourth starts tomorrow." This is followed next day with: "My own canoe set off with my family and baggage." Then, two days later: "At nine o'clock I set off on horseback with Messrs. Bethune and Rowand . . ."

Encumbered with women and children, and traveling in "ugly, gloomy country" through storms of rain and snow, the party moved slowly. But on the sixth day it came within sight of the mountains. Henry filled his pipe and enjoyed a smoke, while he sat beside his grazing horse and had his first look, in all his days in the West, at the Rockies:

> Here we had a grand view of the Rocky Mountains southward, apparently running E. and W. The valley through which the Saskatchewan winds appears to form a great gap in the mountains, about S.S.W. from this spot.

Three days later he descended the trail along the Rivière à L'Eau Claire and looked down on Rocky Mountain House. What he saw struck him with amazement:

> Upon coming in sight of the old fort, we were surprised to see some people standing at the gate, and smoke coming

from within the stockades; on nearer approach, our surprise increased when we observed them to be whites and Indians.

Henry had good reason to be astonished. For Rocky Mountain House — which had been built by John McDonald of Garth in 1802 — had long been abandoned!

X

The Haunt of the Mammoth

THE MYSTERIOUS occupants of Rocky Mountain House turned out to be David Thompson's people — the canoe brigade with which he had set off almost a month ago for the Columbia. They had been stopped by the Piegan, the guide said. The Piegan, indeed, had tried to kill them; but the voyageurs had fought them off from behind a little breastwork of stones.

While this was happening, David Thompson and William Henry were upriver, ahead of the canoes, in search of game. Where were they now? Nobody knew. Perhaps the Piegan had got them!

Henry decided they were probably still upriver, waiting for the canoes. He ordered the guide to load up and rejoin his bourgeois. Before the brigade could take off, however, a band of Piegan arrived, upsetting everything. If these obviously hostile Indians saw the canoes leave, they would simply follow and plunder them upstream at their leisure. There was nothing to do but wait them out.

The Piegan left, at last, but other Indians arrived. With liquor and laudanum Henry put them fast asleep, and finally got the canoes off under cover of darkness. But next day William Henry showed up with the news that he and Thompson had not been upstream after all! They had been downriver, near the North Branch, where Thompson still remained.

After hunting all day, William explained, he and Thompson had ridden back to the river to join the canoes. But none were to be seen. After a while they discovered a place on the riverbank where there was a little rampart of stones, and there was blood on the stones. So he and Thompson decided the brigade had got away, after a fight with the Piegan, and had gone downriver. As for themselves, they lost no time in mounting their horses and getting out of there. They had fled downriver, where Thompson was encamped — waiting for his canoes.

Next morning Henry set out to find Thompson. Late in the afternoon, he spotted his camp "on top of a hill 300 feet above the water, where tall pines stood so thickly that I could not see his tent until we came within 10 yards of it." Thompson was brooding about the Piegan attack on his brigade. Now, more than ever, he was certain of one thing — a new route would have to be found to the Columbia, one that avoided the Piegan warlands. He returned to an idea he had already expounded to Henry: there was such a route — north to the Athabasca River, then over the mountains, then down to the Columbia and to the Coast. Some Nipissing and freemen had made it that way a few years ago, he had heard. So why couldn't he? Anyhow, he'd have a try at it. There was nothing else to do. He had to be on the Pacific by August . . .

They talked about it far into the night, watching the snow fall in great, wet flakes through the pines. At seven o'clock next morning, Henry was ready to leave. He shook Thompson's hand, promised to see that his canoes rejoined him immediately, and set off. He expected never to see the great geographer alive again. To take a train of dogs and pack horses over the mountains, by an unknown path, in the dead of winter — that was asking too much, even of David Thompson.

2

ROCKY Mountain House, to which Henry now returned, was the post at which all the Nor'westers' expeditions over the mountains outfitted. As early as 1790, a trader named Peter Pangman had got his first view of the mountains from a nearby hill, and had carved his name on a tree to commemorate the event. Henry went out to see it:

> I rode up the river about three miles to a rising ground on the N. side, where Mr. Pangman cut his name on a pine in 1790. This spot was then the utmost extent of discoveries on the Saskatchewan toward the Rocky Mountains, of which indeed we had a tolerable view from this hill.

Unlike Fort Vermilion, a "pemmican post," Rocky Mountain House was important for furs. The trade was brisk, and early in November Henry could report a store of 720 beavers, 33 grizzly bears, 20 buffalo robes, 300 muskrats, and 100 lynxes. The Piegan also had other merchandise to barter:

The Piegans and Sarcees traded; the latter set off, but the former remained, on purpose to offer their women to my people, which is very common amongst the Slaves; a mere trifle is sufficient payment. But the Fall Indians are the most lavish of such favors, and actually a nuisance in offering their women; anything satisfies them . . . The Piegans set off, having had several customers for their ladies during the night.

In other respects, however, the Indians around Rocky Mountain House were much less troublesome than the tribes that had made Henry's life miserable at Fort Vermilion. While there was the usual niggling annoyance about liquor, the post was never threatened, and no lives were lost. By late October, Henry had settled down to a calm existence, at peace even with his Hudson's Bay Company neighbors.

Twice men from David Thompson's party arrived. The first of them, two men with three horses, had left Thompson's camp on a branch of the Athabasca River, far to the north, near what is now Jasper National Park:

They had left him, with all his property, on his way to the Columbia, cutting his roads through a wretched, thick, woody country, over mountains and gloomy muskagues, and nearly starving, animals being very scarce.

Thompson, the men reported, had given up the idea of going any farther with horses, and was preparing to cross the mountains on snowshoes, with dog sledges. But the Canadians had beaten so many dogs to death that only eight sledges were left. Things were not going well; the men from Thompson's camp were content to be free of it.

It was the devil's own country, one of them said, and full of mammoths. No, he hadn't seen the mammoths himself —

he was only telling what he had heard. And he was, in fact, repeating a very old legend — possibly passed down from the age of ice itself? — that Thompson had also noted in his own journal: "We are now entering the defiles of the Rocky Mountains by the Athabasca River . . . strange to say, here is a strong belief that the haunt of the mammoth is about this place."

Almost a month later, seven more of Thompson's men arrived at Rocky Mountain House. They had been starving for seventeen days, having eaten only "an old horse and five dogs" on their journey. But Thompson, they reported, was in still worse straits on the Athabasca.

Over snow fields seven feet deep, in blizzards that howled incessantly through the stark passes, his party sometimes made no more than four or five miles a day. "Such was the despondency of the men," Thompson recorded, "that when night came we had only wood to make a bottom, and on this to make a small fire, which soon burnt out, and in this exposed condition we passed the rest of the long night without fire, and part of my men had strong feelings of personal insecurity."

Their fear mounted as they toiled upward in the thin, scentless air, sometimes giving way to mutinous panic, sometimes finding an outlet in the brutality that was never far beneath the surface of the Canadian dog-driver's gaiety: "One of my men named Du Nord beat a dog to death. He is what we call a 'flash' man, a showy fellow before women but a coward in heart."

But despite the steadily closing grip of terror, the men were not insensible to the unearthly beauty of the high, silent world through which they were toiling. "Yet, when night came,"

Thompson wrote of them, "they admired the brilliancy of the stars, and as one of them said, he thought he could almost touch them with his hand."

They were in the glacier fields now; and, like all men before and after him, Thompson marveled at "an enormous Glacier, the eastern face of which, quite steep, of about two thousand feet in height, was of a clean, fine green color." He noted in his journal each wonder of the dazzling, deadly scene that now lay everywhere below them — for they had reached, at last, the Height of Land: "I found part of my men with a pole twenty feet in length, boring the snow to find bottom . . . On looking into the hole they had bored, I was surprised to see the color of the sides a beautiful blue; the surface was of a very light color, but as it descended the color became more deep, and at the lowest point was of a blue almost black."

Thompson returned to his fire that night in an odd mood of exhilaration mixed with despondency. Having examined the country around their camp, he found that they "had now to descend the west side of the mountains." He had found a new way to the Pacific.

But it was a way filled with terrifying uncertainties and, he could be sure, grave dangers. "Many reflections came to my mind," he wrote. "A new world was in a manner before me, and my object was to be at the Pacific Ocean before the month of August. How were we to find provisions, and how many men would remain with me, for they were dispirited? Amidst various thoughts I fell asleep on my bed of snow."

The seven men who had made their way back from David Thompson's camp sat long before the fire in Alexander Henry's quarters, nursing their dram of rum, and answering the bourgeois' questions. They were a dull, small-minded run of men, talkative as children; and they had caught not even a small spark from the fire that burned in the stout, adventurous soul of their great master.

But as Alexander Henry followed his friend on his lonely journey through those far, lost places, he must have felt that he himself could wait no longer to see what lay beyond the snowy peaks he viewed each day from the west gate of his fort. For suddenly he decided he would begin preparations — even though it was the dead of winter — for his own trip to the Height of Land.

3

BUT a month passed before he could record the start:

> *Sunday, Feb. 3, 1811.* Clear and calm, thermometer 12 below zero. At 5:30 A.M. I set out on my journey, accompanied by two men, each of us with a sled and dogs.

This, like his Mandan journey, was a pleasure trip for Henry; and he writes about it with zest and color. For example . . . the wintry charm of this small vignette:

> Having passed the fort and fallen upon the track leading above, we drove briskly on until sunrise, which found us at the *bas fond* where our horses were wintered. The noise of our bells and the cries of the men and dogs so alarmed the gang of horses that we saw only the smoke and snow that arose in their flight from the river.

His description of the mode of travel by dog sledge in the Northwest is concise and vivid:

> The road which lay before us could be traveled with expedition, having hardy, able-bodied men, and sleds not too

heavily loaded, with three stout, active dogs to each . . .
My own was a kind of cariole made by stretching a wet
parchment of mooseskin over a few timbers, to which
it was well secured with a line. This forms a comfortable
voiture, prevents the snow from gathering in the sled,
and keeps a person snug and warm, wrapped in a buffalo
robe.

Snug and warm in his buffalo robe, with the bells of his
cariole making frosty music, Henry and his men whirled up
the river ice, through thick forests of pine and aspen, toward
the mountains. Now and again, beyond the long reach of the
Saskatchewan, the Rockies thrust up their snow-covered peaks
against the pale winter sky: they seemed hardly an hour's
march away.

That night they camped beneath a huge pine. Before the
cries of the dog-drivers started the expedition off next morning — *"Marche! Marche! Sacré chien mort!"* — Henry took
a precaution that travelers in the Northwest observed: he
cached part of their provisions for the return trip:

> Here we stopped to lay up some provisions for our return,
> which was done by cutting a large hole in the ice to contain
> them, and piercing a small hole to let the water rise and
> cover them.

Shortly after arranging this deep-freeze, Henry was suddenly taken ill with a colic that made him weak and faint for
some time; but a few peppermint drops relieved him, and the
journey was resumed at a brisk pace:

> At 11 A.M. we reached the entrance of the mountains,
> where the river is 60 yards wide . . . The gap in the
> mountains does not seem to be more than half a mile wide
> . . . Both sides rise to an immense height of solid, barren

rock, with a few stunted pines scattered at the base, and thence about half way up.

Unwell again, Henry was forced to make camp early; but he was not too ill to record his first real physical contact with the Shining Mountains:

> We were in full view of the mountains, and a grand sight it was — the main body of the Rocky Mountains ahead of us, upheaved in all shapes and directions.

After a sleepless night, he was still very weak and exhausted from running behind the dogs; so the party laid over for a day, which was spent in hunting meat. At dawn the march was resumed. Although "scarcely able to crawl about camp," Henry took careful note of the geological features of the stupendous peaks under which the river was now forcing its ever-narrowing way:

> The adjacent mountains are very high and craggy, consisting of solid rocks, destitute of verdure or soil. These are all shapes, with some of the strata, or veins, horizontal, some perpendicular, others oblique, others winding and bending in lines that correspond with the shape of the mountain.

At times the prose of this sick and exhausted fur trader, toiling in subzero cold over a man-killing trail on broken river ice, attains a kind of rough majesty:

> *Feb. 7th.* At dawn I sent three hunters ahead to kill sheep, and at sunrise left camp with the others. The weather was clear and calm; but soon after getting upon the ice, I observed some thick clouds rise in the N. E.. which in a short time enveloped the mountain tops in obscurity . . . By degrees the clouds appeared to descend within 300 feet above our heads, and there hovered for some time, while

the upper part of the mountains became visible; there the sky was perfectly clear, and the rays of the rising sun shone with their usual luster, while below we were in the clouds.

He did not neglect to make note of the wild life of the high places, and he was particularly fascinated by the mountain sheep, with their great curving horns:

Shortly after leaving camp we saw a herd of about 30 rams feeding among the rocks. They did not seem to be shy, though the noise of our bells and dogs was sufficient to have alarmed a herd of buffalo two miles off. The rams stood for some time gazing at us, and did not retreat until some people with dogs climbed up to fire at them, when they set off at full speed, directing their course up the mountain.

But he takes time, also, to sketch quick vignettes of the small, humble creatures along the way; here a flock of dippers:

I observed several flocks of birds hovering about those ponds; they alighted upon the edge of the ice, and instantly hopped into the water, where they plunged and frisked about for some time before they flew away. These birds were very small, of a brownish color, with short, erect tails.

At the entrance of the Little Mirliton River, Henry paused to gaze up at a mountain that was extraordinary even in that world of marvels:

Along this river I observed a high, steep mountain of singular shape, like a wall surrounded by a moat and ramparts, with an elevated central summit resembling a citadel, the whole having the appearance of a commanding fortress.

On the fourth day of their journey they arrived at the great valley called the Kootenay Plains. This, a notable stopping place on the route to the Columbia, was a level, mountain-ringed flat, "about two hours' walk in length, and nearly a mile wide." Here the canoes were left behind and trade goods and provisions loaded on horses for transportation over the Height of Land. Many old Kootenay camps stood in the shelter of the surrounding rocks:

> Formerly that nation frequented this place to make dried provisions, for which purpose it must have been conveni-ent, as buffalo and sheep are always more numerous than in any other place. Moose and red deer are also plenty; jumping deer, grizzly bears, and other animals peculiar to this country are also found here. We saw a flock of up-wards of 100 white partridges on this plain. They are very beautiful birds, and very good eating.

It was snowing when they broke camp the next morning, and they were obliged to take to snowshoes, with one of the men going ahead to beat a road for the dogs:

> The face of the country altered . . . The mountain was covered with vast bodies of snow . . . Some of the high-est remained all day enveloped in clouds which were not dispersed for several hours after the wind arose, and even then hovered about the summits, as if loath to leave, until torn away by the violence of the wind.

At noon they arrived at the last forks of the Saskatchewan, and suddenly the staggering panorama of the glacier fields opened before them:

> Upon the top of a mountain N. W. of us, whose summit appeared level, I observed an immense field of snow, of which a part seemed lately to have separated and fallen down. This frequently happens during the winter, when vast quantities of snow accumulate until the mass projects beyond the rocks and then gives way. The noise occa-

sioned by the fall of such a body of snow equals an explosion of thunder, and the avalanche sweeps away everything movable in its course to the valleys.

On the sides of some mountains S. of us, where the rays of the sun never reach, are vast beds of eternal snow, or, more probably, bodies of ice. Their bluish color plainly distinguishes them from the snows of this season; some parts have recently given way and fallen into the valleys, while the remainder presents a perpendicular face of ice."

Next day, a week after the start from Rocky Mountain House, Henry reached the source of the Saskatchewan:

When we came to within about half a mile of the end of the river, we left it to our right, and entered the thick forest of pines, whose branches were heavily loaded with snow. We went on about two miles through these thick woods, and at nine o'clock came to a small opening, where three small streams of the Columbian waters join."

Henry was over the Continental Divide. The rill he mentions was Blaeberry Creek, the first westward-flowing stream beyond the mountains. Only one day's portaging from here took one into the navigable waters of the Columbia . . . and so to the Pacific Ocean.

Having attained his goal, Henry did not spend much time on this windy, snow-piled top of the world:

After staying here about an hour, I gave a hearty dram to the Indians who were going to the old Kootenay House . . . At 10 A.M. I bade farewell to the waters of the Columbia. I got on my sled, sent my men ahead on snowshoes, and at noon arrived at camp.

The return to Rocky Mountain House was uneventful. Henry drove his men unmercifully all the way. On the last day he aroused them at eleven o'clock at night to prepare for the next day's march!

> As they had not slept more than two hours, fatigue was still heavy upon them. Their motions were therefore slow; but what grieved them most was having nothing to eat before starting. This made them surly; they first quarreled among themselves and then gave full vent to their ill humor upon the poor dogs, which they beat most cruelly. It was 2 A.M. before we left camp . . . As we approached home, both men and dogs seemed to acquire fresh vigor; we drove at full speed, and at 2:30 P.M. reached the fort.

Between the time of this return to Rocky Mountain House in February and Henry's departure in the fall for Fort William — as the New Fort at Kaministiquia was now called — we learn nothing from his journal about his activities. To fill the gap, he leaves us only an ethnological discussion of the Rocky Mountain tribes and a long vocabulary of the Flathead language!

After that, there is a routine log of his trip down to Terre Blanche House. And when we next pick up the thread of the journal of Alexander Henry the Younger, it is two years later, and Henry is on the Pacific Coast.

XI

Astoria

BETWEEN the spring of 1811 and the fall of 1813, Henry was on the Saskatchewan; but the manuscript of his journal has been lost, and so we have no record of his activities until the entry for November 15, 1813: "Arrived at Astoria, as per Journal from Fort William." We do know, however, that the years skipped by the published journal were eventful and even anxious ones. In 1811 the very existence of the North West Company was suddenly threatened by two gigantic figures: Lord Selkirk, the Scotsman; and John Jacob Astor, the American.

This was the year in which the youthful Earl of Selkirk, having got a controlling interest in the Hudson's Bay Company, obtained a Crown grant of forty million acres in the Red River valley — with the idea of founding a settlement of

Scottish farmers near the site of Winnipeg and squarely athwart the North West Company's communications with the West!

This was also the year in which Astor outflanked the Nor'-westers beyond the Rockies by building a post at the mouth of the Columbia River. He named the post Astoria, but it might more appropriately have been called Fort Disaster.

For ill luck dogged Astor's enterprise from the beginning. His first supply ship, *Tonquin*, which sailed from New York with thirty-three men aboard, was commanded by an incredibly stupid and bullheaded martinet named Jonathan Thorn. Thorn's ideas of discipline were pure man-o'-war: in the Falklands, he set sail and left behind on a barren island eight of Astor's men who, in his opinion, did not respond with proper alacrity to the signal for embarkation. After rowing frantically after the ship for three and a half hours in a heavy sea, the men saw the island growing smaller behind them and the ship disappearing ahead. If the wind hadn't suddenly shifted, they would have been lost; for Thorn wrote Astor: "Had the wind (unfortunately) not hauled soon after leaving the harbor's mouth, I should positively have left them."

After landing the Astoria "settlers" at the mouth of the Columbia, Thorn coasted north to trade pelts in competition with the Russians. He mortally insulted a band of Chinooks who came aboard the *Tonquin* to barter, and was then unwise enough to allow them to return on the following day and trade for knives! In the ensuing massacre, everybody was killed except the ship's clerk, who blew up the *Tonquin* with her decks full of looting Indians.

Astor's second ship, *Lark*, was lost in a gale off the Sandwich Islands. A third from New York, *Beaver*, touched at

Astoria to unload supplies, then went coasting off toward Sitka. With it went Wilson P. Hunt, commander of an overland expedition to Astoria, and now in charge of the post. He promised to return in two months, but more than a year passed without word from the *Beaver* — a long and anxious year, naturally, for the Astorians stranded on a strange and hostile coast.

The overland expedition from St. Louis had not fared much better than the sea ventures. It straggled into Astoria, a few men at a time, starving and half dead from exhaustion — a cheerless and not very useful addition to the fort's already underfed population.

And now, climaxing all of Astor's difficulties, war had been declared between the United States and England, putting a complete stop to any further contact with Astoria by sea.

Yet, in spite of its misfortunes, the Pacific Fur Company had dug in on the Pacific Coast. Trading parties were pushing out from Astoria into territory that hitherto had been the Nor'westers' exclusive preserve. American posts were being built farther and farther up the Columbia. Coastwise trading, particularly for the sea otter so highly valued in Canton, was being developed. And the rich trade with China was being successfully interdicted.

It would have been quite unlike the Nor'westers to have watched all this with equanimity. To Selkirk's threat to their lifeline they reacted promptly and violently, both in the law courts and on the prairies of the west. In Henry's old Red River department, open warfare led to the destruction of Selkirk's settlements, finally, a pitched battle at Seven Oaks, and the seizure of Fort William by the young laird's soldiers.

In this fierce struggle the Nor'westers won the battles of

both briefs and bullets, but in the end they lost the war. For the Hudson's Bay Company, aroused as never before, forced the North West Company into "Union" at last — a coalition that turned out to be nothing more, in fact, than defeat and financial ruin.

But before they went down, the Nor'westers struck some hard blows against their two rich and powerful enemies. Astor they attacked by land and sea. In the minutes of the North West Company's deliberations at Fort William in the summer of 1811 is a short paragraph that set the counteroffensive against the Americans in motion: "Mr. Donald McTavish is appointed to set out immediately & proceed in the Columbia business by sailing from England for the South West Coast as soon as possible & conduct that business in conformity with the resolve of the Company last Year."

In plain words, these guarded phrases meant simply that McTavish was to go by ship to the Pacific Coast and take Astoria by force. Accompanied by John McDonald of Garth, he sailed without delay from Montreal in the armed ship *Isaac Todd*. In England he disposed of a cargo of pelts, then set sail for the Columbia. In order to evade American naval action, McDonald transferred to a sloop of war, the *Raccoon*. This led to an awkward situation, for in rounding the Horn the two ships became separated and lost touch with each other for the rest of the journey. Nothing to do with Astoria, it seemed, ever went smoothly.

For Alexander Henry the Younger, however, a later paragraph in the minutes of the 1811 Rendezvous was of special interest: "Mr. Alexander Henry, having been appointed by the Agents at Montreal to take the place of Mr. Hughes in the charge and conducting of the Canoe for the Columbia in case

of Mr. Hughes' health not permitting him to proceed . . .
was appointed for this duty."

Henry, in short, had his orders to hurry to the Columbia
and there join a considerable force of Nor'westers converg-
ing from various points of the *pays d'en haut*, as well as by
sea, on Astoria.

2

FROM Henry himself we learn nothing about how he crossed
the mountains: all that is in the lost pages of his journal. But
he undoubtedly followed David Thompson's old route, now
regularly traveled by the Nor'westers — up the Saskatchewan, over Howse Pass, down Blaeberry Creek, and down the
Columbia to the sea.

Only a handful of Nor'westers had ever followed the route
all the way; and Henry was to find much that was strange,
and sometimes frightening, before he had finished the long
descent of the rapids-filled stream. Below the magnificent
falls that Thompson called Ilthkoyape and are known today
as Kettle Falls, he found Indians who lived, not in bark or
leather lodges, but in great houses made of planks, with grotesque carved figures guarding the doorways. These Indians
were hunters of the salmon that every fall made their mysterious return from the sea to the place where they had
spawned, there to be speared by the Indians. Henry, no
doubt noted, as David Thompson did, that the women of
these salmon killers "had no beauty to spare, and wanted the
agile step of those that dwell in tents."

Leaving the Upper Columbia, Henry cruised down the

great stream through the settlements of other Indians who greeted him with dances of friendship and gave him roasted fish and dried marmot meat in return for a little tobacco, a few blue beads and hawk bells, half a dozen buttons — trash and trinkets at which the haughty Indians of the plains would have looked down their haughty noses.

Farther down the river he found the Wenatchee Indians living in great plank lodges. They were better-looking and cleaner than the tribes upriver, and no less friendly. He had now reached that country of lofty, snow-covered mountains and lovely valleys in which the Americans from Astoria had built trading posts.

At the mouth of the Snake River he came to a village where, two years before, David Thompson had tied a half sheet of paper to a pole. On the paper he had written: "Know hereby that this country is claimed by Great Britain as part of its territories."

From now on, all the way to the Pacific, his route coincided with that of Lewis and Clark. It passed through the country of the Walla Walla tribe, and then into the land of the Chinook. Henry, we cannot doubt, noted with disgust the change in the people that even the kindly Thompson reported after clearing the raging, hissing ten-mile stretch of the Columbia known as the Dalles. They were a race, he could see, distinctly different from the people above the rapids — short, fat, brawny, with round faces and flat noses. They were all naked. "The women," Thompson had observed, "had scarcely a trace of the decency and modesty of the women of the upper country." When they offered their favors, Henry's men, like Thompson's, were probably uninterested.

Besides being unappetizing, the Indians between the Dalles

and Astoria were far from friendly. They had already been
spoiled by the Americans — as others had been spoiled by
the Nor'westers — and a party of traders on the Columbia
had to be strong indeed to feel secure from pillage and even
death by the poisoned arrows of the Chinook. Henry, however, succeeded in running a gantlet of hostile villages and
arrived unscathed at Astoria on the fifteenth of November,
1813.

Rather dourly, the event was noted by Gabriel Franchère,
a young clerk who had come to Astoria on the *Tonquin*:
"Messrs. Alexander Stuart and Alexander Henry, both partners of the N. W. Company, arrived at the factory in a couple
of bark canoes manned by sixteen voyageurs. . . They
brought us Canadian papers, by which we learned that the
British arms had so far been in the ascendant. They also
confirmed that an English frigate was coming to take possession of our quondam establishment; they were even surprised not to see the *Isaac Todd* lying in the road."

Henry had arrived too late to take part in the "capture" of
Astoria. But there would have been no need for his help in
any event, nor for the *Isaac Todd*'s either. By this time, the
main force of the Nor'westers, under John George McTavish,
were on the ground and in full possession of the post. They
had not been required to do any fighting for it, however;
they had simply bought it from the Americans!

3

THERE was something dismally comic opera about almost
everything that happened in connection with Astoria. And
not the least ludicrous was the finale of the great land-and-sea

expedition against this supposedly formidable stronghold on the Columbia.

When McTavish and his force arrived on the scene, the Astorians were in deep trouble. They had waited a full year for their supply ship *Beaver*. Now they could only look forward to a winter of starvation. They were worried, too, because many of them were former Nor'westers and British subjects — now in the embarrassing position of trading under the American flag while their own country was at war with the United States. "All of us," Franchère wrote fervently, "wished ourselves in Canada!"

They began to think about abandoning the post, then to talk about it openly. Some, indeed, set off up the Columbia and over the mountains, finally reaching St. Louis after incredible suffering. The rest decided to postpone their return to the United States until they could scrape together enough provisions to last through so long and perilous a journey.

It was at this point that two birchbark canoes flying the Union Jack arrived at Astoria with J. G. McTavish, Joseph Larocque, and nineteen voyageurs. They landed under the guns of the fort and made camp. They settled down to await the arrival of the *Isaac Todd*, from England, with Donald McTavish, generalissimo of the Nor'westers.

The Astorians generously allowed them to remain under their guns, while they went on gathering provisions for their trip back home. An unexpected windfall of thirty-two bales of dried venison gave them a renewed sense of security, however, and the fur harvest from the upper posts was proving very rich; so they decided to postpone evacuation of the fort for another year. It turned out to be a rather good summer for the Astorians, in fact; and it became an even better one

when an American schooner, *Albatross*, arrived out of nowhere with thirty-five barrels of salt meat, nine tierces of
rice, and a great quantity of the Sandwich Islanders' staple,
taro. Aboard was Wilson P. Hunt, who had sailed away a
year ago in Astor's ship, *Beaver*, promising to return in two
months. Hearing of the outbreak of war, he explained, he
had prudently sent the *Beaver* on to Canton, after chartering
a smaller ship, *Albatross*, in the Sandwich Islands.

Hunt was disturbed to find Astoria under siege, so to speak,
by the Nor'westers; and most unhappy to learn that the
Astorians had all but decided to abandon the post. He reminded them that John Jacob Astor held this venture dear to
his heart; and nothing would pain him more than capitulation
to the British. "Were I on the spot," Astor had written Hunt,
from a safe distance, "and had the management of affairs, I
would defy them all."

When Hunt sailed away on the *Albatross*, however, he
had come to a reluctant agreement with the rest of the Astorians. Bowing to the inevitable, he had consented to sell the
post to the North West Company, and had delegated author-
ity to close the deal to Duncan McDougall, a former Nor'-
wester who had joined Astor's venture and was in charge of
his operations on the Columbia. He could hardly have made
a worse choice. McDougall all but gave Astoria away to the
Nor'westers. So unfavorable a bargain did he strike for his
employer, indeed, that the mild-spoken Franchère called him
a traitor. And it is not easy, in fact, to understand the easy
terms on which he surrendered such an important post to the
enemy.

For the Nor'westers were not doing very well. Although
a second detachment of voyageurs had now joined the original

party, bringing the total up to seventy-five men, their strength was illusory. Camped at the bottom of a dreary little bay, they were destitute of provisions. Indeed, they had to beg handouts from the fort they had come to conquer! The summer wore on. The *Isaac Todd* did not arrive. The Nor'westers' situation deteriorated rapidly.

Soon they were completely without food. Or goods to trade for provisions. Or ammunition with which to hunt game. The Indians, friendly to the Americans, were waiting only for word from the Astorians to kill them. They could not stay where they were, and they could not return to Canada. And how did they decide to get themselves out of this hopeless predicament? They would buy Astoria from the Americans!

Improbable as it may seem, they actually proposed to purchase the whole establishment; and after a certain face-saving delay, McDougall accepted the offer. He sold out Astor at forty cents on the dollar — $40,000 for the post and all the furs and supplies on hand. Franchère, pointing out how easy it would have been to "get rid of the land party of the Northwest Company, who were completely in our power," was bitter about the whole matter. "Those at the head of affairs," he wrote, "had their own fortunes to seek . . . but that will not clear them in the eyes of the world."

The world, however, has long forgotten McDougall's perfidy — if such it was; and even at the time there was not enough indignation among the Astorians to prevent the transfer of Astoria to McTavish and his handful of voyageurs. The American colors were hauled down and the British run up; and the first settlement at the mouth of the Columbia became a Crown property.

It was a month after this that Alexander Henry and Alexander Stuart arrived and were astonished to see the Union Jack flying above the post.

4

HENRY found the former masters of Astoria and the new owners living happily enough together. Most of the Astorians had been recruited from the North West Company; and many, in fact, had re-entered the Concern's service. Some had already left to man the old Pacific Fur Company posts at Okanaga, Willamette, and Spokane.

Henry strolled about the environs of Astoria, observing everything with his usual curious eye and noting all that interested him in his journal. The sea, "rolling in like small hills, all afoam" from Chinook Point, fascinated him. Of the resident Indians he took a dim view. The Chinook impressed him no more favorably than they had Lewis and Clark, who had not allowed them in their fort. With their flattened heads and filthy habits, they seemed somewhat less than human to him; and their language — a gibberish invented for trading along the coast and sprinkled with English words, mostly obscene — hardly a language. Their greeting, he noted, sounded something like, "Ho-ah-ya-clahk." It was derived, he learned, from Captain Lewis' habit of saluting his fellow-officer with, "How are you, Clark?"

But little as he fancied the Chinook, Henry took the time out to write a conscientious description of one of their flea-infested villages:

I measured an inhabited house and found it to be 70 feet long and 25 feet wide; the entrance in the gable end, as usual, was cut through a plank 5½ feet wide, and nearly oval. A board suspended on the outside answered for a door; on the other side of the broad plank was rudely carved a large figure of a man, between whose legs was the passage . . . The houses are exceedingly filthy, sturgeon and salmon being strewn about in every direction. The men seemed brutes and the women devoid of shame or decency.

It is plain enough that he was struck by his first sight of the Chinook chief, Comcomly, as he swept across the Columbia in his great high-decked fighting canoe, with its flaring bows and grotesque, painted figures carved at prow and stern, "alongside one of his favorite women, La Blanche." But he found him somewhat less impressive than did Lewis and Clark, David Thompson, and other visitors to the mouth of the Columbia. For Washington Irving's "Mephistopheles of Astoria," he has only the dry comment: "He is a troublesome beggar."

The great King Comcomly figures prominently in all accounts of Astoria. Like Le Borgne, of the Mandan, he is constantly in the background of improbable events. Strutting in his scarlet coat and silken cravat, driving impossible bargains with the frustrated traders, selling his daughter to McDougall for an exorbitant price, he is a bizarre but by no means miscast player in the crazy drama of Astoria.

But Henry gives little space to the Chinook chief in his journal. He is much more interested in the little scenes encountered on his daily strolls and canoe trips across the bay:

We walked down to the beach to see the *Dolly*, a small vessel of 10 tons, built at this place by the late Pacific Fur

Company, with timber brought from New York . . . In
the cabin of this vessel we found a Chinook woman alone
with the usual covering — a kind of petticoat of cedar
fibres, reaching nearly down to the knee, and a small robe
of wood rat skins. She had just been bathing in the river
and was by no means shy.

We walked along the beach gathering shells of various
kinds. We saw several canoes containing dead bodies.

We saw some small green frogs. Immense quantities of
driftwood lay on the beach, in general of extraordinary
size. We observed many of their dead; some lying on the
ground covered with mats, and a canoe over all . . . they
all seemed much neglected by the living.

Walked down to Point George; collected a few pebbles
and some petrifactions bearing the prints of small fishes.
Saw some wrens and other birds.

I observed in the hands of a fellow from towards Gray's
harbor a musket of Russian manufacture.

We walked out to see the old American winter quarters of
Captains Lewis and Clark in 1805-06, which are in total
ruins.

We had this evening for supper some taroo root, made into
excellent pancakes.

Henry, with little to occupy him after his arrival, killed
time and waited for a house to be readied for him and his
companions from Fort William. On November 26, he and
Stuart and Bethune moved into winter quarters, with a Sandwich Islander called Dick as their major-domo.

5

ALTHOUGH Astoria had been depicted to the British government as a large, strongly-fortified, heavily-garrisoned fort, it was actually a ramshackle sort of post by Nor'wester standards.

Situated on a high point of land, it consisted of no more than a stockade about ninety feet wide and a hundred long, with feeble bastions at the north and south angles, each mounting small brass cannon. The warehouse and dwelling-house, both built of logs and covered with cedar bark, formed two sides of the stockade; the other buildings — blacksmith shop, powder magazine, miscellaneous sheds, and later on a hospital of sorts — were jammed in wherever they would fit. The quality of the construction may be judged by the fact that the whole establishment was thrown up in six days.

In this small, penlike enclosure a hundred and fifty men or more milled about on ordinary days — American traders, French-Canadian voyageurs, Scottish Nor'westers, and natives of the Sandwich Islands, not to mention the Chinook and Clatsop. About half of this motley population was American by birth, the other half Canadian. Counting the original Astorians stationed at the upriver posts, the total roster of Astoria now comprised about a hundred and forty Americans and half that number of British nationals . . . all men.

For, unlike the big establishments of the North West Company in the Interior, Astoria was almost without women. Except for the wives and families of a few of the bourgeois — and Henry's was not among them — none lived inside the stockade. This, however, did not mean that large numbers of females did not frequent the post. Women, indeed, were one of the major problems at Astoria.

In the spring, when the fur brigades arrived from upriver, they poured into the area from all quarters and set up for business in small huts "from which it was difficult to keep the men." Ross Cox, the Astorian clerk, was reminded of home. "They besiege our voyageurs," he wrote, "much after the manner which their frail sisters at Portsmouth adopt when attacking the crews of the newly arrived East India fleet. Mothers participate with their daughters in the proceeds arising from prostitution; and in many instances husbands share with their wives the wages of infamy. Disease is the natural consequence of this state of demoralization, and numbers of unfortunate beings suffer dreadfully from the effects of promiscuous intercourse."

This is an observation that Alexander Henry confirms over and over. When he himself became master of Astoria, the traffic with the Chinook women appears to have been one of his constant worries:

> A canotee of prostitutes came here this morning, but were not allowed to land on pain of being put in irons; this threat, I hope, will keep them off.

But it didn't, apparently, and the inevitable aftermath is made clear in this obviously nettled passage:

> I informed the men that if any of them should be disabled by venereal disease, I would deduct the time lost from their wages, and insisted that no woman should sleep in any of our houses.

To what extent venereal infection had become prevalent at Astoria is indicated by a roster of the post prepared by

Henry, in which he notes that out of fifty men eight were confined to their rooms with the sickness, and eleven others were more or less disabled. He concludes hopelessly:

> But the fellows are so incautious or blind to their health that they make light of my advice on the subject, although they have the glowing example of 10 comrades now laid up in the hospital in a very bad state, under a course of mercury. Others are infected more or less, few, if any, being entirely exempt; and proper medicines for the foul disease are very scarce here.

But women were not the only source of trouble at Astoria. A good second was the crowded quarters in which so many men of two different nations — and those nations at war — had to live. Friction was inevitable. The Americans, Washington Irving observes, "were exceedingly galled by the tone and manner assumed by the clerks and retainers of the Northwest Company, who ruffled about in that swelling and braggart style which grows up among these heroes of the wilderness; they, in fact, considered themselves lords of the ascendant and regarded the hampered and harassed Americans as a conquered people."

What the Nor'westers, on the other hand, thought of the Astorians is more briefly summed up by Henry:

> Most of the men brought overland by the late P. F. Co. are undisciplined, impertinent, ill-behaved vagabonds, devoid of that sense of subordination which our business requires.

As one might expect, frequent quarrels and occasionally physical violence resulted from the irksomeness of close quarters. In an altercation over hoisting the flag, one of Henry's voyageurs received a knife wound from an Astorian. At Spokane House, Ross Cox witnessed a little trouble between two fiery clerks: "Mr. Pillet fought a duel with Mr. Montour of the North-west, with pocket pistols at six paces; two shots were fired, both hits; one in the collar of the coat, the other in the leg of the trousers. Two of their men acted as seconds, and the tailor speedily healed their wounds."

The marvel is that things ran as smoothly as they did at Astoria, considering the powerful irritants to tempers that were always present. Among these were long stretches of nothing to eat but sun-dried fish, often rotten; the rainy seasons, which bogged the post down in a sea of mud, interdicting even the small pleasure of an occasional stroll; and, it might be added, the monotony of waiting without end for the *Isaac Todd*, a ship that some came to believe would never arrive.

It had been more than a year, now, since the *Isaac Todd*, with Donald McTavish and John McDonald of Garth aboard, had left Montreal; ten months since she had sailed from England for the Columbia. The Nor'westers had spent a whole round of seasons waiting for her to appear — time used in building new posts far up the river, enlarging and strengthening the Astorians' flimsy fort, amassing furs and provisions . . . and waiting.

Then, on November 30, almost exactly a year after Henry's arrival at Astoria, this entry in his journal:

At twelve o'clock, being about half tide, a large ship appeared in sight, standing in over the bar with all sail spread, under a light breeze from the N.E. We could observe no flag flying. We fired three shots from a four-pounder but received no answer.

Was this, at last the *Isaac Todd*? Or was it, perhaps, an

American sloop-of-war? For the rest of the day, Astoria remained in a state of almost frantic suspense:

> At half-past twelve she came to anchor in Baker's Bay
> . . . At one, Mr. McDougall and Mr. Halsey left in
> a birch canoe, with six men, to go aboard, while we prepared for flight, should she prove to be an enemy . . .
> At three I observed a white flag at her fore — our signal;
> but Joseph Ashton tells us the American ships on the N. W.
> coast have the same signal — in short, we are at a loss what
> to think . . . At five, Mr. Thompson embarked with all
> our packs, 92 in number, and a stock of arms, ammunition,
> and provisions in one large boat and a canoe . . . At six,
> Mr. McKenzie set off with another boat with our baggage,
> etc. The night was uncommonly dark, and our situation
> nowise enviable. Messrs. S., B., and self remained to see
> the result of matters.

Finally the anxious Astorians heard singing on the water, and soon afterward the familiar sounds of a canoe approaching land. This proved to be Mr. Halsey, dead drunk. He brought the welcome news that the mystery ship, although not the *Isaac Todd*, was one of His Majesty's sloops-of-war, *Raccoon*, 26 guns, Captain Black commanding. The whole Halsey party was in rather a bad way: "The men were all intoxicated with wine given them aboard, and had shipped much water in the canoe; in any squall of wind, they must inevitably have perished."

Guns were immediately fired, summoning the canoes up-river to return, and before daybreak all packs, arms and ammunition were once again safely in the warehouse of the fort. At ten o'clock Henry and several men embarked in a large boat for the *Raccoon* and were welcomed aboard by Captain Black and none other than John McDonald of Garth!

Garth was a pitiful sight. His famous long red hair had been cut short, his great bushy beard was gone, his face was blistered and disfigured, his arms — including the withered one — were wrapped in oily bandages. He explained how he had parted from Donald McTavish and taken separate passage on the *Raccoon* to lessen the chance of their both being captured by the Americans. Off Rio, Captain Black had decided to scale the ship's guns. At the tenth discharge something had gone wrong. Explosions ran from gun to gun and to the powder horns of the marines. Some died. A score had been burned so severely that they lay for weeks in excruciating pain, groaning pitifully and, Garth said, surpassing all previous records for sea profanity. He himself was lucky to be alive, since he had been burned worst of all. Indeed, he was still in poor condition; Captain Black and his first mate had to support his huge figure as he walked slowly across the deck to meet Henry.

But five days later Garth came ashore to take command of Astoria, and was saluted with five guns as he landed. The next morning the *Dolly*, with a new flag at her maintop, sailed out to the *Raccoon* to fetch supplies; she was saluted by three guns as she left. No guns boomed when Captain Black came ashore a few nights later; but the approach of his officers, as they reeled up to the fort, was announced by some of the heaviest profanity yet heard on the Columbia:

At 11 P.M. Captain Black, Mr. A. Stuart, and Mr. Clarke arrived by land, having broken the canoe running ashore at Point George . . . The gentlemen and men came here by land, along the beach, in feeling darkness, over slippery stones, through pools of water, and among embarrassments of driftwood. Fortunately for them, the tide was out.

which favored them with a wide though rugged beach. Having got supper, it was 2 A.M. before we went to bed.

On the morning after, the captain had his first good look at Astoria; and what he saw seems not to have impressed him. "Great God Almighty!" he is reported to have exclaimed. "Is this the fort I've heard so much about? Why, damn me, I could knock it down in a couple of hours with a four-pounder!"

That afternoon Captain Black presented the fort with a new Union Jack. This seemed to call for some sort of formal ceremony, so one was arranged:

> We collected all our men, armed with muskets; the marines were drawn up in uniform under arms, and the sailors, with Quartermaster Hill, attended to the guns. The captain in full uniform, broke a bottle of Madeira on the flag-staff, and took possession of this country and place in the name of His Britannic Majesty, calling this post Fort George. Three cheers were then given by us all, and three rounds of musketry were fired by our men and the marines. One of the latter had a narrow escape from shooting himself in the face, his gun having flashed and then gone off on being grounded . . . Eleven guns were fired from our four-pounder. We drank His Majesty's health, and a speech to Comcomly's son was made by Mr. Franchère. The ceremony ended by taking a few extra glasses of wine.

And so, with the firing of guns and musketry, toasts, speeches, cheers, and a marine almost shooting himself in the face, Astoria passed formally from American possession and became Fort George. Only Comcomly — absent from the festivities — appears to have dissented. He considered the whole affair an outrage, offered to exterminate King George's men singlehanded, and announced that McDougall, his son-

in-law, was an old woman for having surrendered so readily
to the British.

From now on, more firing of guns was heard than ever
before or since, perhaps, at the mouth of the Columbia. Each
time that Captain Black left Fort George for his ship, he was
given a five-gun salute — and welcomed aboard with another.
The *Dolly*'s comings and goings were marked by three-gun
salutes, as if she were a man-o'-war. When heavy gunfire was
heard at sea, it was supposed at first that the *Isaac Todd* had
at last arrived. But . . .

> The shots our people heard proved to be a morning and
> evening gun fired by the *Raccoon* in honor of the Union
> Jack which had been given us by the captain. The gentle-
> men and crew of the boat [which had arrived from the
> *Raccoon*] were all intoxicated.

Morning and evening guns continued to be fired by the
Raccoon in honor of the new Union Jack. Days passed, and
one is led to suspect from the tone of Henry's journal that
the pace set by the ship's officers — excepting Captain Black,
who seems to have been a temperate man — began to wear on
even such seasoned bottlemen as the Nor'westers.

It was not until a month after her arrival that the *Raccoon*
finally upped anchor and cleared the bar on New Year's Eve.
Fort George gave her a farewell salute of seven guns and
watched her slip behind Point Adams with no vast regret. An
awful lot of powder had been wasted in salutes during the
Raccoon's visit, and an unconscionable quantity of rum consumed.

"Famous fellows for grog, they are!" was Henry's final
comment on the officers and crew of His Majesty's Sloop-of-
war *Raccoon*.

6

McDonald of Garth made one thing clear at once: until Donald McTavish arrived, he would be in command at Fort George. There were some objections, it would seem, despite Garth's clear claim to senior partnership:

> A long correspondence took place between Messrs. John McDonald, Alex. Stuart, John Stuart, and myself, and Mr. J. G. McTavish, on the subject of Mr. McDonald's right to assume the management of affairs at this place, which he has taken upon himself; a long altercation ensued this evening, which ended to the satisfaction of none present.

Garth, however, was a very large and forceful man, with a habit of flourishing a couple of pocket pistols he habitually carried; and he appears, at least temporarily, to have won his point. Almost immediately, as the new commander of Fort George, he was confronted with a situation that demanded action:

> At 9 A.M. a canoe arrived from above, with Messrs. David Stuart, John Stuart, and Donald McKenzie, and 12 men. They brought the unpleasant news that Indians had attacked them in camp between Seal Falls and Grand Rapids during the night.

The only casualty was one man shot through the ear by an arrow. But three days later, more canoes arrived from the Upper Columbia with more serious news. The Indians had again attacked at the Rapids. A hunter had been killed, and Henry's friend, Alexander Stuart, was badly wounded. Worst of all, everything had been looted. The loss was heavy. It ran into thousands of items, including 50 new guns, 140 pounds of powder, 213 copper kettles, 44 blankets, 200 axes. Unless recovered, the blow to the upper posts would be crippling.

Garth, of course, was for immediate and bloody reprisal; but others remembered that they were in hostile country, and their number was small. A series of consultations with the more-or-less friendly Chinook and Clatsop Indians ensued. Even the wife of Coalpo, the Clatsop chief, was consulted. She agreed with Garth: she was in favor of wiping out practically everyone on the upper river. Volunteers for a punitive expedition were called for, and everyone responded gallantly:

> They all heartily agreed to accompany us on any expedition, and act in whatever manner we thought proper — war or peace was the same to them; they were ready to the last man.

Muskets were distributed, and next day the warlike party set out with Henry at its head.

> At noon we embarked in four birch-rind canoes and two large wooden canoes — 51 men and 11 passengers. Coalpo and his wife went with us in their own canoe, paddled by eight of his slaves. She was to act as mediator.

Rather a bloodthirsty mediator, one might think; but many aspects of this foray could strike one as a trifle odd. For instance, nobody seems to have looked after its provisioning. On the second day out, Henry wrote:

> This afternoon we finished our stock of dried salmon and meat, being thus left without one mouthful for 65 of us and four Indians, on the eve of encountering enemies.

From now on, the party lived on dogs and horses — when the Indians cared to provide them. Cold was added to the discomfort of hunger; and a generally unpleasant situation is summed up in such passages of Henry's journal as:

We traded nine dogs and one horse for food; the dogs were knocked on the head with an ax, and the horses shot through the head. Here we lay three hours, exposed to a heavy rain.

Picking up a Willamette chief named Casino to serve as interpreter, the expedition continued up the Columbia, with Mount St. Helens and Mount Rainier towering against the sky. They passed through villages from which the Indians fled at their approach, or else lurked behind trees "with bows bent and arrows across them, ready to let fly." Occasionally, Casino and Coalpo's wife went ashore and, by dint of threats and cajolery, recovered a few of the stolen guns.

On the fifth day, the Nor'westers arrived at the Rapids (now the Cascades) where, as Henry expresses it, "the scuffle took place." Blood was found on the rocks — some of it Stuart's, Henry surmised, some of it the blood of two Indians who had been killed in the "scuffle." A strong camp was made and a guard set round the clock.

The Nor'westers held counsel and decided to capture Canook, the chief of the pillagers. When this great plan fell through — Canook proving un-cooperative — they compromised on the kidnapping of an obscure chief, who had come trustingly into Henry's tent for a smoke. This caused a "great bawling and harrying about in the village," and Henry ordered the swivel gun to be fired off, "to show them there was such a thing."

The idea back of all this was to frighten the Indians into

returning the stolen goods. Perhaps, it was suggested, a formal show of the white man's power would expedite their recovery:

> We paraded our people on the field facing the village, fired a round of musketry, and marched and countermarched, Mr. Franchère acting as drill sergeant. We then called out to the Indians that we were ready for peace or war, as they saw fit . . . We fired the swivel and sent up two skyrockets, which must have alarmed the natives, who had never seen or heard anything of the kind.

All this marching, countermarching and pyrotechny resulted in the appearance of two wives of the prisoner with three guns and thirteen copper kettles as ransom for their husband. A few more pieces of bale goods were brought in the following day, after which the Indians swore they had given up all the plunder. The expedition was running out of food again. All hands were put on an allowance of one meal a day — when it could be come by. Henry notes ominously that "some extraordinarily large vultures were hovering over our camp." As a last resort, Franchère was sent to harangue the village. He returned a beaten man:

> Mr. Franchère returned with their answer, which was that we must be a bad lot, to want all our property back after killing two chiefs, and they would give no more. Canook encouraged his people by telling them we were _____, whom their arrows could kill. This closed the business.

What Canook called the whites must have been colorful indeed, for Henry was not in the habit of using dashes in place of plain English; and it seems to have taken the starch out of everyone. The prisoner was given two blankets and, to his natural astonishment, a North West Company flag, and turned loose. The expedition started back:

> We pushed off, not less pleased to be on our way home than the natives must have been to get rid of such troublesome visitors.

The dreamlike quality of the whole episode is epitomized in the next sentence of the journal's account:

> We put ashore at our camp of the 13th, to search for two pairs of handcuffs and my umberella, which had been forgotten there.

Henry did not return to Fort George with the expedition. At the Willamette River he remembered that he had not seen his cousin William Henry for a long time, and cut out to visit his post upstream. Others, too, found excuses for not returning to the fort at once. McTavish timed his arrival to take place at night.

Nobody was eager to face John McDonald of Garth with the story of the expedition's farcical denouement. When Henry showed up, at last, he found that even Mrs. Coalpo had spoken her forthright mind about it:

> Coalpo's wife has given out that our pacific measures at the rapids were due more to timidity than humanity, and says we ought to have killed them all.

This was probably the first time that the bourgeois of the great North West Company had ever suffered that ultimate humiliation — revilement by a squaw for cowardice. What, we may wonder, had happened to the Nor'westers who, whatever their other human failings, had never, at least, shown themselves to be either fools or cowards in their dealings with the Indians? We do not know. All we know is: at Astoria anything could happen.

7

Subsequent events, indeed, made hardly more sense than the great punitive expedition against the river pirates. The year 1814 opened with the Partners wrangling about the management of Astoria, now Fort George. But whereas everybody had previously sought command, now nobody wanted it. In order to put themselves on record with the Partners at Fort William, the disputants began to write letters to each other, and to answer them, and then to answer the answers. In the end, "Mr. McDonald agreed to continue the management of affairs . . ."

Henry found some escape from it all in jotting down those brief notes on his environment that had sprinkled his journal so profusely since that far-off autumn of 1799, when we first found him scribbling in his big rawhide-bound book, "with a candle burning in my tent for some time after the fires had been put out":

> During my absence, one of our goats produced three kids, two of which were trampled to death; a hen had a brood of chickens, all of which the skunks destroyed; and a sow had 17 pigs, all of which she ate up herself.
>
> The P.F. Co. gentlemen are daily practicing at the mark with pistols and rifles; some of them are excellent shots.
>
> Mr. McDonald brought a bunch of beautiful small red flowers . . . In the woods the fern is as green as last fall . . . This evening the frogs were merrily croaking.
>
> A boat with 10 Sandwich Islanders, and a canoe with 10 Canadians and Mr. Matthews, set off to clear away the underbrush and rubbish on Tongue Point for the purpose of building a new fort.

I observed more women on the ground than I have ever seen before — 70 at one time.

A canoe arrived from the Willamette with three American freemen, Milligan, Flanagan and Baker.

He adds to the considerable file of nature notes that he has accumulated in his wanderings over half a continent. It is probable that he saw an albatross — with a wingspread of 94 inches. He also reported great sea lions in the Columbia, of a species probably never seen there before or since: "the hair is like that of a horse in summer, of a chestnut color."

He gives us one of the best descriptions of the Clatsop's great war canoes that has come down to us:

> The Clatsop chief was in his war canoe — the first of the kind I had seen. She was about six fathoms long and wide in proportion, the stem rising upright about six feet, on top of which was a figure of some imaginary monster of uncouth sculpture, having the head of a carnivorous animal with large erect ears, but no body, clinging by arms and legs to the upper end of the canoe. The ears were painted green, the other parts red and black . . . The stern also rose about five feet in height, but had no figures carved on it. On each side of both stem and stern, broad strips of wood rose about four feet, having holes cut in them to shoot arrows through. She had a high spritsail of handkerchiefs and gunahs, forming irregular stripes.

The sturgeon season opened, with immense quantities of the great fish strung between stakes in the villages along the river. The importance of sturgeon on the Columbia was comparable to that of buffalo on the prairies, or whitefish in the forest belt. It was the staple food of the traders:

Our party, when all together, numbers 60 men, who consume 13 sturgeons per day, weighing from 25 to 250 pounds each . . . One of the largest we have seen measured 10 ft. 7 inches over all, the head 3 ft. 10 inches in circumference; it weighed, after the guts were out, 395 pounds.

As spring approached, the routine activities common to every fur-trading post, no matter where located, gathered momentum. Canoes were built and given out. Accounts were settled and new engagements signed by the voyageurs. Goods were packed for the Interior, orders for the 1815 Columbia outfit prepared for dispatch to England, dried provisions traded with the Indians, letters for the Fort William spring express written and signed . . .

Then, on the last day of February, the familiar pattern of springtime bustle and stir was interrupted by a shout from the lookout: *"Ship ahoy!"*

8

EVERYONE, of course, supposed the ship at the mouth of the river to be the long-awaited *Isaac Todd*, but nobody could be sure. The watchers on the firing platform were kept in suspense:

We fired three shots from our four-pounder. Once when she turned broadside on, heading for Cape Dissapointment, some of us imagined we made her out to be a brig . . . We all conjectured what ship she was, and whether friend or foe; bets were made of skins and hats; but all rejoiced at the sight of a vessel.

Next day it was determined that she was a brig, all right —
but a brig flying no colors and making no signals — and the
natural conclusion was that she must be an American:

> Measures were therefore taken for defense; we being
> determined to risk all rather than to send off the packs; for
> if she were an enemy and took the fort, what benefit
> would our few packs be to us, destitute of resources? We
> could not remain here long, nor had we means to cross
> the mountains . . . We took all the men from their several
> occupations and manned a kind of battery, our two four-
> pounders fronting the fort, to command the anchorage
> and landing.

But, although the brig turned out to be American, with
Wilson Price Hunt aboard, she made no hostile moves. Hunt
sent the Nor'westers a present of yams, coconuts and sweet
potatoes, and invited them aboard his ship. He himself, however, prudently remained outside the range of Fort George's
guns. He sent word: "I do not consider it safe for an American subject to come to Fort George."

Later, he grew bolder, and there followed a great deal of
visiting back and forth between the fort and Hunt's ship,
Pedlar. Hunt soon got down to business. He wanted to take
away as many Americans as he could persuade to leave, and
all the Sandwich Islanders. During the dickering, he engaged
in a few side activities: he got the Fort George voyageurs
fighting drunk on Sandwich Island rum — a noxious distilla-
tion, according to Henry, "clear in its natural state, with a
smoky taste, something like whisky or bad gin" — and he did
his best to subvert the Indians:

> While I was on the brig, Comcomly and his second son
> came in his six-oared boat. He was cloathed by Mr.
> Hunt with a red coat, New Brunswick Regiment 104th,

a Chinese hat, white shirt, cravat, trousers, cotton stockings, and a fine pair of shoes, and two guns were fired on the occasion.

The negotiations continued, with occasional violent altercations, for eighteen days. In the end, a final settlement was made between the Pacific Fur Company and the North West Company; and the *Pedlar* sailed away with all the Americans who had not entered the service of the Nor'westers. They were not very many.

And now Fort George prepared for the most important event since Captain Black broke the bottle of Madeira on the flagpole and took possession of the post in the name of George Third: the departure of more than half of the fort's population on a great overland trek to Fort William.

9

IT HAD never been the Nor'westers' idea to turn Astoria into a military strong point. They were not interested in war or politics, except as it affected the fur trade; and they viewed Astor's occupation of the Columbia not as a phase of American territorial expansion, but simply as an encroachment on their beaver preserves west of the mountains, and a threat to their communications with the Pacific. As soon as Astoria was firmly in their possession, therefore, they turned their attention to putting the post on a paying basis.

The first step, obviously, was to get rid of a lot of idle hands. In the spring of 1814, more than 150 men were quartered at Fort George, including nineteen of the Partner or Clerk grade, about eighty voyageurs, fifteen Sandwich Islanders, two idiots, two hunters, two cooks, two blacksmiths, and a few freemen. Fifty of these, it was decided, were enough to staff Fort George and the upriver posts. The rest — including the original Astorians who had joined up with the Nor'westers — would return to Canada. The post would be left in charge of Alexander Henry. With him would remain Duncan McDougall, William Henry, Angus Bethune, thirty-six Canadians and nine Sandwich Islanders.

The overland brigade, under command of John McDonald of Garth, would include fourteen Partners and Clerks, and sixty-one canoemen and their families. Oddly enough, half a dozen Sandwich Islanders elected to make the harrowing trip over the mountains to Canada — with little, if any, chance of ever returning to their own flowery home in the Pacific.

Nine canoes were made ready to carry the expedition on the first leg of its journey up the Columbia. About fifty kegs, bags and bales of meat, flour, grease, rice, corn, molasses, potatoes and other concentrated foodstuffs made up the brigade's provision list. When that was gone, the expedition would barter trade goods with the Indians for beat meat, dried fish, dogs and horses.

To avoid the warlike Piegan, it was decided to take David Thompson's northern route, over Athabasca Pass, instead of the usual Howse Pass road to the Saskatchewan. It would be a long, perilous, grinding trip — which, as it turned out, all would not finish alive. They would be lucky if they made it back to Fort William by the middle of July.

The fort's guns boomed farewell as the nine cedar canoes pushed off on their long and hazardous journey, and all on shore shouted the familiar, *"Bon voyage! Bon voyage, mes voyageurs!*" And Alexander Henry, watching the last of them vanish down the wide reaches of the river, and observing the dark faces of the Indians who had flocked in to see the best part of the white men leave, was far from cheerful. That night he wrote in his journal:

> Here we are left to the sport of fortune, at the mercy of chance, on a barbarous coast, among natives more inclined to murder us for our property than to assist us, and during a war which may at any moment strip us of our all. Any retreat up the river would be folly, as the falls would be an insurmountable barrier in our weak condition. The N. W. Company could expect no lenity from an American armed vessel. Thus, with the natives on one hand and the Americans on the other, our situation would be wretched indeed.

And this, somehow, does not sound in the least like Alexander Henry the Younger. Can it be, one wonders, that he was softening under the strange and baleful influence that seems to have shaped the sometimes tragic, often farcical, and always unpredictable course of events on the Columbia? It is difficult to decide. We can only know that within two months Henry himself would be past caring.

10

AFTER the "confusion and rummaging" of the overland brigade's departure, it took several days to restore order at Fort George; and then began once more the monotonous, now almost hopeless, waiting for the *Isaac Todd*. The chance of everybody's dying before her arrival seemed very real. Astor's venture on the Columbia had already taken a heavy toll of lives: eight lost when the ship's boat capsized at the first landing; five lost on the overland expedition to St. Louis; twenty-seven murdered on the *Tonquin;* eight lost on the *Lark;* nine killed by Indians on the Snake River; with another here and there, and some who went mad. Now, it seemed to Henry, the Nor'westers might well add to the list.

To deepen the general despondency, the rainy season had set in; and rations were so bad that they almost drove the men to mutiny:

> Men complain of their food, and declare they cannot subsist on dried smelt. I opened two casks of California beef to give them a portion to eat with their fish, but found it very bad — lean, dry and tasteless; some spoiled, and all as salt as it could be.

News came that the American party that had left Astoria in June, 1812, six men in all, had been murdered by the Indians on the east side of the mountains. It was an erroneous report, but no less depressing because of that.

Rumors of gunfire at sea began to trickle into the fort; but the Nor'westers resolutely closed their ears to them. The Indians were always circulating such tales, hoping for a reward. Or Joe Ashton spread them, simply because he was a natural liar. Yet, it was hard not to listen. "We are on tiptoe with expectation," Henry confessed, "in hopes of seeing a sail. But the tide flows, the breeze blows, the tide ebbs, and our hopes vanish . . ." So he tried to concentrate on the dull chores of post-keeping, performing all the pointless duties of his job; and noting with a kind of fetishlike faithfulness the smallest happenings in his journal:

> Men all at work, as yesterday. Roussel making four fine square-headed axes for the mechanics, to replace the same number taken away by our gentlemen.

A Chinook canoe came to trade, but they cannot make up their minds to the alteration in the price of the small Canton beads, the only kind now in fashion; the first and second sizes they will not take.

Our sick, having taken mercury enough, were this morning put on a course of corrosive sublimate.

Comcomly brought three baskets of clams; they are tough eating.

I saw several humming birds this morning . . . A whale was cast ashore yesterday . . . A canotee of prostitutes came here this morning, but were not allowed to land, on pain of being put in irons.

Battle between Mrs. McDougall and Ignace's woman regarding the latter's children, who were playing with some trifling things, when the former lady, who is haughty and imperious, took the playthings from them and set them bawling; the consequence was a slap from the mother. Royalty was offended, and a dreadful row ensued.

More and more reports of ships at sea began to reach Fort George; and some of them had a certain ring of authenticity. Comcomly reported three vessels having been in port somewhere near Cape Flattery, two of them Russians, which sailed after trading, the other still there and trading sea otter. A pair of pistols was offered as a reward to the Indian first sighting an actual sail; and this, of course, led to any number of spurious claims. On the twenty-first, however, the reports began to take solid form:

About 4 P.M. some workmen in the woods cutting poles heard the report of three cannons, which they imagined to be on the river, and came to the fort. A canotee of prostitutes from the Clatsop village arrived and said they also had heard three reports; but we gave no credit and ordered them away . . . About six o'clock a canoe with four men from Chinook Point, paddling very hard, passed near the *Dolly*, and informed Joe they had seen a ship at sea. Joe cheered and waved his hat to give the news to us, who were standing at the gate.

The ship, the natives said, was a large, black, three-masted craft, standing off Cape Disappointment. They had been able to make out the men aboard her; and — obviously a bit of Chinook embroidery — *a woman with yellow hair*.

The news, however, did not bring much joy to Fort George. Instead, it threw the whole post into something near panic. For the old question came up again: was she friend or foe? Henry suddenly realized the awkwardness of his situation. He had no craft in condition to carry his property up the river and into hiding, should the strange ship turn out to be hostile. And more than half his men were in hospital. He proceeded, however, to take whatever measures he could:

> I sent a boat for all our people to come from Tongue Point, packed our papers, blankets, beads, strouds, etc. and put our guns in order. At 8 A.M. Mr. McDougall set off to see the vessel and find out who she is, if possible, so we may be able to send off the most essential articles, should she prove to be an enemy . . . Mr. Bethune, myself and Cartier are to await our fate at the fort, with the sick and disabled.

That same afternoon the watchers at the gate saw the ship for the first time. She was half lost in the haze, but could be followed with the glass as she passed Cape Disappointment and entered Baker's Bay, where she dropped anchor.

Henry, taking no chances, got off two boatloads of furs and provisions for the Willamette. Four boxes of bar lead were buried in the ground. McDougall returned from his scouting expedition with little to add to what was already known. He had not, apparently, ventured very close to the ship. Henry sent him back in a temper.

Toward evening the ship fired three guns and the fort replied with three. Through the glass, Henry could make out the anchored craft; and what he saw only added to his puzzlement:

> She appeared to be a large vessel; at the foretop she flew a white flag, apparently with a cross on it, nothing at her maintop, at her mizzentop a pennant, and at her peak a red flag. She appeared black, with a narrow yellow stripe, and a figurehead on her bow.

The night passed, and morning brought nothing new. McDougall did not return, and Henry cursed him for a bungling incompetent. His nerves were on edge. "It is unpleasant," he fretted, "to remain in such a state of suspense, not knowing whether she is friend or foe."

A little before ten o'clock he hoisted the agreed signal, a white flag. For half an hour there was no response from the ship. Then a white flag, the proper answer, was run up to her foretop. Two puffs of smoke issued from her ports, and the boom of guns rolled across the bay.

And so, at last, it was the *Isaac Todd*.

At noon, Lamsoi, the Chinook who had taken McDougall out to the ship, arrived with a note confirming this. It was a short note, written in the large, unmistakable hand of J. C. McTavish: *"Isaac Todd Ship, London. Mr. McDougall has come aboard."*

Henry instantly lowered the signal flag, hoisted the post's Union Jack, and fired five guns. Like a housewife tidying up for unexpected guests, he set everyone to putting away the packs, clearing the stores, and throwing out the rotten sturgeon that, ever since Astorian days, had stunk up the post. As if in approval, the ship then fired eleven guns, and Donald McTavish's personal envoy, J. C. McTavish, came ashore to invite Henry aboard the *Isaac Todd*.

II

FROM this point on, the trend of events at Fort George becomes curiouser and curiouser. Next morning, Henry was up at dawn. By six o'clock he had shaved, dressed, and was off in the ship's jolly-boat. At eight he climbed aboard the *Isaac Todd* — to find the decks empty.

This was both a disappointment to Henry and an affront to his dignity. As master of Fort George, he had expected to be welcomed with some degree of ceremony — even Mc-Dougall had received a two-gun salute. But his pique turned to astonishment when Donald McTavish finally put in an appearance.

The Chinook reports about a yellow-haired woman on the ship had not been mere Indian hallucinations, after all. For there she stood. There she stood in broad daylight, clinging to McTavish's arm and gazing at Henry with bold, blue eyes.

McTavish introduced her as Miss Jane Barnes. He had found her in a bar at Portsmouth, and had offered to take her to Montreal with him — by the somewhat circuitous route around the Horn and across the whole continent of North America. Miss Barnes had good-naturedly accepted. It mattered little to Jane, apparently, where she went, or how she got there. (She was to wind up in Canton, as a matter of fact, the chatelaine of a wealthy nabob of the East India Company.)

Her impact on Henry must have been shattering. For Jane Barnes was the first white woman — with the exception of Marie Gaboury and the unfortunate Orkney girl — that he had seen in fifteen years. And, from all accounts, she was an eyeful. To Ross Cox she was "a flaxen-haired, blue-eyed daughter of Albion," a lively, good-looking wench, with a seductive figure, an engaging line of conversation — full of amusing malapropisms — and physical charms that even the Chinook braves found irresistible.

"The Indians daily thronged in numbers to our fort," another Astorian, Alexander Ross, wrote later, "for the purpose of gazing on and admiring the fair beauty . . . She had rather an extravagant wardrobe, and each day exhibited her in a new dress, which she always managed in a manner to display her figure to the best advantage." It can hardly be doubted that she made the most of her charms when McTavish presented Henry; and if, from now on, a certain note of fatuousness is to be detected in the journal of Alexander Henry the Younger, it is perhaps understandable.

Introductions over, an hour passed "in smoking and chatting." Nobody offered Henry breakfast. Finally, he asked for a cup of tea, and "a glass of Noyeaux cordial was produced, in another half hour a slice of cold salt beef and pork, and a cup of salt water tea, all very bad, with brown biscuits." Hardly the way to treat a gentleman of his importance on the Columbia, Henry thought; for his irritation shows through in his journal. "I had several times expressed a wish to be introduced to the captain," he complains, "but it has been as often put off . . ."

At last, however, everybody went on deck, and Henry was properly presented to the ship's doctor, Mr. Swan, and then to Captain Smith. There seems to have been nothing very genuine in these amenities. The captain was decidedly uncordial. Even Jane had little to say. Henry's annoyance moved him to a rare attempt at sarcasm:

> We looked about and gaped on deck for some time; the doctor being the only person who came near us. A few words were exchanged, a solemn silence ensued, and nothing answered me but the noise of the cocks and hens.

What Henry did not know was that not only Captain Smith but the whole crew of the *Isaac Todd* hated Donald McTavish — and perhaps by analogy all Nor'westers — so heartily that his person was actually unsafe aboard the ship.

12

IGNORED on deck, Henry went into the cabin again and demanded something to eat before returning to Fort George. After a long time, "a bit of cheese, brown biscuit, and some port wine were brought, of which the doctor, Mr. McTavish, Mr. McDougall and myself partook. A vile discourse took place in the hearing of Jane on the subject of venereal disease and the Chinook ladies."

Immediately after lunch, everybody piled into the jolly-boat and set off for Fort George. At two o'clock the first white woman ever to set foot on the banks of the Columbia went ashore. She did not remain long — only long enough to stun the Indians and voyageurs and to sow the first seeds of demoralization in the receptive soil of Fort George.

When she and the others had returned to the *Isaac Todd*, Henry sat down to his journal and tried to record the experiences of an eventful and not altogether satisfying day. He closed with this notation:

> Mr. D. McTavish and Captain Smith are on bad terms. One messes in the after cabin, and the other with his officers in the gunroom; the first mate being in disgrace with the captain, the latter objects to sit at the same table with him.

Well, he might have reflected, the *Isaac Todd* had been thirteen months on her way from England . . . a long time on a ship with one woman aboard.

13

FROM this point, it is difficult to trace the course of events at Fort George. For now Henry's journal, hitherto so explicit, often becomes vague and even mysterious — particularly when dealing with Jane Barnes; and one can discern a growing irritation, and perhaps a certain puzzlement, on Henry's part with the trend of affairs — and, at last, with his own somewhat peculiar conduct.

He seems to have nursed a nagging grudge against Donald McTavish, the new bourgeois of Fort George. He was full of resentments at fancied slights, larded his journal with sarcasm, and complained bitterly about McTavish's "want of common politeness." And Jane Barnes, quite plainly, was at the bottom of his touchiness, just as she was probably responsible for the breakdown of discipline and morals — as morals were understood at Fort George — that followed the arrival of the *Isaac Todd*.

Donald McTavish — taking no chances! — brought her with him every time he came ashore; and her flamboyant arrival at the fort was always an event. The voyageurs stopped work, the Indians swarmed in, and Henry himself made a holiday of her visits. "In the jolly-boat came Mr. McT., the doctor, and Jane," he wrote on one occasion. "I opened a cask of bottled porter, and also a cask of rather mouldy biscuits. Many Chinooks and Clatsops came in, some to trade, and others to visit." And, of course, to gawk at Jane.

The Chinook and Clatsop bucks became madly infatuated with her. King Comcomly's son, according to Ross, offered a hundred rare sea otters for her hand. Not only that. "He would never ask her to carry wood, draw water, dig for roots, or hunt for provisions . . . he would make her mistress over his other wives, and permit her to sit her ease from morning to night . . . she would always have an abundance of fat salmon, anchovies, and elk, and be allowed to smoke as many pipes of tobacco during the day as she thought proper."

But, although Jane's morals may have been strictly of the Chinook variety, her tastes were her own. She looked down her nose at these and many other tempting offers. Then Comcomly's son changed his tack: he formed a plan with his friends to carry her off while she was taking her customary evening stroll along the beach. He also declared that he would never again come near the fort while she was there — which, we may assume, was quite all right with Jane.

Her effect on the voyageurs and young gentlemen of Fort George was, of course, no less devastating; and Henry began to discuss measures for her "protection" with McTavish. In the meantime, evidence of an alarming deterioration of affairs at Fort George began to pile up. Drunkenness, which

during the visit of the *Raccoon* had been restricted mostly to
the officers of the ship and fort, now began to incapacitate
the whole post for days at a time. In the *pays d'en haut*, an
entire establishment drank itself stiff only on such high holidays as Christmas, New Year's, St. Andrew's Day, and All
Saints' Day. But at Fort George no excuse — except, perhaps,
the radiant presence of Jane — seems to have been needed.

Rum fired up the already smouldering hostility between
the Fort George voyageurs and the *Isaac Todd* seamen:

> When the longboat brought a load, Duchesne and Le
> Prine quarreled with some of the sailors, who had used
> them ill on the *Isaac Todd*, and pushed off with the boat;
> our men followed in a canoe, overtook, and attacked
> them . . . Our men were drinking and feasting all day.

The voyageurs, made bold by grog, began to flout the
post's discipline. Thus the blacksmith, who had come to
Astoria on the *Tonquin:*

> While we were at supper, Roussel, the blacksmith, came
> into the hall, was impertinent to Mr. McDougall, hurrahed
> for the Americans, and thus insulted us all.

The habit of insolence spread to the Indians, who became
pushing and arrogant. Comcomly himself made a display of
his contempt for the whites:

> Comcomly and his suite came over. I had a misunderstand-
> ing at dinner with the troublesome old fellow, who would
> not accept a piece of goose; he said it was not fit for a
> Chinook dog, and went off in a pet. When he came back,
> I gave him a whole goose, and made him a speech on the
> proprieties. He ate his goose, drank his wine and porter,
> and seemed to care little about us.

Comcomly followed through with an outrageous demand on Duncan McDougall for the remainder of his daughter's purchase price:

> Mr. D. McDougall this afternoon completed the payment for his wife to Comcomly, whose daughter she was; he gave 5 new guns, and 5 blankets, 2½ feet wide, which makes 15 guns, besides a great deal of other property, as the total cost of this precious lady. This Comcomly is a mercenary brute, destitute of decency.

A few days later, while Henry was at dinner, McDougall's wife was seized by her brothers, forced aboard a canoe, and dragged back to the Chinook village. The prestige of the white man on the Columbia had little farther to fall.

14

THE *Dolly*, the skiff that Astor's men had brought from New York, had been rechristened the *Jane*, and we find this reference to it in the *Journal:*

> The *Jane* came over with a load; the sailors were intoxicated, and we suspected they had broken open a cask of porter.

During the month of May, 1814, Henry's journal is full of such revealing entries — little asides that leave no doubt about how things were going at Fort George:

> The crew of the *Isaac Todd* begin to feel the effects of their communications with the Chinook ladies; several of them are laid up already.

> This evening Mr. A. Bethune, Mr. William Henry, and old Joseph Cartier took each of them a Chinook woman, with the approbation of Mr. D. McTavish.

Mr. J. Cartier discharged his lady, she being far gone with the venereal disease, and on examination the doctor gives it as his opinion that he is in a very bad way.

Quarrel between Mr. D. McTavish and Mr. Wm. Henry. Orders from Fort William produced, etc. Poor William!

We began to examine and assort goods, opening all bales, casks, etc. Things are in bad order; there is no correct account of the several packages, and the cargo is mixed up with the ship's stores.

Mr. McTavish treated the sailors with biscuits, cheese and rum. Much disturbance took place this morning on board ship between him and the captain, which may be attended with serious consequences . . . Mr. McTavish's person is not safe on board the ship; the captain could raise the crew in a twinkling, and they would be happy to vent their spleen on Mr. McTavish, as they detest him beyond all measure.

One of our goats had two kids, and a cat kittened. Our men purchased rum and molasses, and had a drinking match all day and night . . . About sunset the jolly-boat took Mr. McTavish on board alone; Jane, of course, remained, having taken up her lodgings in my room.

For in the meantime, "of course," *l'affaire Jane* had progressed along somewhat mysterious lines to a singular conclusion.

15

FOR two weeks Jane was a frequent visitor at Fort George, sometimes staying the night at the post, more often returning to the *Isaac Todd* with McTavish. The return trip, often made in the darkness, was a trying one, however; and steps were taken to provide comfortable overnight quarters for the pair: "Duschene and La Framboise put a room in order for Mr. D. McTavish and Jane." Less than a week later, she came ashore bag and baggage — and, as his journal coyly informs us, moved in with Henry!

But not, however, before some rather odd preliminaries. By this time, apparently, Jane's generous nature had included Henry in her affections; but the situation was by no means simple. It was decided to hold a conference to clear matters up. Jane was thoughtfully invited to attend.

Negotiations were conducted under the euphemistic pretense of providing the lady with protection against the Indians and the ardent young men of the post. Henry, it must have been decided by all three, was a more logical protector than the older McTavish. And yet, the Governor of Fort George, having brought the girl all the way around the Horn, surely had a valid claim to her companionship. The outcome was a compromise, perfectly acceptable to Jane: they would share and share alike.

A few days later, Henry and McTavish took a walk along the beach and worked out the final details of their "arrangement." The Governor must have assumed that giving up a share of Jane justified him in making up the loss elsewhere; for a week later he "took in tow" the Chinook widow of a Pacific Fur Company clerk; and we find him "dressing his *tête platte* in fine broadcloth which costs 25 shillings sterling a yard, and his *belle mère* also received a present."

Thus, with the good-natured co-operation of the lady herself, the matter of Jane Barnes' affections was settled to the satisfaction of everyone — except, perhaps, the woman-hungry "young gentlemen" about the post.

16

DURING this whole mad period, Henry never failed to put down in the big book a record of each day's sometimes improbable events. Sick or well, drunk or sober, he kept his journal.

Curiously, however, he has nothing more to say about Jane Barnes; and it is only from the young clerk, Ross Cox, that we get an occasional glimpse of her, "one day, her head decorated with feathers and flowers; the next her hair braided and unconcealed by any covering." But always a disturbing presence in the already restless fort.

Yet, if Alexander Henry henceforth ignores Jane Barnes in his journal, he does not neglect — as if impelled by a force of habit too deep for anything to alter — the careful recording of daily life at Fort George. And sometimes, in the midst of chaos, he succeeds in reporting a normal interlude so clearly and explicitly that historians have ever since been indebted to him. Thus his description of the departure of the Fort William Express:

> *May 1st.* All hands up early, preparing for the departure of the express for Fort William . . . At 10:30 the two canoes set off light — Messrs. D. McDougall, A. Bethune, A. McTavish, and A. Fraser, with 12 men in one canoe and eight in the other, provisioned for 12 days with beef, pork, flour, peas, rum, etc.

Then, with all his old-time passion for detail, he gives us the exact lading of each canoe, "it being their intention to make the portages light." And thus we get, more circumstantially than from any other source, an idea of just how the North West Company's famous expresses prepared for their great dashes across the continent.

Even more important from the standpoint of the professional historian, perhaps, is Henry's account of how Coniah, the Clatsop chief, brought him a writing left by Captains Lewis and Clark, with a roster of the American expeditionary force to the Columbia. This list included an Indian woman and child, who, of course, was Sacajawea, "the Bird Woman," and her baby. Henry with his usual meticulousness, copied down the names in order — then gave Coniah a new writing, and threw the priceless American document into the fire!

Scattered through the record now are those small observations that, no matter how disjointed the times, never failed to find a place in the journal of Alexander Henry the Younger:

> The *Jane* unloaded a cargo, including a large Spanish sow that had been hurt, on removal, by the slings giving away. The poor brute was let fall from the ship to the shallop's deck, and as she was heavy with pig, she littered on the deck.
>
> One of our goats had a kid which died. I wrote to Fort William.
>
> The tailor cut coats for Mr. Bethune and myself . . . a corbeau carried off one of our Spanish sow's pigs.
>
> Sowed a large quantity of early York, sugar-loaf, and red cabbage seed.
>
> The baker made a very bad batch of bread, having no yeast to leaven . . . The women brought in a quart of excellent large yellow raspberries. Swallows are numerous.

The shallop brought a load of coal . . . I put my curtains up.

One evening Alexander Henry sat down to write the last page of his journal. It had been fifteen years ago that, as a young man on his maiden venture into the *pays d'en haut*, he had written the first:

> *Autumn, 1799.* While building at Riviere Terre Blanche, near the foot of Fort Dauphin mountain, my Russia sheeting tent was pitched in a low place on the lower branch of a little river, sheltered from the wind among some tall elms and oaks. I was accustomed to sit up late at night, with a candle burning in my tent, for some time after the fires had been put out . . .

Never since that faraway time had he laid aside the pen. Wherever he went, with a faithfulness that amounted almost to a compulsion, Henry wrote in minute and precise detail of all he had seen and experienced in his continent-wide travels: almost, one is led to feel at last, with a kind of dogged insistence that there really was some meaning in life, even for a trader in the *pays sauvage*, and that writing it all down might help, in some small way, to make it clear.

And so, on the night of May 21, 1814, he sat down as usual, and wrote out a full account of what had happened that day at Fort George — ending for some unknown reason, but with a kind of symbolic fitness, in the middle of a sentence:

> *May 21st.* Coniah and other Clatsops brought back some stolen things. We clothed the chief and gave him a writing in lieu of the American one, which I threw into the fire before him. Finished examining the goods, arranging the garret, etc. Now all is in readiness and order, and a bedstead put up . . . There has been a misunderstanding on board the ship with Mr. McKay, regarding the bread

given out to the crew, and an appeal made to the captain. The weather cleared up——

When Henry laid down his pen in the middle of this sentence — or perhaps had it plucked from his hand by an impatient Jane — it was for good. With "all in readiness and order," he had written all he was ever to write in the journal of Alexander Henry the Younger. Next day, while sailing in the *Jane* to the *Isaac Todd,* he and Donald McTavish and five voyageurs were capsized and drowned in the Columbia.

17

For almost a century and a half, Alexander Henry the Younger has been lost in the company of dead and forgotten men, and the journal he so meticulously kept during all the years of his wandering is known to only a few scholars and specialists.

He is not remembered, as are Captains Lewis and Clark, Sir John Franklin, and his fellow Nor'westers Alexander Mackenzie and Simon Fraser, for dramatic explorations. Despite the prodigious range of his travels, he made no great discoveries, established no "firsts"; and so he has no mountain, river or pass named for him.

Nor did he ever reach the peak of power and wealth attained by such giants of the Concern as Simon McTavish, William McGillivray, and, again, Mackenzie. He was never more than a simple Wintering Partner, managing the affairs of his post and living with an Indian wife and their children among the savages of the *pays d'en haut.*

He wrote no popular account of his experiences — in the rhetorical and moralistic fashion of the time — as did Ross

Cox and Alexander Ross. Nor does he figure in the writings of his contemporaries. Even the account of the disaster in which he lost his life — written by Ross Cox — oddly omits any mention of him at all:

> This gentleman [Donald McTavish] had embarked in an open boat with six *voyageurs*, to proceed to the opposite side of the Columbia. It blew a stiff gale; and about the middle of the river, owing to some mismanagement of the sail, a heavy wave struck the boat, which instantly filled and went down. With the exception of one man, they all perished: he succeeded in gaining a snag which was a few feet above the water, and on which he remained for nearly two hours, until he was rescued in a state of great exhaustion by two Chinooks, who proceeded to his assistance in a small canoe. Thus perished the respected Mr. Donald McTavish, one of the oldest proprietors of the North-West Company, and for many years the principal director for managing the affairs of the interior.

But his death did not go unnoticed — nor, in the laconic fashion of the Northwest, unmourned — by such old "Wolves of the North" as Daniel Harmon and John McDonald of Garth. For he was one of them. He was a daring and enterprising trader; master of some of the North West Company's biggest, most remote, and most dangerous departments; a bourgeois respected for his fairness and courage by whites and savages alike.

If he was not a great man, he did not, at least, lack some of the qualities of greatness: bravery, endurance, steadfastness, and a dogged loyalty to the rough ideals of his harsh and lonely world. He possessed, it might be added, a sense of pity and justice that was rare in the *pays sauvage*. His weaknesses were the common ones . . . Perhaps it is enough to say of him: he was a Nor'wester.

The Sources

Most of the contemporary sources for *The Savage Country* will be found in the fort journals and other writings of the Partners and Clerks of the North West Company. By far the most important, of course, is the journal of Alexander Henry the Younger himself, published in 1897 under the title of *New Light on the Early History of the Greater Northwest.*

Edited by Dr. Elliott Coues, with a copious critical commentary — the footnotes sometimes occupy nine tenths of the page — *New Light* is a monumental work of scholarship and a superb — and warmly human — job of editing. Dr. Coues worked from a 1642-page manuscript, in the Library of Parliament at Ottawa, copied by one George Coventry from Henry's original in 1824. Henry's journals in his own handwriting are not extant.

Among other published writings of the Nor'westers, the most important are: Alexander Henry the Elder's *Travels and Adventures;* Sir Alexander Mackenzie's *Voyages from Montreal;* L. R. Masson's invaluable *Les Bourgeois de la Compagnie du Nord-Ouest,* which contains the journals, letters and memoirs of Roderic McKenzie,

François Antoine Larocque, Simon Fraser, Ferdinand Wentzel, George Keith, Aeneas McDonald, John McDonald of Garth, John McDonnell, François Malhiot, and others; Daniel W. Harmon's *Travels and Adventures;* David Thompson's *Narrative* (ed. J. B. Tyrrell); Gabriele Franchère's *Narrative* (ed. R. G. Thwaites); John Long's *Voyages and Travels* (ed. R. G. Thwaites); Duncan McGillivray's *Journal* (ed. Arthur S. Morton); Ross Cox's *Adventures on the Columbia River;* Alexander Ross' *First Settlers on the Oregon;* Peter Pond's *Narrative,* and the *Diaries* of John McDonnell, Archibald Norman McLeod, Hugh Faries, and Thomas Connor in *Five Fur Traders of the Northwest* (ed. Charles M. Gates).

Other published journals and memoirs, not written by Nor'westers, but more-or-less contemporary, include: Nicholas Garry's *Diary* (*Proceedings Royal Society of Canada*); *Journals of the Lewis and Clark Expedition* (ed. R. G. Thwaites); Sir John Franklin's *Journey to the Shores of the Polar Sea;* John Tanner's *Narrative* (ed. Edwin James); John J. Bigsby's *The Shoe and Canoe;* William H. Keating's *Narrative of an Expedition to the Source of St. Peter's River;* Matthew Cocking's *Journal* (ed. L. J. Burpee); Selkirk's *Sketch of the British Fur Trade;* R. M. Ballantyne's *Hudson Bay;* Jonathan Carver's *Travels;* Samuel Hearne's *Journey from Prince of Wales Fort;* Paul Kane's *Wanderings of an Artist;* George Catlin's *North American Indians;* Henry R. Schoolcraft's *Sources of the Mississippi; Cumberland and Hudson House Journals, Publications of the Hudson's Bay Record Society.*

The Champlain Society's *Documents Relating to the North West Company,* with a magnificent introduction by Editor W. Stewart Wallace, is, of course, a primary source on the formation, organization and personnel of the North West Company.

Among the important unpublished manuscript journals, letters and reports are those in the *Masson Papers,* Canadian Archives, Ottawa. They contain, among many other interesting items, a fair copy of Roderic McKenzie's first chapter of his projected work, *An Account of the North West Company;* an anonymous *Sketch of the Fur Trade;* John Johnston's *Account of Lake Superior;* fragments of journals by Ferdinand Wentzel, J. Thompson, Charles Chaboillez, William Henry, William McGillivray, and Henry Monk. In the Canadian Archives are also to be found manuscript *Minutes of the North West Company.*

Of non-contemporary books dealing with the North West Company or related subjects, the following were useful in writing *The Savage Country:* The Rev. Edward D. O'Neill's *History of the Ojibways;* George Bryce's *Remarkable History of the Hudson's Bay Company;* William H. Drummond's *The Voyageur and Other Poems;* H. H. Bancroft's *History of the North West Coast;* Washington Irving's *Astoria;* Grace Lee Nute's *The Voyageur;* L. J. Burpee's *The Search for the Western Sea;* Harold Innis' *The Fur Trade in Canada;* Harold Innis' *The Fur Trade of Canada;* Charles Gordon Davidson's *The North West Company;* Marjorie Wilkins Campbell's *The North West Company;* Wayne Stevens' *The North West Fur Trade;* J. N. Wallace's *Wintering Partners on the Peace River;* V. Steffanson's *The Fat of the Land;* John F. Spargo's *Two Bennington-Born Explorers;* M. Dugas, Ptr., *Legends du Nord-Ouest;* Harold Innis' *Peter Pond;* Frances Densmore's *Chippewa Customs;* Alexander Ross' *Fur Hunters of the Far West;* Charles Lanmann's *Adventures in the Wilds of the United States;* Capt. Thomas G. Anderson's *Narrative,* in *Wisconsin Historical Collections,* Vol. IX; Henry John Moberly's *When Fur Was King;* Francis Parkman's *The Old Regime in Canada;* H. M. Robinson's *The Great Fur Land;* Diamond Jenness' *Indians of Canada, National Museum of Canada, Bulletin 65, Anthropological Series No. 15.*

A great deal of material has also been drawn from the publications of various historical societies, among which may be mentioned: *Canadian Archives Publications, Minnesota Historical Collections* and *Minnesota History, Wisconsin Historical Collections, Michigan Pioneer and Historical Collections, Manitoba Historical and Scientific Transactions, Proceedings of the Royal Society of Canada, The Geographical Journal* of the Royal Geographical Society. And to these must be added the Hudson's Bay Company's fascinating magazine, *The Beaver.*

Index

Albatross, schooner, 255
Antelope, 161
Ashton, Joe, 280
Askin, John, 109
Assiniboine Indians, 76, 86, 104, 151, 161, 190, 206, 208, 211-12, 219-20; women, 112-13
Assiniboine River, 4
Astor, John Jacob, 224, 247, 248, 255
Astoria, 260-63; "capture" of, 253-56; passes to British, 266. *See also* Fort George
Athabasca House, Rainy Lake Fort, 63, 158, 193
"Athabasca Library," 31
Auneau, Father, 69

Baker, Mr., 274
Barnes, Jane, 284-88, 289, 291-93
Bas de la Rivière, 62, 73-74, 134, 147, 148
Basswood Portage, 46

Battle River, 207
Beaver, search for, ix-x; hats, x-xi; hunting for, 82-83; trading with Indians for, 83-86
Beaver, ship, 126, 248-49, 254, 255
Bethune, Angus, 229, 259, 278, 282, 290, 293
Big Belly Indians, 165, 174, 176-79
Big Man, 172
Black, Captain, 264, 265, 266, 267
Black Cat, 165, 171
Blackfoot Indians, 76, 211, 212, 215; women, 113
Blaeberry Creek, 244
Blood Indians, women of, 113
Bonaparte, Napoleon, 143
Bonga, Pierre, 53-54, 91; wife, 98
Bras Croche. *See* McDonald of Garth, John
Bread, 128
Buffalo, 94-95, 138-39, 161; meat, 123-24; tallow, 124; running, 138-40

Cadot, Jean Baptiste, 35, 218
Caldwell, James, 177, 193
Cameron, Duncan, 111, 129
Cameron, John, 80, 82, 96, 98, 99; wife, 98
Cannibalism, 121
Canoes, 16-17; north, 43-44; crews, 52-54; races, 71
Canook, 270, 271
Canots du maître, 15-17
Capot Rouge, 104
Caribou Portage, 56
Cartier, Joseph, 282, 290, 291
Carver, Jonathan, 8
Casino, 270
Catlin, George, 167, 169, 170, 181, 182-83
Chaboillez, Charles, 32, 159-60, 165, 178
Chamanau, 86
Chamard, 98
Charlo, 98, 99
Cherry portages, 56
Cheval de Bois Portage, 46, 58
Cheyenne Indians, 184-92
Children, diet of, 129-30
Chinook Indians, 248, 252, 253, 257-58, 269; women, 261
Chipewyan Indians, 26
Chippewa Indians, 26, 40
Chokecherry, 185
Chouart, 3
Clarke, John, 219
Clatsop Indians, 269, 274
Clement, 221
Clothing, voyageurs', 26, 45
Coalpo, 269; wife of, 269, 270, 272
Columbia River, posts on, 248-49
Concomly, King, 258, 266, 276, 281, 289-90
Coniah, 294, 295
Conolly, William, 115
Construction, Rainy Lake houses, 63-64
Corn, lyed, 130
Corne, Commandant de la, 205
Coteau du Missouri, 162, 164
Coureurs du bois, 6

Coventry, Vermont, 115
Cox, Ross, 261, 263, 285, 293, 297
Crebassa, 90, 153
Cree Indians, 73, 75, 76, 82, 86, 104, 151, 206, 207, 211, 213, 216, 217, 221; at Eagle Hills, 105-6; women of, 112
Crooked Lake, 46
Crops, at Pembina, 125-26
Crow Indians, 76
Cumberland House, 62, 134, 204
Cyr, Joseph, 96

Dalles, the, 252
Dancing, 37-38
Décharges, 51
Dégrades, 55
Demarais, 80, 82, 87
Dérouines, 82
Desrosiers, 222
Detour, the, 202
Diet. *See* Food
Dog sledge, travel by, 239-40
Dog's Den, 162
Dogs, 95-96; as food, 127
Dolly, skiff, 258, 265, 267, 290
Down River Fort. *See* Bas de la Rivière
Duchesne, 289, 292
Dugas, Abbé, 118, 214

Eagle Hills Fort, 77, 105-6, 207
Elbow, the, 207
Explorers, French, 3-7
Expresses, 141-44, 293

Falcon, Pierre, 67
"Falcon, the." *See* Tanner, John
Fall Indians, 77, 212
Faries, Hugh, 143
Fish, 122, 274-75
Flanagan, Mr., 274
Flathead Indians, 201
Flour, 128
Fond du Lac, 126
Food, problems of, 119-30; on the march, 130-32, 133
Forks, the, 77, 148, 205

Fort à la Corne, 5
Fort Alexandria, 133
Fort Astoria. *See* Astoria
Fort Augustus, 211, 221
Fort Bas de la Rivière. *See* Bas de la Rivière
Fort Brule, 212
Fort Charlotte, 43, 44
Fort Chipewyan, 31, 134
Fort de la Frenier, 160
Fort de la Montée, 62, 133
Fort de l'Isle, 134
Fort des Prairies, 211
Fort Esperance, 134
Fort George (Astoria), 266, 267, 268; wrangling over management of, 273; departure of large group from, 277-79; Henry in charge of, 278-95; deterioration of affairs at, 288-90
Fort George (Fort des Prairies), 123, 133, 211
Fort Gibraltar, Great Hall at, 64
Fort Maurepas, 73
Fort Nipeween, 205
Fort Paskoyac, 203
Fort Providence, 134
Fort Resolution, 134
Fort St. Charles, 4
Fort St. Louis, 205
Fort St. Pierre, 4, 62
Fort Vermilion, 133, 197, 208; as rendezvous for Indians, 211-12; Henry decides to abandon, 220, 222, 223-24
Fort William (New Fort), 146-47, 215, 245; seizure of, 249; Fort George personnel leave for, 277-78
Forts, French, 5
Fowl Portage, 56
Franchère, Gabriel, 23, 73, 253, 254, 255, 256, 266, 271
Franklin, Sir John, 111, 124, 296
Fraser, A., 293
Fraser, Simon, 36, 144, 296
French explorers, 3-7
Frobisher, Joseph, 10, 203

Frobishers (Joseph and Thomas), 203
Fruit, 128-29

Gaboury, Marie, 117-18, 119
Game, 127
Games, Indian, 138
Gardens, post, 125-26
Garry, Nicholas, 67, 74, 111, 122
Garth. *See* McDonald of Garth, John
Gass, Sergeant Patrick, 222
Gaultier, Pierre, Sieur de la Vérendrye. *See* Vérendrye
Graham, Andrew, 53
Grand Portage, 1-2, 4, 5, 7, 9, 24; 1801 Rendezvous at, 15, 21, 24-40; annual ball at, 37-39
Grand Portage Bay, 19
Grand River canoe. *See Canots du maître*
Grande Allumette, 1
Grande Gueule, 91, 93, 104, 149
Grandes Fourches, 80
Grant, Peter, 26, 32, 62, 65
Grasshoppers, 195
Grease, importance in diet, 124
Great Carry. *See* Grand Portage
Great Hall, Fort Gibraltar, 64
Great Map of the West, Thompson's, 147, 199, 200, 226
Great Plains, 206
Grey Coat School, 199
Greysolon, Daniel, Sieur Duluth, 3
Gunflint Lake, 46, 58

Hair Hills, 80, 82, 86
Hallett, Mr., 228
Halsey, Mr., 264
Hamel, 86
Harmon, Daniel, 143, 297; on Grand Portage, 20; description of dance, 37; on Rendezvous ball, 39; on Canadian voyageurs, 53, 107; marriage, 114-15; on food, 120; on sturgeon, 122
Harmon, Elizabeth, 115

Harmon, Polly, 115
Harmon, Sally, 115
Harrison, Edward, 137
Hat Point, 19
Height of Land, 238, 239; frolic at, 57-58
Henry, Alexander, the Elder, 7, 73, 74, 122, 127, 203
Henry, Alexander, the Younger, at 1801 Rendezvous, 11, 18, 22; course of career, 11-12; journal, 12-13; promoted, 35, 36; journey over Northwest Road, 44-62, 65-77; at Rainy Lake House, 65; loses canoe and man, 72-73; finishes fort at Pembina, 81; life at Pembina, 82, 137-41, 143, 144-46, 153, 194-95; trips to outposts, 87-90; relations with Indians, 90-93, 144-46; threats against life, 91; detailed nature of journal entries, 93-99; as physician, 99-101; takes wife, 108, 116-17; trips to Kaministiquia, 147-48; death of mother-in-law, 150; trip to the Mandan, 153-55, 157-75, 180-84, 192-94; among the Big Belly, 176-79; goes to Cheyenne camp, 184-92; appointed to Lower Fort des Prairies, 195; journeys to new post, 197-208; encounters David Thompson, 198, 201-2, 203; at Fort Vermilion, 214, 215; at Fort William, 215; at Terre Blanche, 224, 225-29; goes to Rocky Mountain House, 229-30, 233, 235-36; trip to Height of Land, 239-45; ordered to Astoria, 250-51; trip to Astoria, 251-53; at Astoria, 257-59, 261-62, 267, 273-77; on expedition against Indians, 269-72; left in charge of Fort George, 278-95; death, 296
Henry, William, 137, 233, 234, 272, 278, 290, 291
Henry House, 11
Hesse, Charles, 98
High wine, 104, 107

Holidays, voyageurs' celebration of, 37, 108
Hominy, 130
Homme au Calumet, l', 77
Horse stealing, 221
Howse, Joseph, 224-25
Hudson's Bay Company, 158, 204, 224-25; post attacked by Indians, 77; struggle with, 80; Thompson in employ of, 199; coalition with North West Company, 250
Hughes, James, 220, 222, 250-51
Hunt, Wilson Price, 249, 255, 276

Illness, 99-101
Ilthkoyape, 251
Indians, trouble with, 9, 76-77, 144-46, 220-22; trading for beaver with, 83-86; drinking among, 103-7; at Fort Vermilion, 211-13, 215-17, 219; punishment of, 218-19; around Rocky Mountain House, 236; blond. See Mandan Indians; of Northwest, 251-53; trouble with at Fort George (Astoria), 268-72. See also names of individual tribes
Irving, Washington, 258, 262
Isaac Todd, ship, 250, 253, 254, 256, 263, 275, 279, 283, 284, 287
Isle Royale, 19

Jane, skiff, 290, 296
Jussaume, 172

Kaministiquia River, fort at, 3, 146
Keith, James, 142
Kettle Falls, 251
Knife Lake, 46
Koo-Koo-Sint. See Thompson, David
Kootenay House, 201, 226
Kootenay Indians, 201, 226
Kullyspell House, 226

La Biche, 105
La Framboise, M., 292
La France, Jean Baptiste, 171
La Plante's River, 208

Lac Bois Blanc, 59
Lac Croche, 46, 60
Lac des Couteaux, 46, 59, 60
Lac la Croix, 46, 60
Lac la Pluie. *See* Rainy Lake
Lac Pierre à Fusil, 46
Lac Winipic, 4, 74, 197, 198, 202
Lacombe, M., 62, 65
Lagasse, 86
Lahontan, Baron, 122
Lajimonière, Jean Baptiste, 142
Lake Athabasca, Pond's fort near, 8
Lake of the Mountains, 56
Lake of the Woods, 4, 68-69
Lake Vermilion, 61
Lamsoi, 283
Langlois, Michel, 79, 80, 82, 87, 89, 90
Lark, ship, 248, 280
Larocque, François Antoine, 31, 85, 158
Larocque, Joseph, 254
Lawrence, Sir Thomas, 28
Le Boeuf, 104
Le Borgne, 180, 184, 187-92
Le Prine, 289
Leech Lake, garden at, 126
Letendre, 227
Lewis and Clark expedition, 143, 158, 165, 171, 172, 179, 222, 226, 252, 257, 258, 259, 294, 296
Little Chief, 149, 151
Little Mirliton River, 242
Little Portage rapids, 51
Little Shell, 104
Livernois, 109
Livestock, 125, 126
Long, John, 121, 122, 129
Long Sault, 68
Longmore, Mr., 219, 221, 222
Louis XV, King of France, 3
Lower Fort des Prairies, 197. *See also* Fort Vermilion

McCracken, Hugh, 159, 162, 164, 165
McDonald, Alan, 160

McDonald of Garth, John, 30, 64, 214, 230, 250, 263, 265, 268, 269, 272, 273, 278, 297
McDonnell, Aneas, 223
McDonnell, "Big John," 30-31, 50; wife, 115
McDougall, Duncan, 255, 256, 258, 264, 266-67, 278, 282, 283, 290, 293
McGillis, Hugh, 35
McGillivray, Duncan, 34, 71, 106, 133; journal quoted, 83; on provisions, 123-24
McGillivray, Farquhar, 35
McGillivray, John, 35
McGillivray, William, 9, 39, 48, 296
McKay, William, 32
Mackenzie, Andrew, 115
McKenzie, Charles, 177-79, 193
McKenzie, Daniel, 32
McKenzie, Donald, 264, 268
Mackenzie, Geddes, 116
McKenzie, James, 35, 110
McKenzie, Roderic, 9, 31-32, 44, 61
Mackenzie, Sir Alexander, 6, 28-29, 81, 143, 296; prowess at drinking, 39; mentions "heavy water," 57; Indian wife of, 115; on health of traders, 121; on lyed corn, 130-31
McLeod, Archibald Norman, 31, 109-10, 133
McLoughlin, John, 100
McNab, John, 225
McTavish, A., 293
McTavish, Donald, 30; ordered to Astoria, 250; arrival awaited, 254, 263; Garth describes parting from, 265; arrives at Astoria, 284; disliked by crew, 286; and Jane Barnes, 287-88, 292; at Astoria, 290, 291; death, 296, 297
McTavish, J. C., 283, 284
McTavish, John George, 253, 254, 268, 272
McTavish, Simon, 10, 296; at 1801 Rendezvous, 18, 27-29, 33-35, 38; death, 143; bust of, 147
Mahliot, François, 24

Mai, the, 61
Mammoths, legend of, 236-37
Mandan Indians, 153-54, 165-75;
    sexual customs, 168; appearance,
    169-70; dress, 170; village, 172;
    huts, 173; ceremonies, 180-83
Mandan Plain, 162, 163
Maple sugar, 127
Maraboeuf Lake, 46, 59
Maraboeuf Portage, 58
Marriages, 108-16
Matootanha, village of, 172-74, 175,
    183, 192
Matthews, Mr., 273
Meat, in diet, 123-24
"Menard, Old," 161
Methye Portage (Portage la
    Loche), 8
Michilimackinac, sack of, 7
Miller, Thomas, 80, 137
Milligan, Mr., 274
Missistaygouine, 92
Missouri Journal, Charles McKen-
    zie's, 178
Missouri River, 162, 163, 164
Monsieur le Chat. *See* Shaw, Angus
Montée, 206
Montour, Mr., 263
Montreal canoes, cargo of, 21. *See
    also Canots du maître*
Montreal *Gazette*, 143
Moose Portage, 46, 56
Mosquitoes, 153, 157, 160
Mountain Men, 202
Mountain sheep, 242

Namakan Lake, 46, 61
Nelson, Lord Horatio, 143
Netnokwa, 152
New Fort, 146-47, 245. *See also*
    Fort William
New Grand Portage, 56
"New Road," 61
Newspapers, 143
Nipissing Indians, 234
North Men, 25-26
North West Company, forts, 2;
    principal trading post, 2; found-
ing, 10; principal fort at Grand
    Portage, 20; Partners at 1801
    Rendezvous, 29-33; coalition
    with XY Company, 143; fort at
    Souris, 158; Cumberland House
    post, 204; existence threatened,
    247; coalition with Hudson's Bay
    Company, 250; purchases Astoria,
    255, 256; settlement with Pacific
    Fur Company, 277
Northwest Angle, 69
Noue, de la, 3
Noyon, Jacques de, 3, 62

Oregon, Father of. *See* McLough-
    lin, John
"Orkney girl," 118-19
Otter, ship, 20, 126

Pacific Fur Company, 249, 277
Pangman, Peter, 235
Partridge Falls, 46
Partridge Portage, 46, 48
Pas, the, 203
Pawnee Indians, 163, 174, 175
Peace River, 8
Pedlar, ship, 276, 277
Pembina, 77, 79-81; size of store-
    house at, 64; trading at, 86;
    Henry's journal records life at,
    93-99; provisions consumed at,
    124-25; crops, 125-26; life at,
    137-46; attacked by Sioux, 148-
    51; decline of, 153, 194-95
Pemmican, 131, 132-35, 223
Pemmican posts, 133, 134
Petit Detroit, 59
Piche, 227
Piegan Indians, 201, 212, 217, 226-
    27, 233-34, 235-36; women, 113
Pigeon River, 2, 48
Pillet, Mr., 263
"Pipes," 55
Pointe à la Framboise, 19, 59
Pointe aux Chapeaux, 19
Pointe Maligne, 198
Poitras, Magdeleine, 31, 115
Pond, Peter, 8, 11, 126, 132

Pontiac, 7
Porkeaters, 22, 25, 40, 50, 62
Portage Bois Blanc, 46
Portage Cheval de Bois, 46, 58
Portage des Gros Pins, 58
Portage la Loche (Methye Portage), 1, 65
Portage la Prairie, 1, 158, 194
Portage l'Escalier, 46
Portage Orignal, 46
Portage Perdrix, 46
Portages: on Northwest Road, 46, 50-51, 56
Portaging, 23-24, 46-48
"Post of the Western Sea," 4
"Potties," 29, 33, 81, 90, 91, 93
Prairie Portage, 48
"Premier, the." *See* McTavish, Simon
Priest, the. *See* McDonnell, "Big John"
Prostitution, 26-27, 261
Provisions. *See* Food
Punishments, 217-19

Raccoon, sloop, 250, 264, 265, 267, 289
Radisson, Pierre, 3
Rain squalls, 59
Rainy Lake, 3, 50, 61; produce, 125; wild rice, 127
Rainy Lake Fort, 4, 50, 61, 62-65, 147
Rainy Lake River, 65-66
Rapid Indians, 212
Rapids, 51-52
Rat River, outpost at, 92
Red Deer River, 208
Red River, 4, 88
Red Tail, 175
Régale, 26
Rendezvous, annual spring, 2; of 1801, 15, 21, 24-40; annual ball, 37-39; at New Fort, 146, 147; of 1811, 250-51
Rice, wild, 127, 131
River of Death, 75
Rivière à l'Eau Claire, 229

Rivière aux Gratias, 80
Rivière la Croix, 61
Rivière la Souris, 158, 160
Rivière Terre Blanche, 13, 295
Rivière Winipic, 72-73
Rocky Mountain House, 230, 235-36
Rogers, Major Robert, 8
Rooptahee, 165, 166
Rose Lake, 57
Ross, Alexander, 112, 138, 285, 288, 297
Ross, John, 9
Roussel, 280, 289
Rowand, M., 229
Rum, traders', 104
Russians, trade with, 248, 281

Sacajawea, 294
Saganaga Lake, 46
St. Gabriel's Street Church, Montreal, 107
Salish House, 226
Salt, 129
Sandwich Islanders, 260, 276, 277-78
Sansregret, 222
Sarcee Indians, 213
Saskatchewan River, 4, 202-3
Saulteur Indians, 82, 86, 87, 90, 104, 144-45, 151, 153; and smallpox epidemic, 76; women, 111; games, 138; Henry takes leave of, 197
Selkirk, Lord, 70, 247
Seven Oaks, battle of, 249
Shaw, Angus, 30
Shining Mountains, Henry's first contact with, 241
Sioux Indians, 69, 76, 145, 153, 162, 194-95; strike Pembina, 148-51; "white-bearded." *See* Mandan Indians
Slave Indians, 208, 211, 212, 217
Small, Charlotte, 115, 200
Small, Patrick, 200
Smallpox, 76
Smith, Captain, 286, 287
Snake's Den, 164, 193

Songs, voyageurs', 17, 66-68
Soulier Indians, 176
Souris. *See* Rivière la Souris
Stairway Portage, 46, 50-51, 58
Stefansson, Vilhjalmar, 124
Stuart, Alexander, 253, 257, 259, 265, 268
Stuart, David, 268
Stuart, John, 268
Sturgeon, 122, 274-75
Sugarloaf hill, 19
Susies (islands), 19

Tabashaw, 86, 92, 153
Tanner, John, 151-53
Terre Blanche, new fort at, 222, 223, 224
Terre Blanche House, 224; life at, 227-28
Thompson, David, disapproval of liquor, 106-7; wife, 115, 200; on pemmican, 132; to establish fort on coast for North West Company, 144, 224; Great Map of the West, 147, 199, 200, 226; on the Mandan, 154, 168; and Hugh McCracken, 159; meets Henry, 198, 203; arrives at Fort Vermilion, 208; leaves for Columbia, 214; rescued by Garth, 214; arrives at Terre Blanche, 225-27; Henry searches for, 233-34; seeks new route to Pacific, 234-35, 236-38; on Indian women, 251, 252; and Concomly, 258
Thompson, Mr., 264
Thorn, Jonathan, 248
Thunder Bay, 146
Times, London, 143

Tonquin, ship, 248, 280
Trade goods, 21, 85-86
Trafalgar, battle of, 143
Treaty of Utrecht, 5
Tripe de roche, 120-21
Trottier, Marguerite, 214-15
Tuberculosis, 99

Venereal disease, 261-62
Vérendrye, Pierre Gaultier, Sieur de la, 4, 5, 62, 73, 158; son, Jean Baptiste, 69
Voyageurs, physical characteristics, 52-53; working day, 54; diet, 54-55; songs, 66-68; drinking, 107-8

Walla Walla Indians, 252
War of 1812, 249
Watab Portage, 56
"Water, heavy," 57
Wenatchee Indians, 252
Wentzel, Willard Ferdinand, 67-68, 120
Western Sea, search for, 3, 4
"White River." *See* Rivière Winipic
Whitefish, 122
Wine, 129; high, 104, 107
Winnipeg, 77
Wolves, 96
Women, traffic in, 109-11; Indian, 111-13, 177, 251, 252; white, 117-19; as problem at Astoria, 260-62
Wooden Horse Portage, 46, 51
Woolwich, Miss, 115

XY Company, 20, 29, 35, 80, 204; post at Rainy Lake, 62; camp near Pembina, 91; coalition with North West Company, 143